Acing

Business Associations

Second Edition

A Checklist Approach to Business Associations

Michael A. Chasalow
Director and Founder of the USC Law School
Small Business Clinic and Clinical Professor of Law
University of Southern California
Gould School of Law

Series Editor
A. Benjamin Spencer

ACING SERIES®

WEST
ACADEMIC
PUBLISHING

Acing Series is a trademark registered in the U.S. Patent and Trademark Office.

© 2010 Thomson Reuters
© 2016 LEG, Inc. d/b/a West Academic
    444 Cedar Street, Suite 700
    St. Paul, MN 55101
    1-877-888-1330

West, West Academic Publishing, and West Academic are trademarks of West Publishing Corporation, used under license.

Printed in the United States of America

ISBN: 978-1-63459-600-8

Acknowledgments

I would like to thank my wonderful wife, Emily for her love and support of all of my "projects" and my personal BJR, Benjamin, Justin and Rachel who inspire me each day and who continually teach me how to be a better teacher.

I would also like to thank all of my students who, over the years, through their quest for knowledge and understanding, have helped me to sharpen my own understanding of the material in this book. I would like to specifically thank my research assistants Amanda McFall, Torin McDonald, Jackson Trugman, Elizabeth Roberts, Tania ElBayar, Morgan Schwartz, Alex Busto, Joseph Sung and Serena Patel for their comments, suggestions and edits of this edition.

Over the years and in preparing the materials in the first edition of this book, I used a variety of other resources which, in addition to the typical primary materials, include articles, essays, text books, teacher's manuals, explanatory materials and other resources, as a means to enhance my own understanding of the material and in an effort to find more effective approaches to present the material to students. Since these materials have influenced my understanding and my teaching, as well as my presentation of some of the materials in this book, I wanted to acknowledge a few of the most significant sources. These include: Several editions of *Business Associations—Cases and Materials on Agency, Partnerships and Corporations* (and accompanying materials including a terrific *Teacher's Manual*) by William A. Klein, J. Mark Ramseyer and Stephen M. Bainbridge; *Commentaries and Cases on the Law of Business Organizations* (and accompanying materials, including *Sample Class Notes and Teacher's Manual*) by William T. Allen, Reinier Kraakman and Guhan Subramanian; *Corporations and Other Business Enterprises—Cases and Materials*, by Thomas Lee Hazen and Jerry W. Markham; *Corporations and Other Business Organizations Cases and Materials* by Melvin Aron Eisenberg; *Business Organization and Finance*, by William A. Klein and John C. Coffee, Jr.; and *Securities Law—Insider Trading* by Stephen M. Bainbridge. I would also like to thank James Gordly, who taught me corporations and showed me that this subject does not need to be complicated in order to convey complex material, and Eric Talley whose notes and guidance were of tremendous help when I began teaching the subject.

Finally, I want to acknowledge my incredible colleagues who comprise the USC Gould School of Law faculty and staff whose feedback, insight and support over the years has been invaluable.

MICHAEL A. CHASALOW

Los Angeles, California
November 2015

Table of Contents

Acing

Business
Associations

Second Edition

Introduction

In my twenty years of teaching about various business subjects, I have interacted with thousands of students. Among these students there are a variety of learning styles and abilities and levels of understanding. One of the most successful approaches to presenting this material is to present the material in an organized and accessible format, so that students can digest the basic principles before moving on to the intricacies. Law school courses frequently focus on intricacies of the law because those areas are often more interesting and challenging. Unfortunately, for students who have not yet established their bearings in the subject, it can be confusing and disorienting to plunge into the complexities. This book is not an effort to explore all the complexities of business associations. Rather, it is designed to provide that foundation of the basics of business associations, so that students will have a better ability to succeed in their studies of the subject. In addition, I have found that the most successful exam answers often have an organization that reflects the student's understanding of the subject matter. Another objective of this book is to help students internalize the organizational framework of the issues that arise in a Business Associations course, so, that students can demonstrate their understanding of the subject matter on their exams in a manner that professors will recognize as that of a student who has a firm grasp of the organizational framework of the subject. It is this ability to demonstrate one's understanding that characterizes the students who "ace" an exam.

The standard Business Associations course in most law schools involves the introduction of a number of concepts. The course is intended to lay the foundation for almost all further business law study. However, unlike many introductory courses, the material covers a vast range of subjects that do not really build upon each other. For example, agency may be related to partnership, but it does not really prepare students for a study of securities laws or mergers. Each topic within a typical Business Associations course has different rules and standards yet will also have some concepts, which overlap with other topics. On the other hand, there is some

1

good news. Most of the rules are not difficult. The hardest part of business law is the vocabulary and learning to translate familiar situations into business concepts. For example, most people have an inherent understanding of conflict of interest. They just need to understand the business situations in which it applies and the structures involved so the concept may be better applied to the facts in a business context. It is not difficult to understand limited liability if a person can grasp the notion of certain property being "off limits." The more challenging questions involve determining the circumstances in which that same property is not off limits.

On the other hand, although the subjects within a Business Associations course cover a substantial range of topics, most of the law of business associations involves some standard questions. This is true because the study of business associations is about the consequences of people working together in an organization. Just a few of the fundamental questions are: What responsibilities does one person have to another when they are working together? What responsibilities does a person have to others when she is working on their behalf in the operation of a business enterprise? What are the features, rules and characteristics of various entities, which are treated as separate "persons" under the law? What are the rights and protections and obligations of the owners of these business entities and what rules protect and govern the transfer of that ownership? The goal of this book is to address these questions in the organization and presentation of the materials that follow.

One key to Business Associations is to learn the language so as not to be intimidated and to be able to translate what appear to be complex concepts into accessible concepts. The intent of this book is to do just that. When appropriate, we have marked in bold some of the concepts and vocabulary that we consider particularly important or useful in understanding a particular topic. While far from an exhaustive list that one might find in a comprehensive dictionary of business terms, the bolded words and phrases generally are intended to highlight certain vocabulary and concepts that many professors in this field would consider important.

This book is a study guide, not a treatise. It is not a substitute for going to class or for reading the cases. In fact, we do not discuss the majority of cases in this subject. This book assumes that the reader has attended class and has been exposed to the material. Unfortunately, a great many "introductory" courses to business associations proceed on a more complex level than many students would choose. Other courses approach the material in a fragmented or selective manner. This often leaves students confused about the basic rules and principles AND how to apply those rules and principles on an exam. This book is intended to demystify some of the more convoluted concepts in the subject and provide students with an organizational framework of the basic rules, so that they can more easily grasp the fundamental concepts and use their enhanced understanding to succeed in the subject of Business Associations. We have also attempted to limit significantly citations to outside materials. Although this book synthesizes general concepts contained in a variety of materials, we did not want to create a guide that required outside research to use.

The law that applies to Business Associations is a patchwork of cases, legislation and regulations at both the state and the Federal level. Often the laws among various states will differ. This book applies general principals of corporate law, primarily those of Delaware, California and New York. We have attempted to note significant variations that might exist among states. However, students should check the particular law in their state for variations.

Since the first edition of this book was published, I have written and published a textbook in the subject, *Experiencing Business Organizations* (West Academic Publishing, January, 2014). While many of the subjects covered in this *Acing* book found their way into *Experiencing Business Organizations*, many students have found that *Acing Business Associations* is still a useful companion to *Experiencing Business Organizations* given its many examples, explanations and model answers and its focus on breaking down the critical elements of many of the more complex legal issues encountered in Business Associations. This *Acing* book is intended to be a useful resource for a wide variety of Business Associations courses and is designed to make the concepts covered in any such course more accessible, regardless of the text used for a particular class.

While students may wish to read this book cover to cover, it may also be used as a reference, so that students may read a particular chapter or even subchapter to help clarify an area of confusion. Where appropriate, we have tried to include examples to illustrate our explanations. Many of these examples were taken from actual exams and are intended not just to provide an illustration of a particular concept, but also the type of questions that students might receive in a particular area. It is our hope that with the concepts, organization and explanations provided in these materials that students experience the success in their studies that grow out of a better understanding of the subject.

CHAPTER 1

Agency

Agency law is about asking when is one party responsible for the actions of another and what rights and obligations do those parties have to one another.

Agency is a fundamental concept in the law. It is central to a number of legal practices and precepts. Because agency involves the most basic example of one person acting on behalf of another, it is often the first area introduced in a Business Associations course. Agency concepts arise throughout the study of Business Associations, and situations in which an officer or employee is an agent for a business are common. The agency principles of whether the agent has the authority to act on behalf of the business, when the business is bound by, or liable for, the actions of its agents, and what duties and responsibilities an agent might have to a business are core concepts that also arise in the study of partnerships, limited liability companies, and corporations.

The first question that a student must resolve when faced with a fact pattern in which one person is acting on behalf of another, is whether a principal-agent relationship exists. "Agency is the fiduciary relationship that arises when one person (a 'principal') manifests assent to another person (an 'agent') that the agent shall act on the principal's behalf and subject to the principal's control, and the agent manifests assent or otherwise consents so to act." RESTATEMENT OF THE LAW (THIRD) AGENCY (the *"Third Restatement"*) § 1.01.

There are three parts to this analysis:

☑ manifestation of consent by the principal that the agent act on the principal's behalf;

AND

☑ subject to the principal's control;

AND

☑ the agent manifests consent.

In order to create an agency there must be some form of agreement or understanding between the parties, but not necessarily a contract between the parties. The existence of the agency may be proved by an evaluation of the facts in each particular situation. We may look at what the parties said, what they did, how they acted, and their course of dealing over time; even silence may be used to show a party's consent. It is not essential that the agent receive compensation.

Once the question of whether a principal agent relationship exists has been answered, one must examine the situations in which agency questions arise. In general we are interested in three "players" in agency questions:

1. The Principal

2. The Agent

3. The Third Party

We want to know what are the rights and responsibilities of each of these parties to the others. There are also some basic principles that govern these agency relationships:

☑ The agent has certain duties and obligations to the principal.

☑ The principal has certain duties and obligations to the agent.

☑ The principal is responsible for tortious acts committed by the agent that fall within the scope of the agency.

☑ The agent has the ability to enter into binding agreements on the principal's behalf, as long as the agreement may be traced to the principal's authority.

☑ The agent's knowledge (in the subject matter of the agency) is imputed to the principal.

When evaluating an agency problem, it is helpful to distinguish between fact patterns that involve tort issues and fact patterns that involve contract issues. In a tort context, we are typically looking to determine: **Who is responsible** for a wrongful act or for harm done? In a contract context, we are typically looking to determine: **Who is bound?**

Agency Materials Tip

Often in presenting agency materials, professors will use names in which the first letter of the name represents the role played by the actor. For example, "Paul" is often the principal and "Alice" is often the agent. While this pattern is not always used and should not be assumed without analysis, students <u>might</u> be able to recognize an agency issue (and possibly the roles played) in a question in which a person whose name begins with "P" and a person whose name begins with "A" (and sometimes a third party whose name starts with "T") interact.

AGENCY PROBLEMS INVOLVING TORTS

When a tort occurs in an agency context, the question is frequently, whether the principal is responsible for the agent's tort. Remember, the issue is not whether the principal was negligent. If the principal was negligent, then he or she is liable under tort law. The question in agency law is **whether the principal may be found liable for the torts of an agent, even though the principal was not negligent**. In evaluating a tort question involving agency, whether a principal is responsible for the wrongdoing of an agent depends upon the nature of the principal-agent relationship. In making this analysis, one must first determine whether an employee/employer relationship existed. **It is critical to determine if the agent was an employee of the principal because the principal is liable for the torts committed by its employee within the scope of that employee's employment**.

When evaluating whether an agent is an "employee" for the purposes of *respondeat superior*, one must assess whether the principal had the right to exert control over the manner and the means by which the agent performed his duty. Note that it is not just the actual exercise of control that is critical; it is also the *right* to exercise control that is evaluated. Various factors are involved in assessing whether a principal has the right to exert enough control over the agent for the agent to be considered an "employee." These factors (set forth in Comment f to the *Third Restatement* § 7.07) include:

☑   The extent of control that the agent and the principal have agreed the principal may exercise over the details of the work (Note that the extent of control that the principal actually exercises is relevant as well.);

☑   Whether the agent is engaged in a distinct occupation or business;

☑ Whether the type of work done by the agent is customarily done under a principal's direction or without supervision;

☑ The skill required in the agent's occupation;

☑ Whether the agent or the principal supplies the tools or other instrumentalities required for the work and the place in which to perform it;

☑ The length of time during which the agent is engaged by a principal;

☑ Whether the agent is paid by the job or by the time worked;

☑ Whether the agent's work is part of the principal's regular business;

☑ Whether the principal and agent believe they are creating an employment relationship; and

☑ Whether the principal is or is not in business.

EMPLOYEES VERSUS INDEPENDENT CONTRACTORS (AKA "NON-EMPLOYEE AGENTS")

The question of whether or not a situation involves an employee/employer relationship with regard to agency is a question of fact. For example, if Paul hires Adam to be the manager of Paul's candy factory, and Adam shows up for work every day, receives a weekly salary, supervises workers and projects and reports to Paul about how things are going at the candy factory, then Adam is an employee. In contrast to Adam's position, consider the following: One day, Paul decides that he wants a mural painted on the front of the factory, and he hires Ivan to do it. Ivan, who regularly paints murals and other works of art for hire, is to be paid $5,000 for painting the mural. Paul tells Ivan that Paul has no artistic taste, so Ivan should just paint whatever he wants as long as it appeals to kids. Ivan supplies his own paints and materials, and completes the job in one week. Ivan is Paul's Agent. However, Ivan is not an employee. Ivan is an independent contractor (or under the *Third Restatement*, a "non-employee agent").

The distinction between employee and independent contractor (also known as a "non-employee agent") is important because **employees and independent contractors create different potential liabilities for their principals**. Under the doctrine of *Respondeat Superior*, employers are **vicariously liable** (i.e.

responsible) for the torts of their employees that arise within the scope of the employee's employment. However, principals are not responsible for the torts of their independent contractors unless the tort (1) arises out of an area over which the principal exercised control, or (2) falls into one of the exceptions such as an inherently dangerous activity or a non-delegable duty.

Franchise Arrangements

A franchise arrangement involves a company or an individual (the "franchisee") selling a product or a service or operating a business pursuant to a license to do so (typically referred to in this context as a "franchise agreement") from another company or individual (the "franchisor"). Even though a franchise relationship is a contractual relationship and not an employee/employer relationship, courts (and Business Associations students) are often asked to evaluate a fact pattern to determine whether a franchisor exercised sufficient control over a franchisee to create an agency relationship that might be characterized as an employee/employer relationship. In order to make this determination, students should evaluate:

☑ The extent of the franchisor's involvement in the franchisee's day-to-day operations;

☑ The franchisor's right to control the franchisee's operations (even if that control is not exercised), which might include provisions in the franchise agreement such as pricing requirements, audit rights and approval of advertising; and

☑ The right of the franchisor to terminate the relationship (which could suggest that the franchisor has the power to control the franchisee's actions, even if explicit rights to control are not articulated.

If the franchisor exercises sufficient control over the franchisee to characterize the relationship as an employee/employer relationship, then the franchisor would be vicariously liable for tortious conduct of the franchisee (or even tortious conduct of the franchisee's employees) that occurs within the scope of that employee/employer relationship.

INTENTIONAL TORTS

Typically, principals (including employers) are not found to be liable for the intentional torts of their agents (including employees). Such actions are usually found to be outside the scope of employment and are committed without any intent to serve the employer. However, there is an exception to this exclusion when the employee's job is such that some part of the intentional tort might be characterized as being done with the intent of "serving the employer." For example, a bouncer who ejects a patron from a club, seriously injuring the patron, might be said to have done so with, at least a partial, intent to serve his employer. Some jurisdictions broaden the evaluation and look beyond the test of whether the intentional tort was committed with the purpose of serving the employer. These jurisdictions would allow a court to find a principal liable for harm done as a result of the intentional tort of an agent if it is *foreseeable* that some harm might arise out of the specific employment/agency relationship, even if the specific harm that occurred was not foreseeable. In an effort to assess whether a particular harm was foreseeable, courts in these jurisdictions will ask whether the tort was of "characteristic risk" associated with the agency relationship.

FROLIC AND DETOUR

Of course there are times when an agent is not acting within the scope of her employment. For example, if an agent has gone home for the evening, is driving to a party and gets into a car accident, that accident has not occurred within the scope of the agent's employment. Sometimes it can be difficult to determine whether or not an agent has "left" employment. When an employee leaves employment to do something for personal reasons, that activity is known as a "**frolic**." If an employee is still engaged in employment but strays only slightly from the direct assignment, that is known as a mere "**detour**." An agent who is driving to the bank to deposit money for the store that employs him and takes a longer route so he can drive by the new sculpture in the park is on a "**detour**." If he gets into an accident while driving by the sculpture, his employer will still be liable. However, if that same agent, instead of going to the bank, goes to see a movie and spills his soda on the person sitting next to him, the person with the soda-stained garment cannot charge the agent's employer for the cleaning bill because the agent's leaving work to attend the movie would be considered a frolic.

ILLUSTRATIVE PROBLEMS

PROBLEM 1.1

In Paul's candy factory, discussed above, where Adam works as a supervisor, there are regular tours of the factory given. One day Adam notices that a big vat of cherry flavored liquid is leaking. He decides that it does not need to be fixed immediately, but can wait until the weekend. Unfortunately, Adam does not remember that there is a tour of the factory scheduled for that afternoon. One of the individuals on the tour, named Clem Zee, slips on the cherry liquid and breaks his arm. Clem sues Paul because it was Paul's factory. Paul's position is that Adam's negligence caused Clem's accident, and, because Paul was not negligent, Paul does not think he is liable. What is the likely result?

Analysis

We have already been told that Adam is Paul's employee. As such, Paul is responsible for Adam's torts that arise out of Adam's job and/or position as manager of the Candy Factory. It was Adam's job to supervise the factory. Adam negligently decided that it was not necessary to clean up the spill immediately. As a direct result, Clem was injured. It does not matter that Adam was not supposed to be negligent in his job. It only matters that, in Adam's employment of supervising the factory, he was negligent. Because Paul is Adam's principal/employer, Paul is liable for Adam's negligence and will be liable to Clem. Note that Paul will have a claim against Adam. So, should he choose to take action, Paul could recover from Adam if Paul is found liable as a result of Adam's negligence.

PROBLEM 1.2

Several months pass following the incident in the preceding problem, and Adam is still working as a supervisor at the Candy Factory. One day Adam leaves work early to go to the local high school football game. At the game he throws a rotten tomato at a fan named Frank, who is cheering for the opposing team. Frank is injured. After the game Adam returns to work until the end of the day. The injured fan, Frank, sues Paul. Does Frank have a claim?

Analysis

Since Adam was not acting as Paul's employee at the football game, and the wrongdoing did not arise out of Adam's employment at the candy factory, Frank would not have a claim against Paul. Adam was clearly on a "frolic" and had left his position as Paul's agent. Therefore, Paul would not be liable, even though Adam is his employee, because the wrong did not occur within the scope of Adam's employment.

PROBLEM 1.3

Adam is still working for Paul's Candy Factory. One day, in the middle of the workday, Adam looks through the front window of the Candy Factory' and sees his childhood nemesis, Cruel Carl, walking across the street. Remembering how mean Carl had been in Grammar School, Adam runs outside, crosses the street, and punches Carl in the nose. It turns out that Carl has become a pacifist and wants to stamp out any violence in the world, so he sues Adam and Paul for his injuries. Does Carl have a case against Paul?

Analysis

Paul is probably not liable for Adam's intentional tort. Adam's action was without any intention of serving his employer—it was a purely personal action. Furthermore, to the extent relevant, such an action is not foreseeable as the type of harm which might arise out of the employment of a supervisor for the Candy Factory. However, if instead of spotting Cruel Carl, Adam had seen a Candy Factory competitor, spying on the Candy Factory in an effort to steal its candy secrets, and Adam had punched the competitor in the nose, then it is likely that Paul would be liable because Adam's action would have been taken with the intent of serving his employer. Of course, Carl would have a case against Adam, but that claim would be discussed in a Torts class, not Business Associations.

NON-EMPLOYEE AGENTS AND INDEPENDENT CONTRACTORS

It is possible to have an agency relationship in which the agent is not an employee. Prior to the *Third Restatement*, those who performed services for another who were not employees were called "independent contractors." The *Third Restatement* refers to these individuals as "non-employee agents." Other sources still use the term "independent contractors." The idea here is that these individuals operate on **a continuum of control**. For some, the principal exercises some control over the subject matter of the agency, but not enough control to create an employer/employee relationship. For others, virtually no control is exercised by the principal, and the relationship involves a third party performing services on a truly independent basis. In most of these "non-employee" instances, the principal is not liable for the torts of the agent or service provider. However, there are a few circumstances in which a principal still would be liable.

Rule:

When a fact pattern involves an independent contractor or a non-employee agent, if the tort occurs in an area over which the principal exercises some control, the principal might still be liable. However, if the tort occurs in an area over which the principal does not exercise control, then there is no liability unless the activity falls within one of the exceptions.

Exceptions:

There are certain situations in which a principal still is liable for the torts of an agent who is not an employee and over whom the principal exercises no control. Those situations are:

☑   Inherently dangerous activities;

☑   Non-delegable duties; and

☑   Negligent hiring

Inherently dangerous activities include any activity that is likely to cause harm or damage unless some precautions are taken. A **non-delegable duty** is one that a person may not avoid by the mere delegation of a task to another person. For example, landlords have certain non-delegable duties to their tenants. Attorneys have certain non-delegable duties to their clients. If something is "non-delegable," it does not mean that an agent may not be hired to perform the task. It means that hiring an agent to perform the task will not discharge or transfer the principal's responsibility or liability. The last category, **negligent hiring**, is not really about vicarious liability. It refers to circumstances in which the principal may be found liable for the torts of an independent contractor. However, that liability is based on the principal's negligence in hiring the independent contractor, not on attributing responsibility for the tortious act of an independent contractor to an innocent principal.

PROBLEM 1.4

Recall from the example above that Paul hires Ivan, an independent contractor, to paint a mural on the front of the factory. Remember that Ivan, who regularly paints murals and other works of art for hire, is to be paid $5,000 for painting the mural, plus expenses. Paul tells Ivan that Paul has no artistic taste, so Ivan should just paint whatever he wants as long as it appeals to kids. Ivan supplies his own paints and materials and is to complete the job in one week. While working on the mural, Ivan spills paint on a Ferrari parked outside of the factory. Fiona, the Ferrari owner, wants to sue Paul for the damage to her car. In a separate occurrence, Paul, who is also being billed for Ivan's expenses, tells Ivan not to buy new ladders, but to use an old ladder from the abandoned firehouse next door to the factory in order to reach the high parts of the building. Ivan does use one of the old ladders, which, unfortunately, breaks while Ivan is on it painting the mural, and Ivan falls on Tom who is walking by and admiring the mural. Tom wants to sue Paul for the damage associated with his physical injuries. Will Fiona and/or Tom be successful if they try to recover from Paul?

Analysis

It is unlikely that Fiona would prevail in a suit against Paul. Ivan is not an employee. He is an independent contractor (also known as a "non-employee agent"). The damage to Fiona's car occurred as a result of an activity over which Paul had no control. Since Ivan was an independent contractor acting outside the scope of Paul's control, and the activity did not involve an inherently dangerous activity, a non-delegable duty or a negligent hiring, Paul will not be liable.

However, it is likely that Tom would prevail in a suit against Paul. Because the selection of the ladder is an area over which Paul exercised control, Paul will not be able to claim that he bears no vicarious liability for Ivan's actions, even though Ivan is an independent contractor. Instructing Ivan to use an old ladder is not sufficient to make Ivan Paul's employee. However, it is sufficient to create liability for Paul if the use of the old ladder caused the damage. Because Tom was injured as a result of the use of the old ladder, and Paul instructed Ivan to use that old ladder, it is likely that Tom will be successful in a claim against Paul.

PROBLEM 1.5

One day Paul decides that he wants to expand his factory. Paul buys the property next door to the factory where the abandoned firehouse currently stands. Paul then hires Allison to demolish the abandoned firehouse so the candy factory can build new facilities. Allison uses exceptionally powerful dynamite to demolish the firehouse, and, as a result, property surrounding the firehouse is damaged. The owners of the damaged property sue Paul for the damage. Will Paul prevail if he exercised no control over the manner or means that Allison used to demolish the firehouse?

Analysis

Paul will not prevail. The activity of demolishing a building is inherently dangerous. Inherently dangerous activities are likely to cause harm or injury to others unless precautions are taken, and the law does not let a principal avoid liability for such activities merely by hiring an agent to perform an inherently dangerous activity. These concerns certainly apply to using dynamite to demolish a building. So, Paul will still be liable for the property damage resulting from Allison's activity because of the inherently dangerous nature of the activity. The fact that Allison is an independent contractor or a non-employee agent will not shield Paul, the principal, from liability in such an activity.

A few other points to remember:

1) **The agent is always liable for his own negligence.** Agency problems focus on the question of whether the third party can <u>also</u> recover from the non-negligent principal.

2) **If the principal is negligent, then the principal is liable for his own negligence, not because of** *respondeat superior*, **and not because of the principal-agent relationship**. For example, if Paul negligently hires Allison and knew or should have known that she did not have the skill to perform the job, then Paul could also be liable because of "negligent hiring."

APPARENT AGENCY

A principal (or alleged principal) could also incur liability for the wrongdoing committed by an agent (or an alleged agent), acting with apparent authority on behalf, or purportedly on behalf, of the principal. (*Third Restatement* § 7.08.) Typically the analysis of a principal's responsibility for the actions of an agent turns upon issues of control and vicarious responsibility and not questions of appearances. The evaluation of the appearances of an agency relationship is usually seen when evaluating an agency fact pattern involving a contract. (*See* below.) In such an evaluation of an agency fact pattern involving a contract, the issue is whether the agent acted with "apparent authority." However, while questions of apparent authority are found more in a contract analysis than a tort analysis, there is one instance in which the concept of the apparent role of the agent (or alleged agent) is relevant to a tort analysis. That instance is known as "**apparent agency**."

Apparent agency arises in situations in which the person committing the tort is not the employee, or perhaps not even the agent, of the principal. Therefore, the principal would not be liable for the alleged agent's tort under the traditional agency analysis discussed above. However, if there are circumstances that led the injured third party to reasonably believe that an employment or agency relationship existed between the principal and the alleged agent, and those circumstances existed because of some action or inaction (i.e. manifestation) on the part of the principal, then the principal might still be liable under a theory of apparent agency, even if no employment relationship existed. Many courts, but not all, will also require that the injury to the third party resulted because of the third party's reasonable—albeit incorrect—belief that the alleged agent was, in fact, an agent of the principal—in other words, some showing that if the alleged agent had been under the control of the principal, then the principal would, or could, have exercised control to avoid the tort which took place.

To summarize, apparent agency involves:

☑ A reasonable belief by the third party that the alleged agent is an agent of the principal (i.e. reasonable reliance);

☑ Some action or inaction by the principal to create (or to fail to dispel) that reasonable belief on the part of the third party; and

☑ Some showing (in many cases) that the third party's injury could have been avoided had the alleged principal exercised control over the alleged agent. In other words, the third party's injury arose out of that third party's reasonable belief that an employee/agency relationship existed.

ILLUSTRATIVE EXAMPLE

A restaurant chain called Super Clean Restaurants allows a restaurant, formerly known as Dirty Dan's, to use the Super Clean Restaurant name, logo and menu. The newly named restaurant is now called DD's Super Clean Restaurant ("DD's Restaurant"). Customers who enter DD's Restaurant make the reasonable (although incorrect) assumption that the restaurant is owned and operated by the Super Clean Restaurant chain. However, in reality DD's Restaurant is owned and operated by Dirty Dan, and Dirty Dan has just paid a fee to Super Clean Restaurants to use its name and logo. While Super Clean Restaurants does provide some optional training to DD's Restaurant personnel, Super Clean

Restaurants does not exercise sufficient control to make DD's Super Clean Restaurant an "employee"/agent.

One day, Olive, Charlie and Dexter ("OC & D") go to eat at DD's Restaurant, reasonably believing that it is owned and operated by Super Clean Restaurants. Unfortunately, Dirty Dan's staff doesn't follow proper sanitation or food preparation procedures, and OC & D all get food poisoning. If OC & D sue Super Clean Restaurants, OC & D will not be able to show that DD's Restaurant was Super Clean Restaurants' agent. However, they might be able to show that DD's Restaurant was Super Clean Restaurants' apparent agent, and had Super Clean Restaurants been the principal, it could have required DD's Restaurant to follow proper food sanitation procedures, and, had the Super Clean Restaurants' procedures been followed, OC & D would not have become sick. Since Super Clean Restaurants allowed DD's Restaurant to use the Super Clean Restaurant name, logo and menu and create the impression of an agency relationship with third parties, Super Clean Restaurants could be found liable for OC & D's injuries under a theory of apparent agency.

AGENCY PROBLEMS INVOLVING CONTRACTS

Other agency problems involve actions taken by an agent to bind the principal to an agreement. When facing a fact pattern where a contract is involved, the question is not whether the principal is "liable." Rather, **in a contract action we want to know whether the principal is bound by the agent's actions**. An agent has the ability to bind a principal to an agreement when the agent has some form of authority.

There are various forms of authority through which an agent may bind a principal to an agreement. They include:

- ☑ Actual Authority (both express and implied);

- ☑ Apparent Authority;

- ☑ Ratification (which is authority granted after the fact);

- ☑ Liability of an Undisclosed Principal (This type of authority used to be included in the concept of "Inherent Authority," but that term has been eliminated in the *Third Restatement*.); and

- ☑ Estoppel (Note that Estoppel is not technically a form of authority; rather, it is a doctrine that (as applied in this context) prevents a Principal from arguing that no authority existed. However, even in circumstances in which the Principal might be bound to an agreement by the doctrine of Estoppel, the doctrine may not be used independently by that Principal to enforce the agreement against a third party.)

Actual Authority

Actual Authority exists when the principal communicates to the agent about the activities in which the agent may engage and the obligations the agent may undertake. This communication may be spoken or written; it may be through silence or implied in the job. There are two forms of actual authority: express and implied.

☑   **Actual Express Authority** involves examining the principal's explicit instructions.

☑   **Actual Implied Authority** involves examining the principal's explicit instructions and asking what else might be reasonably included in those instructions (i.e. implied) to accomplish the job. Implied Authority includes actions that are necessary to accomplish the principal's original instructions to the agent; it also includes those actions that the agent reasonably believes the principal wishes him to do, based on the agent's reasonable understanding of the authority granted by the principal.

ILLUSTRATIVE EXAMPLE

Patty hires Andrew to work in her toy company and places Andrew in charge of toys for little girls. Patty tells Andrew to purchase 1,000 stuffed dogs for sale in Patty's store. Andrew does. He is acting under Patty's *actual express authority*. If Andrew also buys 1,000 leashes to sell with the dogs, he is acting pursuant to *actual implied authority*. Patty did not tell Andrew to buy the leashes, but they are an accessory item that accompanies the toy. Andrew's authority is implied from Patty's instructions.

Apparent Authority

Apparent Authority is not about what the principal wants the agent to do. It **is about what a third party reasonably believes the principal has authorized the agent to do**. Because of this dynamic, in evaluating whether apparent authority is present, we do not look at communications between the principal and the agent; instead, we look at manifestations between the principal and the third party. Apparent authority is created when a person (principal or apparent principal) does something, says something, or creates a reasonable impression (a "manifestation") that another person (the apparent agent) has the authority to act on behalf of that apparent principal. For example, Patty calls up the toy manufacturer and tells the manufacturer that Andrew is coming over to buy 1000 stuffed animals for her. However, Patty tells Andrew, "Don't buy bears. I hate bears." If Andrew buys bears anyway and brings them back to Patty saying, "but these bears are cute," and Patty tries to return the bears, the manufacturer does not need to accept them because the manufacturer reasonably relied on Patty's statement that Andrew had authority to buy "stuffed animals." Andrew did not have actual authority to buy the bears, but he did have apparent authority.

Ratification

Ratification is authority that is granted by the principal after an agreement has been made. It involves situations in which an agent enters into an agreement on behalf of the principal without any authority (actual or apparent) to do so. There are two questions to ask in determining if there was a valid ratification of such an agreement:

1) Did the principal, through word or deed, manifest his assent to ("affirm") the agreement?

2) Given the facts and circumstances of the situation, will the law give effect to that assent?

Affirmation may be express or implied. (It is often implied by a principal accepting the benefits of the transaction.) Once an agreement or transaction has been ratified, the law treats it as if the agent with actual authority originally did it. Both parties to the agreement are bound.

Limitations on Ratification

Note that there are only certain circumstances in which an agreement may be ratified. Some of the limits on ratification include the following:

☑ For a ratification to be valid, the principal must know or have reason to know, **at the time of the alleged ratification**, the material facts relating to the transaction.

☑ A principal may not partially ratify a transaction. It is all or nothing.

☑ If the third party manifests an intention to withdraw from the transaction prior to the ratification, the principal may not then ratify the agreement.

☑ Ratification will be denied when necessary to protect the rights of innocent third parties. (This usually happens when there has been some material change in the circumstances between the time of the transaction and the time of the purported ratification.) For example, Annie, without any authority from Pat, enters into an agreement with Ted to sell Pat's house on day one. On day two, Pat's house burns down. Pat cannot ratify on day three and say, "Ok, I accept the agreement; I will sell you my house" because that would be unfair to Ted. Ratification might also be denied if the passage of time affects the rights or the liability of a third party. For example, Mary enters into an agreement with Matt that Herb will sell Matt Herb's concert tickets for a concert taking place on July 1st. Assuming Mary did not have authority from Herb to enter into the agreement with Matt, Herb cannot ratify on July 2nd.

Once a contract has been ratified, it generally creates retroactive authority. In other words, the law treats the agreement as though the agent who entered into the agreement had actual authority at the time the agreement was made, even if the agent lacked authority at that time. One significant exception to this treatment occurs when the principal had no capacity to enter into the agreement at the time it was made. For example, if an agent enters into an agreement on behalf of a minor, and the minor does not ratify the agreement until she becomes an adult, the agreement is effective with respect to that former minor upon ratification, not the date of the original agreement.

Liability of an Undisclosed Principal

There are certain situations in which a principal authorizes an agent to act on the principal's behalf with respect to third parties, but the principal is undisclosed. In such situations, the third party is unaware that the principal exists. If the agent acts with the principal's actual, express, or implied authority then the principal is bound, as discussed above. There are other situations in which the agent of an undisclosed principal acts without actual authority. In some of these situations the agent's actions would have bound the principal under apparent authority had the principal been disclosed. However, because an undisclosed principal cannot, by definition, have made any manifestation to the third party, there can be no apparent authority with an undisclosed principal. These situations are covered under the concept of **liability of an undisclosed principal** (formerly "inherent agency"). Under this concept (set forth in *Third Restatement* § 2.06.), the law will sometimes hold an undisclosed principal liable for certain unauthorized transactions of his agent when:

1) a third party has made a "detrimental change in position;"

2) the principal had notice of the agent's conduct;

3) the conduct might induce third parties to change their positions; AND

4) the principal did not take reasonable steps to notify the third parties of the facts.

Liability of an undisclosed principal most often arises in situations in which the agent acts in a manner consistent with the authority that a third party would reasonably believe the agent to have under the same circumstances had the principal been disclosed.

Estoppel

As mentioned above, **estoppel** is not really a form of authority. Estoppel is an equitable doctrine that prevents the principal from denying that an agency relationship exists. Estoppel generally arises in agency situations in which the principal has done something improper. As used in agency, estoppel involves:

☑ Intentional, negligent or otherwise culpable acts or omissions by the principal, which create an appearance of authority in the purported agent;

☑ A third party who reasonably, and in good faith, acts in reliance on that appearance of authority; and

☑ The third party changes her position in reliance upon that appearance of authority.

Students often want clarification of the difference between apparent authority and estoppel. While it is certainly possible that both conditions exist in the same fact pattern, **estoppel requires that the third party alter his or her position in reliance on the purported authority**. However, there is no requirement of detrimental reliance for apparent authority. In addition, apparent authority requires a manifestation *by the principal* (directly or indirectly) to the third party. No such manifestation is required for estoppel, merely some culpable act or omission by the principal.

Estoppel might arise when the principal takes some improper action even if that improper action is not sufficient to amount to a "manifestation" to the third party. Therefore, it would be difficult to show apparent authority. Note that while estoppel is used in a variety of contexts in different areas of the law to bind various individuals, in the agency context estoppel is not used to create a binding contract that may be enforced by both parties. Estoppel is used to prevent one party (typically the principal) from denying a purported agent's authority when the third party wants to enforce that contract.

PROBLEM 1.6

Penny lives in a small town and owns a bookstore called Better Books. Better Books has been in business for several years and has always had a reputation of hiring well-informed employees who provide excellent book recommendations to customers. One employee, named Astrid, has worked at Better Books for several years. Astrid sometimes helps with inventory and places orders for new books when Penny gets too busy. One day Astrid notices that the store is running low on a book called "The Best Cookbook." Astrid orders 25 more copies. However, unbeknownst to Astrid, Penny had tried the book, thought it was the worst cookbook ever, and does not want to order any more. Penny tries to cancel the order, but the publishing house refuses. Will Penny prevail if she argues that Better Books should not have to pay because she never ordered the book and did not tell Astrid to order the book?

Analysis

No. This is an example of a classic agency problem involving a contract. Astrid was Penny's agent because Astrid was an employee. Astrid either had actual express authority to order books and ordering more copies of "The Best Cookbook" fell under that authority, or, at a minimum, Astrid had actual implied authority to order more books for the store and ordering more copies of "The Best Cookbook" fell under that implied authority. It is reasonable for Astrid to understand her authority to include ordering more copies of a particular book. If Penny did not want Astrid to order more copies of "The Best Cookbook," Penny should have communicated that to Astrid. Furthermore, even if Astrid lacked actual authority, she probably had apparent authority. Because Astrid had placed orders for Better Books in the past and, presumably, the publishing house had dealt with Astrid before, it is reasonable to assume that Astrid had the authority to order more books for the store in, what seemed to be, the ordinary course of business. Under any of these approaches, Penny would be bound.

PROBLEM 1.7

One day Penny's good friend Dan comes into the store and notices that Penny is working really hard. Dan invites Penny to go to lunch, but Penny says she is too busy. Dan says, "I'll tell you what. I will help you, and then you will have time to go to lunch with me." Penny says "O.K., but if you help me, I'm paying for lunch." Dan says, "You've got a deal."

Penny tells Dan to go through a big stack of new books and put them back on the designated shelves. Dan is putting the new books on the shelves when a customer named Sue starts talking with Dan. Dan tells Sue that the best book he ever read is called *Yellow Lollipops Are Best*. Sue looks skeptical, and Dan says, "Go buy it. I'll bet you double your money back that you'll love it." Sue buys the book.

Penny is in the back room and is not aware of any of this. Dan does not tell her because he is embarrassed. A few days later Dan leaves the country to explore the world for an indefinite period of time. A week later Sue comes in to the store and demands double her money back because she HATED *Yellow Lollipops Are Best*. Penny refuses. If Sue sues, is it likely that she will get double her money back?

Analysis

In this situation, we first must ask whether Dan was Penny's agent or just a friend putting a few books on the shelves. The definition of agency is very simple: all that is required is a manifestation of consent by the principal that the agent act on the principal's behalf and subject to the principal's control, and the agent manifests consents to so act. Here, Penny "manifested consent" that Dan shelve books. (In fact she bought him lunch in exchange for his help.) Penny tells Dan what to do and how to do it, and Dan agrees, either verbally or impliedly from his taking on the task requested. That makes Dan Penny's agent. However, we still need to ask what authority Dan has to act on Penny's behalf. There does not seem to be a claim of actual authority here. Penny did not tell Dan to talk with customers or to sell books. She just asked him to help put books on the shelves, and authority to interact with customers probably cannot be implied from those instructions.

However, there is a question of whether Dan had apparent authority. By having Dan perform work on behalf of the bookstore, Penny may have created the impression that Dan was a store employee. If store employees typically have the authority to make double your money back guaranties, Dan might have had apparent authority for his action, and Penny might be bound by it. In order to evaluate this problem, we would want to know additional facts, such as whether store employees have uniforms or nametags to identify them as store employees—in other words, whether it was reasonable for Sue to assume that Dan worked for the store based on the fact that Dan was performing a task for the store. If so, AND if store employees occasionally convey money back offers, Penny will be liable to Sue under apparent authority. Even if there are not enough facts to show that Penny and/or the bookstore created a reasonable inference of Dan's authority, it is possible that Penny might still be liable under an estoppel argument. Asking Dan to shelve books for the store might negligently create some appearance of authority or might allow for a situation in which Dan could misrepresent his authority to Sue. Furthermore, Sue could argue that she relied on the appearance of Dan's authority AND changed her position by buying the *Yellow Lollipops Are Best* book in reliance on that appearance of authority. In that instance, it is quite possible that a court would find that Penny was estopped from denying Dan's authority and would have to pay Sue. Note that there is no allegation the Penny ratified Dan's agreement with Sue, so that would not be an issue here.

AGENCY ANALYSIS SUMMARY FOR PRINCIPAL'S LIABILITY IN TORT AND/OR CONTRACT

In addressing an agency question involving a principal's responsibility for an agent's actions, it might be helpful to use the following questions as an analysis flow chart:

☑ Is there a Principal-Agent relationship?

☑ If so, does the issue involve a tort or a contract?

Tort

If the issue involves a tort, then in order to determine whether the principal is liable, students should evaluate the following questions:

☑ Is there an Employee ("EE")/Employer ("ER") relationship?

- Did the Principal have the right to exert control over the means and manner in which the Agent performed the task(s)?

☑   If the Agent is an EE, did the tort occur within the scope of the employment or was it clearly outside the scope ("frolic or detour")?

- If the tort was intentional with no purpose to serve the ER, was it foreseeable (characteristic of the risks that arise from the employment)?

☑   Even if there is not an EE/ER relationship, is there sufficient control to create a "non-employee agent," and, if so, did the tort occur within the scope of that control?

☑   Even if there is no control exercised over the Agent, does the event fall into an exception such as an inherently dangerous activity, a non-delegable duty, or negligent hiring?

☑   Even if there is no liability for the Principal under a control analysis, is there a claim for Apparent Agency because the third party reasonably relied on the appearance of agency and was harmed as a result of that reliance?

Contract

If the issue involves a contract, then in order to determine whether the Principal is bound, students should evaluate the following questions:

☑   Did the Principal give Actual Authority to the Agent (either express or implied)?

☑   Did the Principal make some manifestation to the third party creating Apparent Authority?

☑   Was the Principal undisclosed, creating liability of an undisclosed principal (formerly Inherent Agency Power (IAP))?

☑   Did the Principal ratify the contract?

- Do any exceptions apply (didn't know all the facts, partial ratification, unfair to third party)?

☑   Is Estoppel an issue?

- Did the Principal do something wrong, or fail to do something, that created an impression with the third party?

- Did the third party rely and alter his or her position to his or her detriment?

AGENT'S LIABILITY

Agent's Liability for Torts

As mentioned above, an agent is liable for his or her tortious conduct regardless of whether the principal is also liable through vicarious liability. (*Third Restatement* § 7.01.) Unless some applicable statute provides otherwise, a person is liable for his or her wrongdoing. The fact that an agent might have been acting as an employee and/or under the authority of a principal does not eliminate the agent's liability. These factors merely impact whether the principal might <u>also</u> be liable for the agent's torts.

Agent's Liability for Contracts

Typically an agent is not liable as a party to the contracts that that agent enters into on behalf of a disclosed principal, unless there are special circumstances and/or the parties agree that the agent will be liable under the contract. However, there are two situations in which the agent will usually be treated as a party to a contract. These situations occur when the agent is acting on behalf of:

☑   An undisclosed principal; or

☑   An unidentified principal (also known as a "partially disclosed principal")

An **undisclosed principal** exists when an agent is acting on behalf of a principal, but the agent does not tell the third party (and the third party does not know) that the agent is acting on behalf of a principal. Because the third party thinks it is entering into an agreement with the agent and no other person is disclosed, the agent is presumed to be a party to the agreement and is bound by the agreement.

An **unidentified principal** (also known as a partially disclosed principal) exists when an agent tells the third party that the agent is acting on behalf of a principal, but the identity of the principal is not disclosed. Because an unidentified party may not enter into a contract, the agent is usually treated as a party to the agreement and is bound by the agreement.

In either of these instances, once the agreement is signed (or otherwise "agreed to"), the agent is bound by the agreement, even if the principal is subsequently disclosed or identified, unless the parties specifically agree that the agent will not be bound, or the original agreement provides that, upon identification of the principal, the agent will no longer be bound. However, **the**

principal might also be bound by the agreement. When both the agent and the principal are bound, if the third party wishes to sue for a breach of the contract, in many states, the third party must often elect whether to sue the agent or the principal. (In other states, the third party may sue both the agent and the principal, but may only recover for damages once.) It is important to note that in most situations in which an agent would be found liable under an agreement entered into for a principal, provided that the agent acted with the principal's authority and did not cause the breach of the agreement, the agent would have a claim for indemnification from the principal.

Students should also be aware that an agent might incur liability if the agent enters into an agreement without the authority to do so from the principal. If the agent enters into an agreement with a third party, purporting to bind a principal, yet the agent actually lacks the authority to do so, the agent could be liable to the third party for breach of the agent's **warranty of authority**. Alternatively, if the principal were to be bound by such an agreement (for example, under an apparent authority claim), the principal might have a claim against the agent for actions that were taken without authority.

To summarize the potential liability of an agent in a contract fact pattern:

☑ If the principal is disclosed and the agent, with authority to do so, enters into an agreement with a third party, then, generally, the principal will be bound but the agent will not.

☑ If the principal is undisclosed or unidentified and the agent, <u>with</u> authority to do so, enters into an agreement with a third party, then, generally, the principal will be bound, but the agent will also be bound.

☑ If the principal is undisclosed or unidentified and the agent, <u>without</u> authority to do so, enters into an agreement with a third party, then the agent will be bound, but the principal is not typically bound unless the circumstances trigger the provisions of the *Third Restatement* (discussed above) for liability of an undisclosed principal, or there is some additional action (such as ratification) on the part of the principal.

☑ If the principal is disclosed and the agent, without authority to do so, enters into an agreement with a third party, then, depending upon the circumstances, the principal may or may not be bound, and the agent (although probably not bound) could be liable to the third party for a breach of the agent's warranty of authority, or could be liable to the principal for the damages caused by the agent's improper actions.

DUTIES IN AGENCY

Duties of the Agent to the Principal

One of the concepts that is introduced in agency (that will arise in the context of partnership and corporations as well as other entities) is the idea that taking responsibility for acting on behalf of another carries with it certain duties beyond the mere completion of the task involved. These duties often relate to the ways in which the task is performed and the responsibilities that accompany the trusted role of the agent. Of course, an agent will have obligations to act consistently with any contractual duties the agent might have to the principal, to act within the scope of the agent's actual authority, and to comply with the principal's lawful instructions. However, there is a long list of additional duties for which an agent is responsible under the *Third Restatement*. While a class on agency and partnership might involve a more in-depth exploration of these duties, we will just address them briefly. These duties include:

☑ **Duty of care, competence, and diligence:** An agent has a duty to the principal to act with the care, competence, and diligence normally exercised by agents in similar circumstances unless the agent has special skills or knowledge, which would require the agent to act at the commensurate, higher level of skill or knowledge. (*Third Restatement* § 8.08.)

☑ **Duty of loyalty:** The agent has a duty to act loyally for the principal's benefit in all matters connected with the agency. (*Third Restatement* § 8.01.)

☑ **Duty not to acquire material benefits arising out of the agency:** The agent may not acquire a material benefit from a third party in connection with transactions or actions taken on behalf of the principal or otherwise through the agent's position. (*Third Restatement* § 8.02.)

☑ **Duty not to act as (or on behalf of) an adverse party:** An agent may not deal with the principal as or on behalf of an adverse party in a transaction connected with the agency relationship. (*Third Restatement* § 8.03.)

☑ **Duty not to compete:** The agent may not compete with the principal or take action on behalf of or otherwise assist the principal's competitors. (*Third Restatement* § 8.04.) (Note that this prohibition does not extend beyond the end of the agency relationship and does not prohibit an agent's preparing to compete, following the end of the agency relationship, provided the conduct is not otherwise wrongful.)

☑ **Duty not to use principal's property:** An agent may not use property of the principal for the agent's own purposes or the purposes of a third party. (*Third Restatement* § 8.05(1).) Moreover, an agent may not mingle the principal's property with anyone else's, including the agent's. (*Third Restatement* § 8.12.)

☑ **Duty not to use confidential information:** An agent may not use or communicate confidential information of the principal for the agent's own purposes or for the purposes of a third party. (*Third Restatement* § 8.05(2).) (Note that this prohibition would typically prevent the use or disclosure of confidential information learned during the agency relationship, even after the termination of that agency relationship.)

☑ **Duty of good conduct:** An agent must, within the scope of the agency, act reasonably and refrain from conduct that is likely to damage the principal's enterprise. (*Third Restatement* § 8.10.)

☑ **Duty to provide information:** An agent has a duty to provide the principal with facts that the agent knows, has reason to know or should know, if the agent knows or should know that the principal would want to know those facts or if the facts are material to the agent's duties to the principal, but only if providing the facts to the principal does not violate a superior duty owed by the agent to another person. (*Third Restatement* § 8.11.)

While the principal may waive some of these duties, such a waiver requires that the principal be fully informed and that the agent still act in good faith and still deal fairly with the principal. (*Third Restatement* § 8.06.) If an agent violates these duties without the consent of the fully-informed principal, the agent will be liable to the principal for damages. In the alternative, the agent could be liable to disgorge to the principal any profit made by the agent in violation of a duty, even if the principal could not have made the same profit.

Duties of the Principal to the Agent

It is also important to be aware that the principal has certain duties to the agent who is taking the responsibility to act on the principal's behalf. These duties include:

☑ **Duty to indemnify:** A principal must typically indemnify an agent for costs, expenses, and/or damages incurred by the agent in the scope of the agency (provided the agent is acting within the scope of the agent's actual authority) or when acting for the principal's benefit and/or in accordance with any agreement between the agent and the principal. (*Third Restatement* § 8.14.)

☑ **Duty of good faith and fair dealing:** A principal must deal with its agent fairly and in good faith. This duty includes an obligation to inform the agent about risks of physical harm or financial loss that the principal knows, has reason to know, or should know are present in the agent's work but are unknown to the agent. (*Third Restatement* § 8.15.)

Problems involving a principal's duties typically involve some damage or wrong done to, or incurred by, the agent and a question about the agent's ability to seek redress from the principal.

In evaluating an agency question involving the potential liability of an agent, students should ask:

☑ Did the agent violate any duty to the principal?

☑ Did the agent violate any duty to a third party?

☑ Did the agent willfully or negligently damage a third party?

☑ For what damages, if any, might the agent be liable?

☑ If the agent has incurred any costs, expenses or damages, does the agent have a claim for indemnification against the principal?

PROBLEM 1.8

Peter hires Alex to drive his classic, convertible car from Massachusetts to San Diego. Peter agrees to pay Alex $500, plus reasonable expenses for gas and lodging, provided the car arrives in San Diego undamaged and within two weeks of Alex's departure. Alex agrees to take the job. As Alex is driving, he realizes that people think the car is "cool," and, as a result, he might be able to make some additional money "on the side." At various points along the way, Alex gives rides to other travelers who pay him for the ride. Occasionally, Alex also stops near various tourist attractions and lets people take pictures posing in the car. Between the pictures and the rides, Alex makes an additional $700. After Alex delivers the car to Peter in San Diego, Peter pays Alex the $500. Peter then says, "Alex, you did a great job. I wish I could pay you more." Alex says, "That's ok. I made $700 using your car to sell rides and photos on the drive out to San Diego." Peter then demands that Alex pay him the $700 even though there was no damage to the car. Will Peter prevail?

Analysis

Because Alex agreed to act on behalf of Peter, Alex is Peter's agent. As an agent, Alex has certain duties to Peter. One of those duties is not to obtain a material benefit from third parties in connection with actions taken on behalf of the principal or otherwise through the agent's use of the agent's position. Another duty is not to use property of the principal for the agent's own purposes. Alex clearly violated these duties to Peter by using the classic car for Alex's own benefit and profit. While Alex might try to argue that Peter did not prohibit such activities as long as Alex arrived in San Diego within two weeks, this argument is unlikely to prevail, especially given the requirement that any waiver of an agent's duties by the principal must be a "fully informed" waiver. Alex might also argue that even if he did violate a duty (or duties) to Peter, the car was not damaged, and thus, Alex does not owe Peter any money. However, the proper remedy in this situation is not based merely on "damages" to Peter. Alex must turn over to Peter the benefit Alex obtained from his breach of duty to Peter. The law would require that Alex hold the benefits/profits of his breach of duty in "constructive trust" for Peter. Therefore, Peter may recover the $700 that Alex obtained using Peter's car in violation of Alex's duties to Peter.

CHAPTER 2

General Partnerships

A partnership is the simplest form of entity. It may be formed by two or more people working together. Partnerships, functioning as business entities, have existed longer than any other entity. In some ways the rules are the most basic, but they form the building blocks for an understanding of other entities. Because more than one person is involved, partnerships must define the rules and principles that govern the relationships among the partners, the relationship between each partner and the partnership, and the relationships between the partnership and outside parties.

A partnership is

- ☑ an association of two or more persons
- ☑ to carry on as co-owners of a business
- ☑ for profit.

"Let's go to the movie together" is not a partnership; "Let's make a movie together" is a partnership. The association between or among the partners must be voluntary, although it does not need to be with the knowledge or intent to form a partnership. The association does not need be in the form of a contract. The association can be an understanding between or among two or more people who are working together. There is no requirement that the "persons" be two individuals. The association may involve any two entities that are considered "persons" under law.

Characteristics of a Typical Partnership

The following is a list of features that are indications of a general partnership. Note that not all of these characteristics are required in order for an endeavor to be deemed to be a partnership; rather, they are used to help evaluate if an endeavor is a partnership.

- ☑ A partnership cannot be another entity (such as an LLC).

☑ Owners in a partnership generally make some contribution (which need not be monetary) in exchange for their share in the partnership.

☑ Partners generally share the profits of the business.

☑ Partners generally share the risk of financial loss.

☑ Partners jointly share the management, but equal votes or control is not necessary.

☑ Note, other individuals can be hired who are not partners (e.g., associates).

There are also features that might be present but do not necessarily create a partnership.

For example:

☑ Joint ownership alone does NOT automatically mean that a partnership exists.

☑ Neither sharing gross returns nor giving capital to an enterprise, independently, is sufficient to create a partnership.

☑ Sharing profits in a business is *prima facie* evidence that a partnership exists, **EXCEPT** where those profits are received as (a) debt service, (b) wages, (c) rent, or (d) annuity. (Note that *prima facie* evidence creates a rebuttable presumption, not a conclusive presumption.)

The best test to evaluate whether a partnership exists is to ask the question: "**Is it the intent of the parties to carry on, as co-owners, a definite business?**" The question of whether an endeavor is a partnership is a question of fact. Students must evaluate the factual circumstances to determine if there is sufficient evidence of the partnership characteristics mentioned above to create a partnership.

Sometimes the question arises of whether a relationship is a partnership or an employer-employee relationship. In such a situation, a court will examine:

☑ **The intent of the parties** (although this is not definitive);

☑ **The language of the agreement**, if any;

☑ **The conduct of the parties toward third parties**;

☑ **The treatment of the returns of the business** (evaluating whether there is a sharing of profits and losses)—As discussed above, sharing profits in a business is prima facie evidence that a partnership exists, rather than an employer-employee relationship, EXCEPT where those profits are received as wages (e.g., a commission); and

☑ **Who bears the risk of financial loss.**

The determination of whether an endeavor is a "partnership" can be critical because, once an entity is classified as a partnership, there are certain attributes that will also be present in the partnership. Many of these attributes arise in the following categories:

☑ **Liabilities—Each partner is jointly and severally liable for the debts of the partnership.** This feature of general partnerships means that if the partnership's assets are not sufficient to cover a debt, the partners are *personally* liable for that debt. In addition, each partner has the power to independently create obligations and liabilities for the partnership.

☑ **Control**—Each partner has the ability to participate in the control and management of the partnership. Under the revised Uniform Partnership Act (1997) ("RUPA"), each partner is entitled to one vote, regardless of how much capital he or she contributed. Alternative voting standards may be established by agreement among the partners.

☑ **Returns**—In a partnership, profits are shared equally among partners. When a partnership is dissolved, the money is divided up among the partners. Most states provide that profits are allocated evenly among the partners, regardless of how much money was contributed by each partner. The partners can also change this feature by an agreement to allocate profits based on the amount contributed to the partnership or using some other measure they might determine appropriate.

☑ **Tax treatment**—Partnerships are not taxed on their income. Instead, the tax responsibility (or credit, as the case may be) for the profits or losses of the partnership is "passed through" to the partners to include on their respective "personal" tax returns.

- ☑ **Fiduciary duties**—Partners owe fiduciary duties to each other and to the partnership. These duties are detailed below.

The Default Rules

Partnerships are generally governed by state law. Most states have adopted some version of RUPA, and the rules in each state's adopted version of RUPA outline the rules that will govern partnerships. These respective codified versions of RUPA are also referred to as the partnership "**default rules**" because these rules typically apply if the partnership is not governed by a partnership agreement, or if the partnership agreement does not cover a particular area. The default rules are intended to fill any (and all) gaps in the partnership agreement. While most provisions of RUPA may be modified by agreement among the partners, there are certain areas that may not be modified. Some significant examples of these limitations are set forth in section 103 of RUPA and may not be limited by a partnership agreement, including that a partnership agreement may NOT:

- ☑ Unreasonably restrict a partner's access to books and records of the partnership;

- ☑ Eliminate the general duty of loyalty (although specific exceptions may be approved) (Note that Delaware permits the elimination of liability for breach of fiduciary duties, including the duty of loyalty, if specified in the partnership agreement. However the actions of the partners are still subject to the obligation of good faith and fair dealing, and few other states allow such complete limitation of the duty of loyalty.)

- ☑ Unreasonably reduce the duty of care;

- ☑ Eliminate the obligation of good faith and fair dealing (although certain reasonable standards by which the performance of this duty is measured may be established);

- ☑ Vary the power of a partner to dissociate;

- ☑ Vary the right of a court to expel a partner under specific circumstances;

- ☑ Vary the requirement to wind up the partnership business in certain circumstances; or

- ☑ Restrict the rights of third parties under RUPA.

Remember, the default rules are not the best rules or even the rules that a particular state's legislature thinks provide the best outcome; the default rules are just the rules that apply in the absence of a partnership agreement. Other than some of the limited areas above, partners often alter the default rules through the partnership agreement.

JOINT VENTURES

A joint venture is a business endeavor undertaken by two or more parties. Joint ventures typically have a limited scope and are usually for a limited time. For these reasons, some people will distinguish joint ventures from traditional partnerships. However, to the extent that any joint endeavor, whether it is called a "joint venture," "partnership" or something else, represents an association of two or more persons to carry on as co-owners a business for profit, then it will be treated as a partnership. Of course, merely calling an endeavor a "joint venture" does not make it a partnership. The factual circumstances surrounding the undertaking will determine whether a joint venture meets the standards to be treated as a partnership. However, students should be aware that a fact pattern involving a joint venture is frequently an indication that the partnership rules should be applied.

PARTNERSHIP BY ESTOPPEL

There are instances when, even if someone is not a partner in a partnership, he or she might still be responsible for the debts of the partnership. The most common situation is known as "**partnership by estoppel**." In partnership by estoppel, if A, B, and C are partners, and X is not a partner, X still can be held liable as a partner IF X acts (or fails to act) in a way that leads third parties to reasonably believe X is a partner. In order to be responsible under partnership by estoppel, X must make some manifestation that creates an impression that allows others outside the partnership to reasonably believe that X is a partner, AND the third party, claiming partnership by estoppel, must rely on that impression to his or her detriment.

Rule

Partnership by estoppel requires:

- ☑ **Actual reliance**—The party claiming partnership by estoppel needs to _actually rely_ on the manifestation. It is not enough for the party to claim that he, she or it would have relied on the manifestation;

☑ **The reliance must have been reasonable**—The third party may not assert that partnership by estoppel exists because (for example) the third party thought X looked like A, B, or C, so the third party assumed they were partners, EVEN IF the third party truly did make that assumption; and

☑ **Some manifestation by the alleged partner**—The alleged partner must act or fail to act in some way, which conveys the (albeit incorrect) message that such individual or entity is a partner. Even if the manifestation is not made directly to the third party, it must be traceable back to some action or inaction of the alleged partner.

A similar concept (which is often taught at the same time as partnership by estoppel) involves situations in which a partnership may be held liable for the actions of a non-partner. In these situations, a "non-partner" is treated as though he or she had the authority of an actual partner to bind the partnership. These situations turn on the agency concept of apparent authority. In these instances, a partnership that creates the (albeit incorrect) appearance that an outside non-partner is in fact a partner may be held liable for the actions of that non-partner taken on behalf of the partnership if the third party dealing with the non-partner reasonably believes that the non-partner is a partner. (This concept is known as the **apparent authority of a purported partner**, although it is almost always taught along with partnership by estoppel.)

In order for an apparent partner to be able to bind the partnership, the partnership must have done (or failed to do) something to make it appear that there was a partnership with the non-partner, and a third party must have reasonably believed that the "non-partner" had the authority to act on behalf of the partnership in the transaction in question.

Partnership by estoppel and the apparent authority of a purported partner are two separate concepts: one involves the possibility that a non-partner will be held liable as a partner by estoppel, and the other involves the ability of a non-partner to bind the partnership. These concepts are not necessarily reciprocal; they exist independently of one another.

The issue in partnership by estoppel is the reasonable understanding of the third party; the understanding of the third party must be traceable back to something the non-partner did (or failed to do) to create that understanding. The issue in the apparent authority of a purported partner involves the same language but, although we are still interested in the reasonable understanding of the third party, it must be traceable back to something the partnership did to create that understanding. Furthermore, there is no requirement that the party claiming apparent authority show detrimental reliance, as is the case with partnership by estoppel.

ILLUSTRATIVE EXAMPLE

Assume that A, B, and C are partners in a telemarketing business called "ABC Partnership." E is not a partner but wants to help A, B, and C with their business. Because E knows a lot about computers, she offers to go with A, B, and C when they purchase a large computer system for their business. If A, B, C, and E sit down with the computer sales company, called "CSC," and act like they are all partners, both the partnership and E will have made manifestations, so they might be able to bind each other. If A, B, and C do not pay the bill for the computer system, and CSC reasonably believed that E was a partner and relied on that information in making the sale and delivery of the computer equipment, E might be liable under a partnership by estoppel theory for the unpaid bill. Under a different scenario, if, after the meeting, E calls CSC and changes the order to a better (and more expensive) computer system, ABC Partnership might be bound by E's actions, even if ABC did not want the more expensive system, because of the apparent authority of E, a purported partner.

Remember, the issue here is whether someone, or some entity, is bound even though he, she or it is not a partner or does not have actual authority to act on behalf of the partnership, respectively.

FIDUCIARY OBLIGATIONS OF PARTNERS ("THE PUNCTILIO OF AN HONOR THE MOST SENSITIVE . . . ")

Each partner has fiduciary obligations to the partnership itself and to the other partners in the partnership. These fiduciary obligations fall within the two general duties, **the duty of loyalty** and **the duty of care.** (See RUPA § 404.)

Partnership Duty of Loyalty

The duty of loyalty encompasses the obligation of each partner:

☑　　To account to the partnership for profits, property, or benefits from the conduct (or winding up) of partnership business or the use of partnership property;

☑ To refrain from acting as or on behalf of a party with an adverse interest to the partnership (e.g., avoiding conflicts of interest);

☑ To refrain from competing with the partnership in the subject matter of the partnership business;

☑ To perform all duties to the partnership and the other partners consistent with the obligation of **good faith and fair dealing**.

Partnership Opportunities

One of the best-known partnership cases relating to the fiduciary duty of loyalty is *Meinhard v. Salmon* (164 N.E. 545 (N.Y. 1928)). This seminal case is about the rights of other partners in a partnership opportunity and the right and/or ability of one partner to seize an opportunity that might rightfully belong to the partnership. In the *Meinhard v. Salmon* opinion, Judge Cardozo coined the famous punctilio of honor phrase. ("Many forms of conduct permissible in a workaday world for those acting at arm's length, are forbidden to those bound by fiduciary ties. . . . Not honesty alone, but the punctilio of an honor the most sensitive, is then the standard of behavior." (*Id.* at 546.)) Even though the holding itself and the subsequent law create a balanced assessment of the extent of a partner's right to take advantage of an opportunity, this phrase is often quoted to support any proposition involving fiduciary duty among partners to emphasize the high duty one partner owes to another.

Partners also have a duty (as part of their duty of loyalty) to not take opportunities that belong to the partnership for their personal benefit. With regard to an opportunity presented to the partnership, often the question is what is the nature of the opportunity. Is the "opportunity" just information about the potential to profit in an enterprise outside the scope of the partnership business? If so, disclosure alone might be sufficient. However, if the business opportunity *falls within the scope of the partnership business*, disclosure alone is probably NOT enough. If the opportunity belongs to the partnership, no partner may take the partnership opportunity for him or herself. When faced with a new opportunity that arises out of, or relates to, the partnership business, the managing partner must:

☑ <u>First</u>, **disclose the business opportunity to the other partners;**

☑ **Second, decide whether or not to act on behalf of the partnership and take the opportunity.** (The partners owe a fiduciary obligation to the partnership, and a decision by any partner whether or not to take advantage of the opportunity must be made in good faith.)

Partnership Duty of Care

The duty of care encompasses the standard by which a partner must evaluate and make partnership decisions. A partner typically does not violate his duty of care for mere negligence. Under the duty of care standards articulated in section 404(c) of RUPA, a partner must not engage in:

☑ gross negligence;

☑ reckless conduct;

☑ intentional misconduct; or

☑ a knowing violation of the law.

In addition, every partner has the obligation to discharge his or her duties to the partnership and other partners (and to exercise any rights that he or she might have under partnership law or the partnership agreement) consistent with the obligations of **good faith and fair dealing**.

The Ability to Waive Fiduciary Duties in a Partnership

Often partners wish to waive or limit certain fiduciary duties in a partnership. While waiver is permissible, there are also limitations regarding the extent to which fiduciary duties may be waived, and, of course, there is variation among the states. In general, partners are permitted to waive specific duties, but not general duties, such as the duty of loyalty. Even when permitted by statute, courts tend to frown upon blanket waivers of rights, such as the duty of care and the duty of loyalty. However, partners can waive specific actions that would otherwise fall under the duty of loyalty, such as the right to start a competing business. In addition, many states will require that the waiver of the duty not be "manifestly unreasonable."

Directly related to a partnership's right to waive duties is the ability to ratify an action that would otherwise violate a duty. In general, waiver occurs before the fact, and ratification occurs after the fact. Because it occurs after an action has been taken, ratification almost always involves a specific action and thus may encompass broader actions than might be allowed in a more general waiver. By definition, ratification, at least in theory, is a more informed action. However, in order to be effective, the partners ratifying an action must be fully informed.

– Attorneys and Their Duties to Their Firms

Several partnership cases involve attorneys leaving law firms. These cases center around two concepts: The first is what lawyers may do with regard to the cases and clients of a firm they are leaving while preparing to leave that firm and after leaving that firm. The second involves the question of what, if anything, the lawyers who leave the firm are entitled to receive with regard to work that remains at the firm and what, if anything, the departing partner's former partners are entitled to receive with regard to clients/cases that accompany the departing partner(s).

With regard to best practices when a lawyer leaves a firm, the ABA has guidelines that include:

☑ Notice must be mailed to each client with whom the lawyer had an active attorney-client relationship.

☑ The notice should not encourage the client to sever relations with the firm.

☑ The notice should be brief, dignified, and not disparage the former firm.

In many of these cases involving lawyers leaving their firms, there are certain actions that are improper, which may get the departing lawyer in trouble. These include:

☑ Communicating with clients before giving notice to the firm that they are leaving;

☑ Taking client files;

☑ Lying; and

☑ Not letting clients know they have a choice about whether to stay with the firm or move with the departing attorney.

Actions that are acceptable include:

☑ Looking for and obtaining office space;

☑ Setting up a merger or an affiliation with another firm;

☑ Negotiating with partners (this is distinct from negotiating with associates to join the departing group which might be questionable and is listed below); and

☑ Reminding clients that they have a right to choose their lawyer.

The gray areas that might get attorneys into trouble, but are not per se improper, are:

☑ Contacting clients after notice to the firm, but before leaving; and

☑ Talking to associates about accompanying the lawyer.

Remember, when evaluating a partner's actions, simply planning to do something improper (i.e., planning to breach a duty) is not actually a breach of duty.

EXPULSION

RUPA provides for the expulsion of partners from a partnership under certain circumstances. They include the following. A partner may be expelled:

☑ Pursuant to the partnership agreement;

☑ By unanimous vote of the other partners if it is unlawful to carry on the partnership business with that partner, if there has been a transfer of all (or substantially all) of the partner's transferable interest, or if the partner to be expelled is another entity that is ending its existence; or

☑ By judicial determination if certain circumstances are satisfied involving the wrongful conduct of the partner to be expelled.

However, the provisions of RUPA may be altered. If the partners agree, the partnership agreement may make it much easier (or more difficult) to expel a partner. In fact, typical partnership agreements will provide for expulsion under certain circumstances. These circumstances may mirror those in RUPA, be more restrictive, or less restrictive. In general, such provisions are permissible. However, **even permissible expulsion provisions (and, in fact, all partnership rights and remedies) must be exercised consistent with the obligation of good faith and fair dealing.** Thus, if the partnership agreement allows for the expulsion of any partner for any reason upon a vote of a majority of the other partners, it is permissible to expel a partner who swears too much. However, it is not permissible to expel a partner because there will be fewer partners to share in the firm profits. Regardless of whether a partner is expelled under RUPA or pursuant to the partnership agreement, if the power to expel is exercised in bad faith or for predatory reasons, the duty of good faith and fair dealing present in every partnership agreement is violated, giving rise to an action for damages the affected partner has suffered as a result of his or her expulsion.

THE NATURE OF PARTNERSHIP INTERESTS

Partnership interests are comprised of two sets of rights: "**economic rights**" and "**management rights**."

☑   **Economic rights** include the right to receive money that is distributed from the partnership to the holder of the economic right.

☑   **Management rights** include the right to vote and participate in management of the partnership.

In general, economic rights are transferable and management rights are not, unless the other partners consent. When a partner transfers economic rights, the recipient, typically referred to as the transferee, has the right to obtain money (or other distributions) that otherwise would have been paid by the partnership to the transferor partner. Note that economic rights do not entitle the holder to any right in any of the specific property of the partnership. In fact, no single partner has an interest in, or right to, any specific property owned by the partnership. Moreover, the transferee does not have the right to vote or to become a partner merely by holding economic rights in the partnership.

Transferees may obtain an economic interest in several ways:

☑   By a voluntary transfer by the transferor partner;

☑   By an involuntary transfer by the transferor partner, which may occur due to the enforcement of a judgment against him or her; or

☑   By the death of the transferor partner.

When economic rights are transferred, the transferor will often still hold management rights in the partnership. This dynamic can create difficult situations for the transferee because the transferee does not have the right to vote or even to enforce fiduciary obligations that might be owed to the transferor partner. The transferee is, therefore, dependent on the transferor to enforce certain fiduciary protections and to vote in the transferor's interest. In the case of an involuntary transfer or the death of the transferor, the "support" of the transferor is not available to a transferee; thus, the transferee is often at the mercy of the remaining partners and can only receive a share of the funds, if any, that the partnership decides to distribute. A transferee of a partnership interest may not become a new partner without the vote of all of the other partners in the partnership. Note that these restrictions may be altered by the partnership agreement that could provide for free transferability or for a different vote on the admission of a new partner.

RIGHTS OF PARTNERS IN MANAGEMENT

Any partner has the authority to bind the partnership in the ordinary course of business (unless the partnership agreement says otherwise). However, the approval of a majority of the partners typically is required for decisions made by the partnership relating to the day-to-day operations of the partnership business. The standard default rule is that each partner will have one vote, regardless of the amount of money he or she contributed to the partnership. Matters outside the ordinary course of business, such as selling all of the partnership assets, typically require unanimous approval. Remember that these standards may be altered by the partnership agreement. Sometimes these requirements can create difficulties, especially with an even number of partners. For example, if there are two partners who each own 50% of the partnership, and one wants to stop doing business with a certain supplier, the consent of the other partner would be required. The other partner's consent is necessary because, even though this matter is in the day-to-day business of the partnership, it would require a majority vote, and 50% is not a majority.

A related management rights issue involves a partner's ability to bind the partnership even though that partner might lack actual authority to do so. Because any partner has the right to bind a partnership, one partner might be able to act with apparent authority to bind the partnership. If such an act was in violation of the partnership agreement, the partnership would have a claim against the partner who acted without actual authority. However, the partnership might still be bound if the third party reasonably believed that the partner was acting with actual authority. Note that because unanimity is required for matters outside the ordinary course of business, it is less reasonable for a third party to rely on the apparent authority of a partner purporting to act on behalf of the partnership with regard to a transaction outside of the ordinary course of business. For example, if a "rogue" partner attempting to act with apparent authority tried to sell all of the assets of the partnership, and the third party knew or should have known that the attempted sale involved all of the assets of the partnership, it might not be reasonable to rely on the rogue partner's authority because the third party should have known that unanimous consent is required for such an action.

PARTNERSHIP DISSOLUTION AND DISSOCIATION

When a partnership ends, it goes through three "phases": **dissolution**, **winding up**, and **termination**. This is a little confusing because we are used to thinking of "dissolution" as the end of something. However, in the partnership world, dissolution signals the end of the prior constitution of the partnership. Most partnership dissolutions are followed by winding up and termination. The winding up phase is a neutral period prior to termination when the partnership must conclude its business, sell its assets, pay creditors, and make distributions to its partners. Once the winding up phase has been concluded, the partnership is terminated. Note that during the winding up phase, the partnership may not embark upon new business. Also, the partners may vote to continue the partnership rather than proceeding to termination. In this instance, a vote of all of the partners is required.

Prior to the adoption of RUPA, whenever a partner left a firm, it was deemed to be a "dissolution," and the remaining partners could vote to either continue the partnership or wind up and terminate the partnership. However, RUPA introduced a new term, "dissociation," to apply to partners who withdraw or otherwise terminate their partner status. When a partner leaves a firm, either voluntarily or involuntarily (by expulsion or even death), that is known as dissociation, and it does not necessarily trigger dissolution. (Dissociation is really just a fancy word for "withdrawn.") If the partner does not have the right to leave the partnership, the dissociation is "wrongful," and the dissociated partner might be liable to the partnership for damages. For example, if the partnership is for a term or an undertaking, dissociation prior to the completion of the term or the undertaking would be "wrongful." (An example of a term might be five years. An undertaking might be, "to buy property, repair the building on the property, lease out the property, and then sell the building." Either would represent a span of time, and dissociation before the term or undertaking was completed would be wrongful.) Also, any dissociation in violation of the partnership agreement would be "wrongful." A partnership that is neither for a term or an undertaking is considered "**at-will**." A partner may dissociate from an at-will partnership at any time, provided the partnership agreement does not provide otherwise.

Whether or not the dissociation was wrongful, the dissociated partner is entitled to receive funds that represent his or her share of the partnership (minus any damages). The biggest questions surrounding dissociation are: 1) to what amount is the dissociated partner entitled, and 2) when is it due. Although partnership agreements may, and often do, provide differently, under RUPA dissociated partners are usually entitled to the greater of their share of the "**going concern**" **value** of the partnership or the **liquidation value** of the partnership. The going concern value is the value of the partnership as an operating entity (without the dissociated partner). The liquidation value of the partnership is the value one could get for selling all of the assets of the business. If the partnership is "at-will," the dissociated partner is entitled to his or her share of the business shortly after dissociating. If the partnership is for a term or an undertaking, the dissociated partner is not entitled to be paid for his or her share of the partnership until the end of the term or the completion of the undertaking. Often there is an exception to this delay in payment, if the dissociated partner can show that payment for his or her share would not create a hardship for the partnership.

The general rule, unless it is altered by the partnership agreement, is that a dissociated partner is entitled to receive:

☑　The value of its partnership interest (measured as the greater of their share of the going concern value or the liquidation value of the partnership); minus

☑　The dissociated partner's share of any liabilities; minus

☑　Any damages for wrongful dissociation; plus

☑　Interest paid from the date of dissociation to the date of payment;

☑　Payable within 120 days provided the partnership is at-will or at the end of the term or undertaking, unless payment would not create a hardship for the partnership.

ILLUSTRATIVE EXAMPLE

Students often struggle with the difference between going concern value and liquidation value. There is no way to have a blanket rule about which valve is greater without information about the specific business. For example, an internet social networking business, which sells advertising and memberships, might have a very small liquidation value, but a larger going concern value. If the business were liquidated, its members would disappear, and it would not be able to sell advertising. It probably has very few assets. However, as a "going concern," it might bring in a great deal of money each year. That business would have a much larger going concern value than liquidation value. On the other hand, consider a business that manufactures diamond drill bits. Diamond drill bits are used to penetrate very hard surfaces without breaking. Imagine that this business has collected a large amount of raw material inventory (i.e., diamonds) when the price of diamonds skyrockets. Because there is a limit on how much people will pay for diamond drill bits, the business does not make very many sales. It probably has a relatively low going concern value. However, if it were to sell its inventory of diamonds, it could make a substantial amount of money. This business has a much higher liquidation value than going concern value.

Liabilities for Departing Partners

When partners dissociate, they are no longer partners in the partnership. Because they have changed status, they are not personally liable for debts of the partnership that arise following dissociation. There is an exception to this limitation for any third party who does not have actual or constructive notice of the partner's dissociation and enters into a transaction with the partnership within two years after the dissociation in reliance upon that third party's reasonable belief that the dissociated partner is a partner. This exception only applies if the third party did not have notice (regardless of his reasonable belief) of the partner's dissociation or is not deemed to have constructive notice based on a notice of dissociation. This structure provides an incentive for dissociated partners to provide notice of their dissociation to third parties. Note that a dissociated partner might also have apparent authority to bind a partnership. This potential provides additional incentive for the partnership to provide notice of the dissociation to third parties.

The dissociated partner is still liable to creditors of the partnership for partnership debts that arose prior to the dissociation. This might seem unfair if the dissociated partner's share of these liabilities has already been deducted from any payments to the dissociated partner. However, the law does not allow an agreement between the partnership and a departing partner to alter a third party's claim or potential claim. Therefore, the dissociated partner remains personally liable for pre-dissociation debts, even after receiving payment for his or her interest from the partnership, but the dissociated partner has the right to seek indemnification from the partnership and, ultimately, from the partners for any claims made against that dissociated partner, following the purchase of that dissociated partner's interest in the partnership.

Liabilities for New Partners

Conversely, if a new partner joins the partnership, that partner is ONLY personally liable for new debts that are incurred once that person joins the firm. (Of course, any capital contribution made by the new partner will be subject to a judgment against the partnership irrespective of whether it arises out of an event that occurred before the new partner joined the firm. However, the new partner would not have personal liability for such a debt.)

Obligations to Dissociated Partners

In general, once a partner has dissociated from a partnership, that partner no longer has an ownership interest in the partnership, and, therefore, is no longer owed any fiduciary duties by the partners or the partnership. However, in certain situations (for example, when there is a delay in the buyout of a dissociated partner's interest in the partnership and the final buyout price will be determined by the future earnings of the partnership), the dissociated partner might still claim that he or she is owed limited fiduciary duties. (Note that partners are owed certain fiduciary duties during the winding up of the partnership business. RUPA § 404.) On the other hand, depending on the specific facts of the buyout, the language of the partnership agreement and the jurisdiction, a dissociated partner (even one with some continuing interest in the partnership) might also only be entitled to the rights of a transferee of an economic interest and would not be entitled to fiduciary claims relating to alleged mismanagement of the partnership.

CHAPTER 3

The Structure of the Corporation

Corporations have certain features. Under the law a corporation is a separate "person." This means it can own property, it has certain "rights," and it can sue and be sued. Let's look at how this "person" functions.

A corporation is owned by shareholders. The shareholders are entitled to the residual value of the corporation after it has paid its creditors. **Shareholders** (at least in their capacity as shareholders) do not participate in the management of the corporation; they merely elect the individuals who serve on the corporation's **Board of Directors**. The Board of Directors then appoints **officers**, such as the president, treasurer, and secretary of the corporation. A typical structure of ABC Corporation might look as follows:

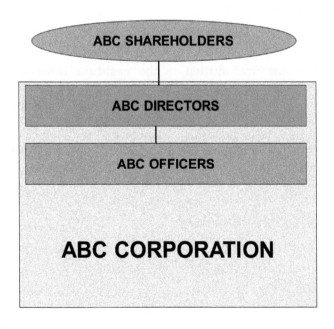

ABC SHAREHOLDERS

ABC DIRECTORS

ABC OFFICERS

ABC CORPORATION

In general, the responsibilities of the three tiers are divided as follows:

Shareholders

Shareholders do not participate directly in the management of the corporation. Rather, corporations are run by a Board of Directors. Directors are elected by the shareholders. This type of structure—where a core group manages the firm—is known as "centralized management." While shareholders do not directly manage the corporation, they do have the right to vote on certain matters. Shareholders typically vote on:

- ☑ The election of directors (While at present, shareholders of publicly held companies do not have the right to nominate directors and typically may only vote on a 'slate' of directors proposed by the Board, the Dodd-Frank Wall Street Reform and Consumer Protection Act of 2010 (the "Dodd-Frank Act") authorizes the Securities and Exchange Commission to create mechanisms through which shareholders may nominate, and solicit votes for, directors.);

- ☑ Amendments to the Articles of Incorporation and (usually) the Bylaws;

- ☑ Fundamental transactions such as mergers and acquisitions; and

- ☑ Miscellaneous matters such as the approval of independent auditors and non-binding resolutions.

Shareholders are entitled to the **residual interest** in the assets of a corporation. This means that upon **liquidation** of a corporation, the shareholders are entitled to receive the value of the assets remaining in the corporation after all of the corporation's obligations have been satisfied. ("Liquidation" refers to the process at the end of a corporation's existence when the corporation's creditors are paid, and its remaining cash and assets (which have not been sold and turned into cash) are distributed to its shareholders.)

Board of Directors

The directors of the corporation are responsible to the Shareholders for managing the corporate assets.

The directors of a corporation:

- ☑ Are elected by the shareholders;

- ☑ Serve for a set term;

- ☑ Typically make the major decisions relating to the operation of the corporation; and

- ☑ Select the officers (who handle the day-to-day affairs of the corporation).

Officers

The officers of a corporation are selected by the Board of Directors and manage the day-to-day operations of the corporation. The typical officers in a corporation are the President (also sometimes called the Chief Executive Officer or "CEO"), the Chief Financial Officer (also sometimes called the Treasurer or "CFO"), and the Secretary. Other officers may include a Chief Operating Officer (also sometimes called the "COO") and various Vice Presidents.

Note that a shareholder may also serve as a director and as an officer, although some states have limitations on the offices that may be held by the same person. For example, some states' corporate statutes provide that the offices of President and Secretary may not be held by the same person.

FORMING A CORPORATION

Corporations are created under state law. In order to form a corporation, **Articles of Incorporation** must be filed with the Secretary of State in the state that has been selected for the corporation's formation. Articles of Incorporation typically include at a minimum:

- ☑ The name of the corporation;

- ☑ The purpose of the corporation (which may be as broad as "any lawful purpose");

- ☑ The number of shares that are authorized for each class of stock of the corporation; and

- ☑ The name and address of the agent for service of process.

There are several optional provisions, which may also be included in the Articles of Incorporation, such as selection of initial directors, limitations on directors' and officers' liability, restrictions on certain transfers of the corporation's shares, dividend requirements, and/or pre-emptive rights for shareholders. These supplemental provisions will vary with the needs and the complexity of the organization.

The person who signs the Articles of Organization is known as the "**Incorporator**." Once the Articles have been properly filed, a corporation is established. If initial directors were not appointed in the Articles of Incorporation, the Incorporator will appoint initial directors who will hold an organizational meeting to adopt **Bylaws**. The Bylaws are the rules that govern the basic internal operations of the corporation and its relations with its shareholders, officers, and directors. At the organizational meeting, the directors will also appoint officers, issue stock, and establish the basic framework for the organization. Assuming the Articles of Incorporation are properly filed, the corporation is known as a "*de jure*" corporation.

DE FACTO CORPORATIONS

Occasionally, corporations are not properly formed. However, the would-be shareholders believe that, and act as though, the corporation was properly formed. In these instances, the shareholders of the organization are sometimes given corporate protection under an equitable doctrine known as "*de facto*" corporation status. In order to assert the protections of a de facto corporation, there are three requirements:

☑ A good faith, substantial effort must have been made to comply with the state's incorporation statute;

☑ The business must have had a legal right to incorporate; and

☑ The parties must have had a good faith belief that, and acted as though, they had, in fact, formed a corporation.

If these standards are met, the organization may be granted de facto corporation status, which means that the principals will have limited liability from the debts of the corporation as though the corporation had been properly formed. Given modern filing procedures, it is unlikely, though not impossible, that de facto corporation status will arise. Because most states provide notice when Articles of Incorporation are properly filed and notice when the Articles of Incorporation are not properly filed, Incorporators will almost always have notice (or constructive notice) of whether the Articles were successfully filed. Therefore, it is difficult to have a good faith belief that the corporation has been formed when it has not.

CORPORATION BY ESTOPPEL

Even when de facto corporation status is not available, it is still possible that the principals of a would-be corporation will be protected by the doctrine of **corporation by estoppel**. Under this doctrine, if a third party treats an organization as though it were a corporation, that third party may be estopped from denying the organization's corporate existence if the denial would result in unjust harm to the principals. Conversely, if an organization holds itself out as a corporation (even though it is not), that organization will be estopped from denying its own corporate existence to avoid an obligation or to obtain an unfair benefit.

In order for the doctrine of corporation by estoppel to apply:

☑ The parties need to have consistently treated the organization as though it were a corporation; and

☑ If one party were allowed to deny the existence of the corporation, that party would obtain an unfair advantage or benefit.

One important feature of the corporation by estoppel doctrine is that it almost never applies in situations involving tort victims. Because the doctrine requires the parties to treat the organization as though it were a corporation, it is unlikely that a tort victim would have prior dealings with the organization in a way that treated the organization as though it were a corporation. The corporation by estoppel doctrine typically arises in contract cases. Note that it can be applied to benefit the owners of an organization or against the owners to prevent them from voiding a contract.

There are many instances in which the corporation by estoppel doctrine will overlap with the de facto corporation doctrine.

ILLUSTRATIVE EXAMPLE

Jamie and David want to form the JD Bicycle Corporation, and they hire a lawyer to file the Articles of Incorporation and organize the corporation. The lawyer tells them that the corporation will be formed in a day, that the lawyer will handle all the paperwork, and that Jamie and David should contact him in a year to make sure that the minutes of the annual meeting are properly drafted. Unfortunately, the lawyer is hit on the head with a heavy law book, develops amnesia, and never files the Articles of Incorporation. However, Jamie and David are never notified of the failure to file, and they assume that JD Bicycle Corporation has been properly formed.

JD Bicycle Corporation orders 100 bicycles from Bike Maker, Inc. However, the bicycle business does not go well, and JD Bicycle Corporation is unable to pay the bill for the 100 bicycles. In investigating its ability to sue in order to collect on the unpaid bill, Bike Maker, Inc. finds out that the JD Bicycle Corporation was never properly formed. Bike Maker, Inc. then sues Jamie and David personally for the outstanding obligation on the bill for the 100 bicycles. However, it is likely that Jamie and David, who have a good faith belief that JD Bicycle Corporation was indeed a validly formed corporation, will be protected by the de facto corporation doctrine. It is likely that Jamie and David will ALSO be protected by the corporation by estoppel doctrine since Bike Maker, Inc. treated the JD Bicycle Corporation as a corporation.

However, imagine that Jamie and David set up a line of bicycles in front of their store. One day, a man named Vic is passing by, and stops to admire the bicycles. Unfortunately, one of JD Bicycle Corporation's employees did not set the kickstands on the bikes properly. When Vic stops at the end of the row of bikes, all of the bikes fall over and land on his foot, breaking two of his toes. If Vic finds out the JD Bicycle Corporation was never properly formed and tries to sue Jamie and David personally, it is likely that Jamie and David will be protected by the de facto corporation doctrine, but not by corporation by estoppel since Vic never dealt with JD Bicycle Corporation as though it were a corporation.

PROMOTERS

Promoters are the people who organize the corporation before it is formed. They will often perform work for the corporation and enter into contracts on behalf of the proposed corporation. While often times the promoter is also the incorporator, this does not need to be the case. Incorporators are the people who actually form the corporation and execute the Articles of Incorporation. Promoters often do work related to laying the "ground work" for the corporation's business or operations, such as entering into contracts, prospectively, on behalf of the yet to be formed corporation. These contracts might be intended to secure or provide important elements of the soon-to-be formed corporation's business, such as potential customers, supplies or inventory, distribution channels, or rental space. Sometimes promoters will also coordinate the investment that is to be made in the new corporation before it is formed.

Promoters have fiduciary duties (both a duty of care and a duty of loyalty) to the corporation they promote and to those who will eventually buy stock in the corporation. These duties are the same fiduciary duties that we have already seen in agency since a promoter is an agent for the proposed corporation.

A question that frequently arises in this area involves the contracts into which the promoter has entered on behalf of the corporation. The basic rules are that the promoter is personally bound by any contract entered into on behalf of a corporation that has not yet been formed (whether the contract was entered into in the promoter's name or in the name of the proposed corporation), unless there is a clear intent that the promoter not be bound or the circumstances are such that the promoter could not perform the agreement. Once the corporation is formed, it may be bound by the contract, but only if the corporation agrees to be bound. A corporation may agree to be bound by adopting the contract, and a corporation may adopt the contract by:

☑ Expressly ratifying the contract (often through a novation (i.e., the substitution of a new obligation for an old one)); or

☑ Impliedly ratifying the contract through the corporation's actions (for example, by paying the rent on a lease) or by accepting or acknowledging the benefits of the contract.

If any of these actions are taken, the corporation will be deemed to have "ratified" (and, therefore, adopted) the contract, and the corporation will be bound. (Note that a corporation might also acquire rights under a contract as a third party beneficiary.)

Ratification by the corporation does not, however, release the promoter from liability. The promoter remains bound under the agreement, unless there is an agreement (a novation) from the other parties to the contract to release the promoter from liability. Typically, such an agreement would provide that only the corporation is bound and not the promoter. If both the promoter and the corporation are bound, and the other party to the contract wishes to sue for breach of contract, that party usually must choose whether it is going to sue the promoter or the corporation. If the corporation has adopted the contract and the promoter is sued, the promoter will usually have a claim for indemnification against the corporation. However, such a claim would be dependent upon whether there were resources remaining in the corporation. If the corporation is never formed, then the promoter is still liable under the contract and has the right to enforce the contract, unless formation of the corporation was an express condition to the contract.

Sometimes there is more than one promoter. In such situations, it is possible that these "co-promoters" will be found to be partners and, as such, will have joint and several liability for the obligations of any one of the promoters that arose out of the activity of setting up the corporation.

CORPORATE CHARACTERISTICS

There are certain important features of corporations:

☑ Being treated as a separate person under the law;

☑ Providing limited liability for its owners;

☑ Creating a division between ownership and control;

☑ Allowing for a flexible capital structure; and

☑ Allowing owners to freely transfer ownership (also called liquidity).

While not an exhaustive list, these represent some of the "hallmarks" of a corporation. These features are explored more extensively below and in the chapters that follow.

THE CORPORATION AS A SEPARATE PERSON

Decisions

A corporation operates through decisions made by its Board of Directors. The Board functions as a "brain" of the corporation. However, because the Board of Directors is not an individual but a group of individuals, it must conduct meetings and make decisions at those meetings. The requirement that a Board of Directors conduct meetings and maintain minutes of those meetings is one of the indications of the functioning of the separate person of the corporation. Other corporate formalities (discussed in more detail below) must be followed as well.

Rights and Lawsuits

A corporation may sue or be sued under the law. It has certain rights, even some constitutional rights. It must also have a "principal place of business," which is typically in the state in which it is headquartered (which may or may not be the state in which the corporation is formed). The corporation must also maintain an agent for service of process in the state in which it was formed so that if someone wants to sue the corporation, there is a public record of where the corporation may be served.

Taxation

The corporation must also file tax returns and pay its own taxes. Corporations are required to pay taxes on the money they earn. (There is an exception to the requirement that a corporation pay its own taxes for S corporations, which are discussed below.) While the corporate tax rate is often (at least slightly) different from the individual tax rate, the concept is the same. In fact, corporations are treated as so separate from their owners that when a corporation wants to take money out of the corporation and distribute it to its shareholders (known as issuing a dividend), the shareholders are typically required to pay taxes on those dividends. Since the corporation has already paid tax on its earnings and the shareholders are taxed again (albeit often at a lower rate), this structure is called "**double taxation**." There are strategies to avoid double taxation such as different entity selection, shifting what would otherwise be corporate income into salary payments to shareholders who are also serving as officers or employees of the corporation, or reinvesting income in, and ultimately selling, the corporation in hopes of transforming ordinary income into capital gains. However, most of these strategies are beyond the scope of this book. Nevertheless, because many structures and transactions are motivated by the shareholders' desire to avoid double taxation, it is important for students to understand.

LIMITED LIABILITY (*HOW TO PRESERVE IT AND HOW PEOPLE LOSE IT*)

The lack of personal liability is the single most important defining feature of a corporation. **The shareholders of a corporation are not personally liable for the debts and obligations of the corporation**. The personal liability of a shareholder is limited to the amount the shareholder has invested in the corporation, which is typically the amount(s) the shareholder initially or subsequently paid to purchase his or her stock. (Of course, if a corporation loses all of its value, the shareholder also loses its rights in the value of the assets of the corporation, but that is not considered "personal" liability since the corporation's creditors do not take that value from the shareholder. The shareholder is merely prevented from receiving that value.)

Limited liability arises out of the fact that a corporation is considered a separate "person" under the law. The corporation's creditors can look only to the corporation's assets for payment, provided that the corporation's owners have adhered to some basic rules. The most important of these rules is that the shareholders must, themselves, treat the corporation as a separate person and not as an extension of themselves. Shareholders do this by following corporate formalities, which include: formal meetings of the shareholders and of the Board of Directors; keeping minutes of those meetings; electing directors; maintaining separate bank accounts for the corporation and not commingling funds; keeping corporate funds and transactions separate from individual funds and transactions; and adequately capitalizing the corporation.

The shareholders of a corporation will want to make sure that the corporation provides notice to clients and customers that those clients and customers are dealing with a corporation so that people who interact with the corporation will be aware that the owners have limited liability. This type of notice can be provided simply by using terms like "Inc.," "Corp.," "Corporation," or "Ltd." in the name of the business and by signing documents on behalf of the corporation in one's capacity as an officer. For example, "Wendy Jones, President, ABC Enterprises, Inc." Finally, the corporation must be a business conducting a business activity, and not merely a liability shield. However, it is **NOT** improper for a firm to become a corporation for the sole and express reason of preventing its shareholders from being personally liable; that is what being a corporation is all about.

There are certain obligations that a corporation must meet in order to have limited liability. Corporations are required to:

- ☑ Follow the rules/formalities;

- ☑ Provide notice to the world that it is a corporation;

- ☑ Treat the corporation as a separate entity from its owner(s) and from sister corporations; and

- ☑ Be a real business, conducting business activities.

EXCEPTIONS TO LIMITED LIABILITY

There are some exceptions to limited liability. Money that was supposed to stay in the corporation, but which was taken out of the corporation as a fraudulent conveyance or an improper dividend, may be recovered by the corporation's creditors (or by a trustee in bankruptcy). However, liability in these situations is only for the amount improperly paid out, NOT for the full amount of the debt. Thus, these situations do not create unlimited liability; they only mean that shareholders might not get to keep money to which the corporation is entitled. In addition, if a shareholder owes money to the corporation for any reason, including for the purchase of stock, that shareholder may be forced to pay that money, even if the corporation has gone bankrupt.

The biggest exception to limited liability occurs when a shareholder loses the protection of the corporation's liability shield and becomes personally liable for the debts of the corporation. When this happens, it is called "**piercing the corporate veil**" because a creditor is able to disregard the protection of the corporation and pursue the personal assets of the shareholder(s).

Piercing the Corporate Veil

If the corporate veil protecting the shareholders from liability is pierced, **a creditor of a corporation can sue the shareholders personally for the debt that creditor is owed by the corporation.**

How Does Someone Pierce the Corporate Veil?

In order to pierce the corporate veil, a creditor of the corporation must have a court rule that the veil may be pierced. In order to obtain this ruling, the creditor must first show that the separate existence between the shareholder(s) and the corporation has not been respected. **If the separate existence of the corporation has been respected, it is extremely unlikely that a creditor will be permitted to pierce the corporate veil.** If the separate existence of the corporation has NOT been respected, the legal standards become more complicated and more uncertain.

If a corporation's separate existence has not been respected, there are a variety of "tests" that different courts apply to determine whether the corporation's veil should be pierced. However, most courts will require a creditor to show that a second category of "wrongdoing" is present, such as "injustice" or "fraud-like" conduct. Some courts find that a total disregard for the separate existence of the corporation is enough. Some courts apply a "sliding scale," and a significant disregard of separate existence between a corporation and its shareholder(s) might be sufficient to warrant piercing, even without a showing of the second "prong" of injustice or fraud-like conduct, or, more accurately, in situations in which there was a complete absence of separate existence, that complete absence might be used to show injustice. Note that courts might also use undercapitalization of a corporation (typically categorized as a failure to follow one of the corporate "formalities") to show injustice as well. However, in most circumstances, (and on most exams) courts (and professors) will require an independent showing of injustice or fraud-like conduct. Students should be aware that there must be some "injustice" beyond the creditor's inability to recover, but how much is unclear.

When a court permits a creditor to pierce the corporate veil, the creditor is allowed to collect on its claim against the corporation from the individual shareholder(s) against whom piercing is allowed. In other words, once the creditor is permitted to pierce the corporate veil of a corporation, the shareholder(s) of that corporation, and the corporation itself, become jointly and severally liable for the debt to the creditor.

Of course, a creditor could also show that a shareholder committed fraud, and that fraud would provide an independent basis to sue the shareholder. However, it is typically more difficult to prove fraud because the creditor would need to show reliance and willful deception, which courts usually do not require a creditor to prove in connection with allegations of a defendant's disregard of formalities.

TEST FOR PIERCING THE CORPORATE VEIL

To summarize the above discussion, in order to pierce a corporation's veil, there are two categories of transgressions that must be established:

☑ First, there must be such **unity of interest** and ownership that the separate personalities of the corporation and the shareholder(s) (whether the shareholder(s) are individuals, corporations, or other entities) no longer exist; AND

☑ Second, circumstances must be such that adherence to the fiction of separate corporate existence would **sanction a fraud or promote injustice**.

The tests for unity of interest take several forms. (California has a list of over 20 formalities, while some other states examine the extent of control and domination by a corporation's shareholders exercised without regard for the corporation's separate identity.) However, actions that demonstrate unity of interest will almost always highlight one or more of the following failings:

☑ **Failure to follow the corporate formalities**—such as a failure to take minutes, a failure to conduct meetings, a failure to elect officers, a failure to maintain separate books and records, a failure to adopt bylaws, a failure to issue stock, a failure to create a Board of Directors, and/or a failure to have the corporation take action consistent with proper procedures (rather than acting through its shareholders).

☑ **Failure to maintain separate accounts ("commingling")**—keeping personal funds (or funds belonging to the shareholders of the corporation) and the corporation's funds together in the same account(s) and/or using the corporation's funds or assets for personal matters.

☑ **Failure to "adequately capitalize" the corporation**—failure to place sufficient funds into the corporation (either through loans, assets, cash, or insurance) to enable it to operate as a viable business, taking into account the type of business and the market. Also, failure to provide the minimum insurance, if any, required for the business.

In order to establish that a failure to pierce the corporate veil would sanction a fraud or promote injustice, courts have looked to a variety of behaviors. However, **the mere fact that the plaintiff will not be paid if the veil is not pierced is not sufficient to justify piercing**. In order to evaluate whether the test for piercing the veil has been met, courts typically look for some improper behavior, such as:

☑ Actions that improperly thwart or undermine the legal rights of others, such as "unfair" business practices;

☑ Intentional misrepresentations, deception, or other fraud-like conduct;

☑ Actions that might incur criminal or civil penalties;

☑ The creation of a corporate structure solely in an attempt to eliminate liability and lacking a true "business operation" or purpose (This element would be similar to showing undercapitalization above if the purpose of the undercapitalization were to avoid liability.);

☑ Unjust enrichment (This behavior might involve looting the corporation at the expense of potential or actual creditors. The idea here is that "undercapitalization" takes place when setting up a corporation. Unjust enrichment involves removing assets from an existing corporation in bad faith, leaving the business undercapitalized.); or

☑   Fraud—If one can demonstrate that some sort of fraud occurred (e.g., false claims about corporate assets, etc.), that showing would certainly suffice. Fraud is, of course, a separate cause of action. If the owners of a corporation engage in fraud, they have already exposed themselves to personal liability. However, actual fraud is often very difficult to prove (which is why fraud is not necessary to prove in a case for piercing the corporate veil). A showing of fraud would certainly be sufficient to meet this element of the test.

While there are many approaches to piercing the corporate veil, and there is no exact science to determine exactly when a court will pierce the corporate veil, it is relatively simple to prevent the corporate veil from being pierced. In order to prevent piercing, those operating the corporation must respect the applicable rules and formalities. The actions to accomplish this include:

☑   Keeping the corporation's business separate (This means separate bank accounts, separate property, separate records.);

☑   Keeping the corporate funds and transactions separate from shareholders' personal funds and transactions;

☑   Holding meetings of the Board of Directors and of the Shareholders at least once a year;

☑   Keeping minutes of those meetings;

☑   Electing Board members;

☑   Issuing stock;

☑   Making sure the corporation is adequately capitalized (Adequately capitalized means that the corporation has funds or other resources that are reasonably sufficient to operate its business when it is formed.); and

☑   Making sure that the corporation carries the minimum amount of required insurance.

The cases that involve piercing the corporate veil frequently arise in situations in which there are only one or two shareholders because in situations in which there are only a few shareholders it is easier to show a unity of interest. Students often ask whether it is possible to pierce the corporate veil in a situation in which there are shareholders who have violated the rules, but also "innocent" shareholders who have not. Most courts will not allow piercing against the shareholders with no involvement in the misconduct, allowing piercing to remove the protection from liability only with respect to the shareholders who have violated the rules, while the innocent shareholders will remain protected. However, there can be no guaranty that courts would apply the rules to protect the innocent shareholders. Note that piercing the corporate veil does not occur in public companies. All piercing cases involve closely held corporations.

PARENT CORPORATION SHAREHOLDERS

Sometimes there is an effort to pierce the veil of a subsidiary corporation in order to get to the assets of the parent corporation. While the standard for piercing is basically the same in these situations, courts are frequently less rigorous in the requirement that fraud-like conduct or injustice be shown. In addition to the other factors, courts will often look for interlocking boards of directors between the parent and the subsidiary as an indication that the subsidiary is not "separate" or independent. Just as a corporation that is not a subsidiary must be separate from its shareholders, a subsidiary corporation must be separate and independent from its parent, or it will risk piercing as well. In *United States v. Jon-T Chemicals, Inc.*, 768 F.2d 686, 691–92 (5th Cir. 1985), cert. denied 475 U.S. 1014, 89 L. Ed. 2d 309, 106 S. Ct. 1194 (1986), the court provided a list of factors to consider in evaluating whether to pierce the veil of a subsidiary:

> The totality of circumstances must be evaluated in determining whether a subsidiary may be found to be the alter ego or mere instrumentality of the parent corporation. Although the standards are not identical in each state, all jurisdictions require a showing of substantial domination. Among the factors to be considered are whether:
>
> - The parent and the subsidiary have common directors or officers;
>
> - The parent and the subsidiary have common business departments;
>
> - The parent and the subsidiary file consolidated financial statements and tax returns;
>
> - The parent finances the subsidiary;
>
> - The parent caused the incorporation of the subsidiary;

- The subsidiary operates with grossly inadequate capital;

- The parent pays the salaries and other expenses of the subsidiary;

- The subsidiary receives no business except that given to it by the parent;

- The parent uses the subsidiary's property as its own;

- The daily operations of the two corporations are not kept separate; and

- The subsidiary does not observe the basic corporate formalities, such as keeping separate books and records and holding shareholder and Board meetings.

REVERSE PIERCING

Reverse piercing occurs when a claim against an individual shareholder is found to be enforceable directly against the corporation in which the individual is a shareholder. One difference of reverse piercing is that it does not enable a creditor to collect on a claim that otherwise would <u>necessarily</u> be unpaid by the party reached by the piercing. It changes the status of the claim holder, enabling the individual shareholder's creditor to be treated as a creditor of the corporation. This avoids a situation in which the corporation's creditors have priority over the individual shareholder's creditor's claim. While the direction of the reverse piercing is different (a claim against a shareholder is treated also as a claim against the corporation), the test is the same. In conventional piercing, a creditor of the corporation may not proceed against the shareholder(s) of that corporation unless piercing is allowed (or some other exception to limited liability exists). However, in a situation in which a creditor has a claim against an individual shareholder, it is possible, even likely, that the creditor could foreclose on that individual shareholder's stock and then become a shareholder of the corporation. As a shareholder of the corporation (especially a controlling shareholder), the creditor could cause the corporation to make distributions to the shareholder(s). Those dividends could reduce the losses of the creditor. However, in that scenario, the creditor of the individual shareholder is not a creditor of the corporation and, therefore, does not have the right to distribute funds before the creditors of the corporation are paid. Some important features of reverse piercing include:

☑   Reverse piercing makes the individual shareholder's personal creditor a creditor directly against the corporation, which puts them higher in line to be paid than if they just had a claim against the shareholder.

☑   If the creditor is able to reverse pierce, then it can collect from the corporation on equal footing with the corporation's creditors.

☑   If the creditor cannot reverse pierce, it may only be able to reach the money that the corporation decides to pay to the shareholder.

☑   The test for reverse piercing is the same as the test for piercing. (But note that some states do not allow reverse piercing.)

☑   There have been cases in which a creditor was allowed to reverse pierce a corporation that had another shareholder who had no obligation to the creditor. According to the test, as long as there is unity of interest, there is the possibility of reverse piercing.

ENTERPRISE LIABILITY

Enterprise liability is often addressed at the same time a course handles piercing the corporate veil. However, enterprise liability (even though it is sometimes referred to as "horizontal piercing") is NOT piercing. In enterprise liability, a creditor claims there are several related corporations and all or some are really part of the same corporation. Enterprise liability involves a creditor's effort to enforce a claim that creditor holds against one corporation against other, related corporations. Enterprise liability is typically claimed when there is common ownership among two or more corporations. These commonly owned corporations are typically known as "sister corporations."

Rule—there is enterprise liability when the sister corporation transgresses the corporation— corporation boundary.

The questions to ask in evaluating a fact pattern for enterprise liability are:

☑   Are two or more nominally separate sister corporations really operating as a single enterprise?

☑ **Are the corporations operated as separate entities with separate accounts, books, and records?**

☑ Are the respective corporations' assets intermingled for use toward a common business purpose?

Enterprise liability is NOT the same thing as piercing. Even if there is enterprise liability and a creditor can reach the assets of other corporations, that does NOT mean that the creditor can reach the shareholders. Enterprise liability is more of an agency theory of liability applied to related corporations.

In order to avoid enterprise liability, separate corporations should:

☑ Maintain separate books and bank accounts for the separate corporations;

☑ Avoid sharing assets, supplies, and other resources; and

☑ If supplies or resources are shared, engage in careful accounting practices that reflect that supplies and/or resources are all being paid for or sold in the manner that would occur between unconnected, independent businesses.

Note that formalities and fraud are NOT relevant to enterprise liability (although a failure to follow certain formalities might provide evidence of a lack of "separateness" between or among sister corporations). Enterprise liability is really just about agency law. Students should also be aware that it is somewhat unlikely that enterprise liability will occur when the corporations are operating in different unrelated industries, because the nature of different business activities makes it unlikely that the corporations could act as a single enterprise.

PIERCING THE VEIL OF LIMITED LIABILITY COMPANIES

Often the discussion of piercing the corporate veil is accompanied by a discussion of piercing the veil of an LLC. Virtually all jurisdictions allow for the piercing of the limited liability veil of an LLC. The cases on LLC piercing tend to follow the principles found in corporate veil-piercing cases, meaning that in order to allow a creditor to pierce the limited liability veil of an LLC, courts typically require the showing of a unity of interest between the LLC owner(s) and the LLC and a showing that a failure to pierce the veil would either sanction a fraud or promote injustice. However, LLCs typically have fewer formalities to follow than do corporations. For example, LLCs are not required to have annual meetings, to adopt Bylaws or to issue stock certificates. Therefore, while it is certainly possible to pierce the veil of an LLC, it also is often more difficult to show the existence of the required unity of interest based upon a failure to follow formalities.

OTHER PERSONAL CLAIMS AGAINST SHAREHOLDERS

As mentioned above, there are other instances in which a creditor of the corporation may also make a claim against the shareholders' personal assets. The most common situations creating such claims involve:

- ☑ Actual fraud;

- ☑ Fraudulent conveyances/transfers;

- ☑ Improper dividends;

- ☑ Negligence; and

- ☑ Personal guaranty of a corporate obligation by a shareholder.

Fraudulent Conveyance and Improper Dividends

In the situation of a fraudulent conveyance or an improper dividend, creditors may be able to recover funds or assets that were supposed to stay in the corporation but were distributed to shareholders, officers, or even third parties. If a person receives money that was not supposed to be paid or distributed by the corporation, creditors of the corporation may be able to make that person give that money back. (While beyond the scope of this book, a fraudulent conveyance typically involves the transfer of money or assets without the receipt of equivalent value, with the knowledge or intent of defrauding one's creditors.) Note that a corporation may not pay dividends if it is insolvent or if the dividend renders the corporation insolvent. Dividends paid under such circumstances are "improper" and may be recovered by, or on behalf of, the corporation. Both of these types of claims are different from "piercing the veil" because they do not allow creditors to collect ALL the money they are owed by the corporation from a shareholder; creditors may only collect to the extent of the fraudulent transfer or improper dividend.

Negligence

In situations that involve the liability of a shareholder that arise out of that shareholder's negligence, the law is not disregarding the protections of a corporation. Instead, the law recognizes that shareholders may play additional roles in the corporation, for which they might incur liability. If a shareholder, on behalf of a corporation, commits a negligent act and someone is injured as a direct result of that act, the injured party may sue the corporation, but may also sue the negligent individual. The fact that the individual also happens to be a shareholder of the corporation will not shield him or her from liability. (Recall the discussion of an agent's liability for that agent's tortious conduct, above.)

Guaranties

Sometimes a shareholder may voluntarily assume liability for the debts of the corporation by promising to pay a debt if the corporation cannot by guaranteeing, bonding, or acting as a surety for the corporation. In these instances, piercing the corporate veil is not necessary. The shareholder is already personally liable under the contractual promise to pay on behalf of the corporation. Third parties (for example, landlords) who do not wish to be subject to the liability limitations of a corporation may negotiate for shareholder guaranties as additional protections of a contractual obligation.

ILLUSTRATIVE PROBLEM

PROBLEM 3.1

John is about to start a rock climbing school. He comes to see you, his attorney, and expresses concerns about personal liability. John would like you to form a corporation for his rock climbing school called "Can't Sue Me, Inc." to protect him from personal liability. John hopes that Can't Sue Me, Inc. will succeed and make profits. However, he has no business reason for operating the business as a corporation other than avoiding personal liability. Assuming that John intends to follow all of the corporate requirements and formalities, but, being exceptionally honest, plans to tell his customers that his only reason for incorporating the business is to shield himself from personal liability, is the corporation likely to be effective to achieve this goal?

Analysis

Yes. Limited personal liability is one of the best reasons to form a corporation. Limited liability is not a secret or a trick. It is the intent behind the design of the corporate structure. By telling his customers about the corporate structure, John is just strengthening his claim that his customers had notice that they were dealing with a corporation and not with John personally. Of course, a corporate structure does not provide a bulletproof vest for liability. John could be liable for his own personal wrongdoing with regard to his customers. For example, if John negligently told a customer that a line was secure, and that customer fell and was hurt, the customer could sue John personally. However, that does not mean that the customer would be able to pierce the corporate veil. Assuming that John treated the corporation as a separate and distinct entity from himself by following the rules and formalities intended to avoid a unity of interest between him and Can't Sue Me, Inc., the corporation would be a strong tool to shield John from personal liability.

CHAPTER 4

Capital Structure of the Firm

S tudents should be aware of the term the "**capital structure**" of the firm. The capital structure of a firm is made up of money that has been invested in the firm *and* money that has been lent to the firm. The various classes of stock that comprise the ownership structure of a firm are only one part of the capital structure, **equity**. The capital structure includes **debt** as well.

EQUITY

The shareholders in a corporation, by definition, own some piece of the corporation. They have made an investment of some kind in the corporation, and, as a result, are entitled to certain rights, and, if they are fortunate, money. As discussed above, these shareholders might own shares in different classes of stock. However, in general, all shareholders have obtained their shares by making an equity investment in the corporation. An equity investment typically has certain features that distinguish it from debt. Equity investments:

☑ May be divided among different classes of stock;

☑ Receive **dividends**, when, as and if declared (Dividends represent payments of money or property (typically representing some portion of the corporation's profits) by the corporation to its shareholders.);

☑ May have specific rights, privileges, or preferences relating to a specific "class" of equity in the corporation;

☑ Are entitled to vote on shareholder matters;

☑ Do not usually have a right to repayment of the amount that was invested or to receive a return on their investment;

☑ Usually prosper as the firm prospers and flounder as the firm flounders; and

☑ Have a residual claim on the assets of the firm, once outside creditors' claims have been satisfied. (Note that there might be different rights or priorities to the residual among different classes of stock within the same firm.)

Historically, stock in a firm was issued for a minimum amount, known as the "**par value**." Par value represented an amount, usually noted on a corporation's stock certificates, below which a share could not be sold. While this concept was intended to assure that stock in a corporation represented some minimum value, it proved to be ineffective in this regard. Today, this concept has been all but abandoned, and par value is almost always set at zero or there is a specific statement of "no par value." However, many stock certificates still have an area to state a "par value," and the concept is often taught in business law courses.

Other Classes of Stock

In the simplest of corporations there is only one class of stock, common stock. However, corporations often create additional classes of stock. Often, those other classes of stock possess a unique bundle of rights designed to attract certain investors to put money into the corporation. Different classes of stock are often (but not necessarily) identified by a letter and are usually called "**preferred stock**." For example, a corporation might have Common Stock, Preferred Class A, and Preferred Class B. Each class of stock will usually have different rights, privileges, and preferences. Preferred stock will often have different features from, or "preferential" to, common stock such as:

☑ **Dividend Rights**—Preferred stock will often have the right to receive a specific dividend before any dividend is paid to holders of common stock. The rights associated with a particular class of stock may sometimes provide that the payment of this dividend is mandatory. Other classes of stock may provide that payment is only required, "when, as and if declared."

☑ **Liquidation Preference**—A right to be paid a certain amount upon liquidation of the corporation before amounts are paid to other classes of stock. Another way to express this idea is to say that preferred stock will often have a liquidation preference that is "senior" to common stock.

☑ **Redemption Rights**—Preferred stock is sometimes subject to repurchase by the corporation for a certain price, meaning that the corporation may force the holder of the preferred stock to sell that stock to the corporation at a set price.

☑ **Put Option**—Sometimes the holder of preferred stock may also possess the right to require the corporation to repurchase the holder's preferred stock for a certain price, meaning that the shareholder may "put" the stock to the corporation, forcing the corporation to purchase the stock at a set price. These options usually arise within or following the passage of some agreed upon period of time, or the occurrence of some event.

☑ **Convertibility**—Preferred stock may also be "convertible" into common stock or even bonds. Conversion is usually at the option of the shareholder, but may also be required upon the occurrence of certain specified events such as an initial public offering.

☑ **Anti-Dilution Protections**—While these protections can take many forms, they generally protect the preferred shareholder from the company issuing stock at a price below the price at which the preferred shareholder possessing the protection purchased his or her shares in the company. These rights usually provide that the preferred shareholder will be protected from "dilution" by an issuance of a number of shares sufficient to make the preferred shareholder's price per share equal to the lower priced issuance that, but for the protection, would have been issued at a lower price. (Note that if the preferred stock is convertible, often the anti-dilution protection will merely increase the number of shares of common stock into which the preferred stock may convert to accomplish the same result.)

☑ **Right of Participation**—Preferred stock holders will often have the right to participate in subsequent financings or investments in the corporation. These rights are sometimes also called "**preemptive rights**" because the holders of these rights may "preempt" others who want to participate in the investments.

☑ **Voting Rights**—Sometimes preferred shareholders will have the right to vote along with common stock shareholders as though the preferred stock were common stock. In other preferred stock structures, the holders of preferred shares will often have different, additional, or superior voting rights to common stock. For example, a class of preferred stock may be entitled to elect a certain number of directors to the Board or exercise a veto right over certain significant corporate actions, such as a sale of the corporation.

In addition to rights that are specific to preferred shareholders, often shareholders in closely held companies will bargain for rights among the shareholders as additional protections. A few of the most typical of these are included below:

☑ **Right of First Refusal**—The right of first refusal is a restriction on the transferability of a corporation's stock. It requires that before a shareholder sells his or her shares in the corporation that shareholder must first offer those shares either to the company, the other shareholders, or both. This type of protection is relatively common in many closely held companies.

☑ **Tag Along Provisions**—A tag along (or "co-sale") provision provides that before a shareholder may sell his or her shares in the corporation, that shareholder must allow other shareholders to participate proportionately in the sale. This type of protection assures that one shareholder will not be able to "cash out" and leave the other shareholders in the company unless that is what they want. It is also a device that might prevent a controlling shareholder from selling his or her shares for a "**control premium**" (defined below) without sharing that premium with the other shareholders.

☑ **Drag Along Rights**—These rights provide that if a majority (or sometimes a super majority) of the shareholders vote for a sale of the corporation, then the other shareholders will agree to sell as well. These provisions eliminate "dissenters" and "hold-outs" and are used to facilitate an easier sale process for the corporation.

DEBT

Debt involves the lending of money to the corporation. Debt may have different features and different rights; however, it usually involves lending money to the corporation and the requirement that the money be repaid, with interest, according to the terms of the loan. There are three basic instruments that are used for loans. All of these may be "securities."

- ☑ **Notes** (including Promissory Notes)—A Note is evidence of a secured or unsecured loan. It involves a promise to repay money on specific terms. Usually banks will use a promissory note to reflect a loan obligation. Notes are usually not traded as bonds whereas debentures might be.

- ☑ **Bonds**—Bonds usually involve a secured loan. The security for the loan may be real or personal property belonging to the corporation. The "holders" of a bond are usually secured creditors. (Note that the term "holder" is used to reflect that bonds might be traded, so the holder, who is entitled to certain rights, might be the original lender or might be someone who obtained the bond that was sold by the lender.) Bonds may be **registered** on the corporation's books or **bearer** bonds. In the case of registered bonds, the corporation's obligations are owed to the owner who is registered in the corporation's books and records. In the case of bearer bonds, the corporation's obligations are owned to the holder (or "bearer") of the bonds.

- ☑ **Debentures**—Debentures are loans that, like bonds, are held by creditors of the corporation. However, debentures are typically unsecured obligations, rather than secured like bonds. This difference means that debenture holders are usually unsecured creditors, rather than secured creditors.

While it is important to understand that there are different forms of debt and different rights and obligations associated with the different forms, it is also important to understand features that are common to most all debt and which distinguish debt from equity. The following are features of debt. Debt:

- ☑ Is typically subject to repayment either over time in periodic payments or at some future date in a lump sum;

☑ Usually includes compensation to the lender for use of the money such as interest payments;

☑ Is subject to repayment regardless of the success or failure of the company (Of course, there might be some extraordinary instances such a bankruptcy in which the debt would not be repaid.);

☑ Has priority over obligations to shareholders of the corporation;

☑ Does not have voting or management rights (although many debt instruments will put restrictions, known as "**debt covenants**," on borrowers, requiring certain practices and limiting other activities or actions of the company (such as the payment of dividends or additional borrowing), until the debt is repaid);

☑ May be secured by specific property or assets of the business (**secured**) or may be a general claim against the business (**unsecured**); and

☑ May involve a personal guaranty by the owners of the borrower business.

The combination of debt and equity create the capital structure of the firm. There are several documents that are involved in the process of building a corporation's capital structure, such as the corporation's charter document (i.e., its Articles of Incorporation) and various contracts such as shareholders' agreements, loan agreements, and other documents relating to either debt or equity being provided to the corporation. These documents (along with any statutory provisions that might apply) will typically define the respective economic rights of the holders of debt and equity of the corporation. These rights may be very basic or they may extremely complex, including many of the provisions discussed above.

While it makes sense in discussing the capital structure of the firm to talk about both debt and equity, students should be aware that the holders of debt and the holders of equity are viewed and treated differently under the law. While it is important for students to recognize the importance of debt in the structure of a firm, the intricacies of all the laws, rules, and regulations relating to lenders and creditors is well beyond the scope of this book and of most business association courses. We therefore, focus on the rights of the equity holders, or shareholders. Remember that the rights that relate to a shareholder receiving money, property, value profit, loss and the like, are economic rights, and these rights capture a shareholder's financial stake in the corporation. However, as "owners," shareholders also have management, or voting, rights as well. These rights are also characterized by rules and structures that must be understood in order to learn how the corporation operates. Furthermore, these rights are not unrelated since shareholders' economic rights are often impacted by the management of the corporation.

CHAPTER 5

Fiduciary Duties (and Other Checks on Corporate Actions)

Before addressing the major fiduciary duties, many Business Associations courses begin this unit with a discussion of the powers of the corporation. The cases that examine the powers of the corporation introduce the concept that there are limits on corporate actions. Initial limits might be set in the corporation's Articles of Incorporation, but even without such limits, there are prohibitions on actions that are beyond the scope of accomplishing the purpose of the corporation, (i.e., to maximize the value of the corporation for its shareholders). The idea behind these limitations arises from the fact that the directors who serve on the Board are not the owners of the corporation (or, in instances in which they are owners, typically are not the only owners). Directors serve in the role of stewards or trustees who are charged with guiding the corporation for the benefit of its shareholders. Because of that role, there are guidelines about the actions that may be taken on behalf of the corporation and guidelines about how the directors perform their roles and the duties associated with those roles.

POWERS OF THE CORPORATION

What Can Corporations Do; What Can't They Do; and How Do They Do It?

The significant actions of a corporation must be authorized or sanctioned by its Board of Directors. These days, corporations are typically authorized to act for any lawful purpose. Often this leads to the question, "What limitations are placed on a corporation or its Board?" Historically, corporations had more limited purposes, so actions taken "outside of the corporate purpose" were considered to be void or voidable as "***ultra vires***." Currently, this doctrine is seldom used and typically is handled under the category of "waste."

However, several professors still cover the types of actions that might fall beyond the corporate purpose. The most common action addressed is an excessive charitable act. This notion of "excessive charity" is perhaps a backhanded way of addressing the question of who the real party in interest in the corporation is. There are many articles and papers that attempt to broaden the constituencies that fall within the parties whose interests are relevant in evaluating a corporation's actions. These groups may include customers, employees, creditors and communities. However, ultimately, the party in interest is the shareholders. While the interests of other constituencies may sometimes be considered, this may not be done at the expense of the shareholders.

The idea behind this concept is that the corporation's duty/purpose is to maximize wealth or value for its shareholders. While the law grants great latitude to the ways in which a corporation may go about maximizing wealth or value for its shareholders, it does not allow corporations to act contrary to that goal. If, for example, a corporation were to donate all of its assets to charity, while the donation might be an act of great generosity, it would not be permitted without the consent of all of the shareholders. Whether the term *ultra vires* or waste is used, the result is the same. Assets must be used within the corporate purpose of maximizing shareholder value, and to accomplish this goal, the company may not engage in "wasteful" acts. In these situations, many shareholders would argue that they should receive the money and make their own decisions about which charity, if any, they wish to support with their portion of the money.

To the extent that students are presented with a charitable act and asked to evaluate that act, the result may vary greatly from state to state, but the underlying assessment involves the question of whether there is some direct or indirect benefit to the shareholders and/or the corporation. Factors that students may want to examine include:

- ☑ Whether the gift was anonymous. (An anonymous gift would reduce the value to the firm if the goal of the gift was marketing or good public relations.)

- ☑ Whether the amount donated was significant when compared to the corporation's earnings.

- ☑ Whether the gift was made to a "pet" charity. (A charity that does not have widespread appeal but is merely an interest of an officer or director of the corporation is more suspect because it is less likely

that such a gift is truly for the benefit of the
corporation.)

ILLUSTRATIVE PROBLEM

PROBLEM 5.1

M. Mouse, Inc. ("MMI") is a company that manufactures
watches. Its annual gross revenue is about $1,000,000. MMI's
president, McKey Mouse, has decided to make a contribution to the
Society to Promote Kindness to Rodents, a charity of which McKey
is particularly fond. The Board of Directors approves the gift in the
amount of $3,000,000. D. Duck is an MMI shareholder who sues to
block the gift. How would a court evaluate this action?

Analysis

It is likely that a court would prevent the gift. A charitable gift
(or for that matter any corporate action) must be designed to benefit
the company and its shareholders. The company has not articulated
any corporate purpose for the gift to the Society to Promote
Kindness to Rodents, and it seems unlikely that it could. The
contribution involves a huge sum of money when compared with
MMI's revenue. It is three times as much as the company receives
each year. The charity seems to be a "pet" charity of McKey's, and it
is difficult to see that there will be a public relations benefit to MMI
even close to the amount of the gift. It seems likely that a court
would find the gift constitutes a "waste" of corporate assets and/or
ultra vires.

FIDUCIARY DUTIES

The most significant guidelines as to how directors should act
in their roles as stewards of the corporation are known as fiduciary
duties. These duties create parameters within which the conduct of
a corporation's officers and directors may be measured. There are
two major categories of fiduciary duties: the **duty of care** and the
duty of loyalty.

DUTY OF CARE AND THE BUSINESS
JUDGMENT RULE

The duty of care requires that each member of the Board of
Directors, when discharging the duties of a director, shall act: (1) in
good faith and (2) in a manner the director *reasonably believes* to
be in the best interests of the corporation. Model Business
Corporations Act § 830(a).

When a director is sued based upon the claim that he or she violated the duty of care, that director is often entitled to the protection of the business judgment rule (the "BJR"). The BJR provides protection for directors from lawsuits that might seek to challenge the business judgment of those directors. The idea underlying the BJR is to give directors wide latitude in taking steps to benefit a corporation. In addition, since many strategic decisions are judgment calls, the law enables directors to use their best judgment, without the fear that a court will attempt to "second guess" their decision. The BJR provides broad protection from such second-guessing by shareholders or by the courts.

While most professors like to describe the BJR as a "shield" that will protect directors, there are some people (and even some courts) who just view the rule as limiting a director's potential liability to acts involving gross negligence, rather than simple negligence. While this shift of the standard of liability may be a useful shortcut, it does not adequately address the subtleties of the rule. Once students understand that the BJR acts as a shield, they can understand that there are circumstances in which the shield of the BJR may not be used or may not be effective. There are several situations in which the broad protection of the BJR is not appropriate. In those situations, the BJR does not apply. The basic rule is that the protections afforded under the BJR apply unless a plaintiff can show any of the following conditions:

☑ Fraud;

☑ Illegality or "Wrongful" Conduct;

☑ Conflict of Interest (duty of loyalty analysis applies);

☑ Bad Faith (duty of loyalty analysis applies (at least in DE)). Bad faith might include several different categories such as:

- "subjective bad faith," which is "conduct motivated by an actual intent to do harm."

- "intentional dereliction of duty, a conscious disregard for one's responsibilities." *In re The Walt Disney Co. Derivative Litigation*, 906 A.2d 27, 66 (Del. 2006).

- "acts with a purpose other than that of advancing the best interests of the corporation." *Stone v. Ritter*, 911 A.2d 362, 369 (Del. 2006);

☑ Egregious/Irrational Decision (a decision with no business justification);

☑ Waste (a transaction that lacks any business rationale to support it or one that is so one sided that no business person of ordinary, sound judgment could conclude "that the corporation has received adequate consideration." *Glazer v. Zapata Corp.*, 658 A.2d 176, 183 (Del. Ch. 1993).);

☑ Uninformed Decision (including a lack of investigation); or

☑ No Decision (for example, no action was taken by the Board, but a plaintiff alleges that some action should have been taken).

PROCEDURAL AND SUBSTANTIVE REQUIREMENTS FOR THE BJR

There are two categories of limitations to the BJR, procedural and substantive.

Procedural Requirements

The last two limitations in the preceding list of exceptions to the BJR relate to procedural limitations. The BJR protects directors when they make an *informed decision*. There is no BJR protection when a Board does not "act" to make a decision, or when it makes an uninformed decision. (As a result, many decisions are challenged on these grounds.) In order to prevail in such a challenge, a plaintiff must show that the Board was grossly negligent in failing to inform itself of all material information reasonably available to it and that the decision itself was grossly negligent.

In order to avoid liability for violating the duty of care on procedural grounds, directors should:

☑ Keep informed about and properly "oversee" the corporation's activities and policies;

☑ Be adequately informed about the corporation's business, its interests and the relevant issues before making decisions;

☑ Possess a minimum level of skill and expertise with regard to the role of director for the specific business; and

☑ Be aware of the financial status of the corporation (e.g., regularly review the corporation's financial statements).

Substantive Requirements

In a situation in which the Board acts in compliance with the procedural requirements, in order to avoid the BJR, a plaintiff must show that there has been a substantive violation. If the BJR does not apply (whether because of a substantive violation or procedural defects), in order for a plaintiff to successfully argue that a fiduciary duty was violated, that plaintiff often must still show a violation of the underlying duty of care. In instances in which there is: illegality, an egregious decision, an uninformed decision, waste, or no decision, it is possible to lose the protection of the BJR but still not to have acted negligently. Therefore, the court must still ask: "Even though this situation does not warrant the protections provided by the BJR, did the defendant violate the applicable duty of care?" If not, then there is no violation. What does this mean? In some instances, for example in the case of an egregious decision, there will be little need to analyze whether the defendant was negligent. The mere fact that there was an egregious decision is evidence of negligence. However, in some of the other categories, there is more room for an action that does not receive BJR protection still to be found not to constitute negligence. Consider the following example:

> If the Board of Directors of an overnight delivery service instructs its drivers to get parking tickets because it is more important to get packages delivered on time, that is "illegality." The Board is saying "Break the law (park illegally) in order to help our business." This decision is, therefore, not protected by the BJR. The decision may also subject the company to fines and perhaps other penalties under the vehicle code. However, it might not necessarily be a violation of the duty of care. A court would need to determine whether that decision was a negligent business decision. One could argue that it might be a good business decision, albeit a violation of other rules.

In the instances in which there is a **conflict of interest or bad faith**, the BJR does not apply. Note that the existence of a conflict of interest does not mean that the duty of care has been violated. It just means that the decision involving the conflict is not protected by the BJR unless the conflict was "cleansed." In instances involving a conflict of interest or of bad faith, a plaintiff would show a breach of fiduciary duty by showing that there was a violation of the duty of loyalty. A duty of loyalty analysis, discussed below, would need to be performed in order to evaluate if there had been a breach of that duty or if the conflict had been cleansed.

Delaware courts have taken the position that instances of bad faith are also subject to a duty of loyalty analysis.

A key point to remember about the BJR is that the **directors are allowed to be wrong or to make mistakes and still have the protection of the BJR.** The directors do not have to pick the best approach to receive protection. They need to act in good faith, to consider their decision, and to have a business reason for their action. The BJR will still protect a bad decision, provided it does not involve fraud, illegality, conflict of interest, bad faith, an egregious or irrational decision, waste, no decision, or an uninformed decision.

AFFIRMATIVE DEFENSES TO DUTY OF CARE VIOLATIONS

Finally, even violations of the duty of care are subject to certain affirmative defenses. A violation might not result in liability if the Board can show that the transaction was beneficial to the corporation, that it was "fair," or that there were no damages. For example, if the Board agreed that it would sell the company to a competitor, and decided it would set the price by letting a monkey throw darts at a dartboard, this would clearly be an egregious decision. However, what if the monkey was incredibly successful and the company sold for a price far in excess of its true worth? The Board, although in violation of its duty of care, would have an affirmative defense that the outcome was "fair" (or not detrimental) to the shareholders.

When we talk about fairness as an affirmative defense, courts will typically look at substantive or intrinsic fairness (i.e., whether the consideration received by the corporation was a "fair" price). An exception to this standard arises in the case of a merger or acquisition in which the courts will look at something called entire fairness. Entire fairness involves **BOTH procedural fairness by which the judgment was made AND the substantive result. (Was it a good deal?) If both of those conditions are met, the decision is protected.** In order to use the BJR, there is a minimum level of care that must be met to show that an informed judgment was made. BUT, if the transaction is judged to have been fair even though good business judgment was not exercised, then there is no liability.

THE BJR AND PROTECTION BY CONSULTING AN EXPERT

If the Board hired or consulted an expert regarding certain matters, the Board's decisions and actions with regard to those matters will later be protected under the BJR as "informed" decisions (provided, of course, that the decision does not violate another requirement of the BJR). Of course, there is some duty of care in hiring the expert (duty of inquiry as part of the duty of care), and the Board should be clear on what is beyond the scope of the expert's competence. For example, an expert hired to evaluate whether a compensation package was fair and consistent with industry practices could not be relied upon to provide advice on whether to acquire a company, unless the expert had expertise in that area as well. In order to have a decision by an expert protected, the expert's opinion must be relied upon. (Thus, if the expert produces a report, that report must be read prior to the Board's action.) Also, reliance on an expert must be reasonable; a Board of Directors may not rely on an expert when the directors know, or should know, that the expert is wrong.

Director's Failure to Act

With regard to instances in which the Board or a director on the Board did not make a decision or did not act, it is important to remember that the BJR protects decisions, not the people who are charged with making them. The BJR requires the director to actually make judgments. If the director fails to make a decision, there is no BJR protection because there has been no "judgment." The BJR does not protect people solely because of their status in a corporation. Directors cannot shut their eyes to corporate misconduct and pretend they did not see the conduct. This does not mean there is automatic liability; a plaintiff would still have to prove a violation of the duty of care.

THE BJR AND FAILURE TO ACT OR TO MONITOR THE FIRM

In some situations where the entire Board is accused of failing to act, the BJR is not available. Recall that the BJR only protects "judgments." It does not apply when the Board has not taken an action (unless the Board has made an affirmative informed decision not to take action). Situations in which a Board is accused of failing to act, often involve instances of corporate wrongdoing that the Board is accused of failing to detect, prevent, or stop. These types of claims are often called "**Caremark**" **claims** for the well-known case in which the rule was established. Even though the BJR does not apply in these "failure to act" cases, the courts still needed to develop a standard to evaluate the actions (or more accurately, inactions) of a Board. In the case *In re Caremark International Inc. Derivative Litigation*, 698 A.2d 959 (Del. Ch. 1996), the Delaware court established standards regarding the Board's duty to monitor the firm. The rule arising out of this case contains both a procedural and a substantive aspect. First, absent suspicion of wrongdoing, there is NO DUTY upon the Board to install and operate a corporate system to find wrongdoing that the Board does not suspect or believe exists. Second, the Board must make a good faith attempt to ensure that an adequate reporting system is in place so that the Board can obtain the necessary information to make informed decisions. One way a Board can ensure it has good information is to establish compliance programs, such as policy manuals, employee training, audits, sanctions for violations, and provisions for self-reporting violations to regulators. Directors do not necessarily have to do a perfect job, but they do have to do their job, and in order to do their job they must be informed. However, as we have seen above, once they inform themselves, their decisions are typically protected. The bottom line is that if directors do NOT have information that something improper is going on, and there is a good system in place for corporate information, the directors are NOT liable for failing to monitor. Once there is some suspicion of wrongdoing, the directors have a *greater* obligation to monitor.

There is some question as to what the applicable standard is to evaluate whether or not directors have adequately informed themselves. Recent cases suggest that, absent a showing of bad faith, a director will not be liable for failure to exercise oversight (". . . only a sustained or systematic failure of the board to exercise oversight—such as an utter failure to attempt to assure a reasonable information and reporting system exists—will establish the lack of good faith that is a necessary condition to liability." *In re Caremark Int'l Inc. Derivative Litigation*, 698 A.2d 959 at 971). However, other cases suggest that once a director is aware of wrongdoing, if the director fails to take adequate action, that failure is evaluated under a gross negligence standard. Of course if the directors do take action, that action should be protected by the BJR.

ILLUSTRATIVE PROBLEM

PROBLEM 5.2

The Sandwich Shop, Inc. ("SSI") owns restaurants all over the country that sell all kinds of sandwiches. After several meetings involving many hours of discussion, SSI's Board of Directors votes to prohibit the use of mayonnaise on any of its sandwiches in all of its restaurants. It does this because the people on the Board all hate mayonnaise and do not think it should ever be used on a sandwich. They have also reviewed substantial research that shows that mayonnaise is bad for cholesterol, and the Board thinks that customers will appreciate a health-conscious organization. The Board also thinks that SSI's mayonnaise-hating customers are more valuable (and will produce more revenue) than SSI's mayonnaise-loving customers. Unfortunately, it turns out that some customers (who apparently like mayonnaise) get very upset about the policy and decide to stop going to SSI's restaurants. An angry shareholder, Matt Mayo, brings a lawsuit against the Board for violating its duty of care. Will the Matt Mayo prevail? Why or why not?

Analysis

Typically, courts will not interfere with the decision of a corporation's Board of Directors, provided that decision meets certain standards. The Board of Directors' actions will have the protection of the BJR. In order to prevail in his action, Matt Mayo will need to show that the BJR does not apply to this situation by showing either: fraud, illegality, conflict of interest, bad faith, waste, an egregious or irrational decision, no decision, or an uninformed decision.

In this instance, there is no indication of fraud, bad faith, illegality or conflict of interest. (Hating mayonnaise is not a conflict of interest. A conflict of interest involves a financial or familial conflict.) In addition, there was an actual decision. This leaves only a few elements on which Matt might make his case. Matt might attempt to argue that the decision to eliminate mayonnaise from the SSI restaurants is irrational, egregious and/or waste. However, the Board of Directors had a business justification for their action. They thought the action would be good for health-conscious customers, and they thought SSI's other mayonnaise-hating customers would appreciate it. It does not matter that the decision turned out to be a bad decision. The BJR will protect bad decisions, as long as there was a rational basis for the decision (and it did not run afoul of the other constraints). Matt would need to show that the business justifications were just a sham and the only reason for the Board's action was the personal tastes of the Board. Such a showing seems unlikely. Finally, Matt might argue that the Board made an uninformed decision. There are cases in which the Board of Directors "rubber stamps" a proposal of the company's presidents without proper consideration. This does not seem to be the case here. The Board discussed, debated, and even read a study. An exhaustive investigation and evaluation is not required, just an informed decision. While Matt might try to argue differently, it is likely that the Board was sufficiently informed. Therefore, it is likely that the SSI Board will have the protection of the business judgment rule, and that Matt Mayo will not prevail in his suit against the SSI directors.

DUTY OF LOYALTY

The duty of loyalty requires that fiduciaries (such as officers and directors) put the interests of the corporation ahead of their own interests. The duty of loyalty is implicated when a director is involved in a situation in which there is a conflict of interest, meaning that there is some aspect of the situation that creates a personal benefit for the fiduciary.

A conflict of interest exists when the director knows that, at the time he is asked to take action with regard to a potential transaction, he or a person related to him (1) is a party to the transaction or (2) has a beneficial financial interest in the transaction, and then exercises his influence to the detriment of the corporation. Model Business Corporations Act § 860.

In evaluating a duty of loyalty situation, one can ask a series of question to determine if there is a problem, whether the problem has been addressed in a satisfactory manner, and, if not, what the consequences are. The typical analysis of a duty of loyalty problem is as follows:

☑   Is there a conflict of interest? (Note that the conflict may be direct or indirect.)

☑   If there is no conflict of interest, there is no duty of loyalty issue.

☑   If there is a conflict of interest, one must determine whether the transaction been "cleansed." (See below for how to cleanse.)

☑   If the transaction has been "cleansed," the transaction is protected and may proceed. (If the transaction is cleansed by a vote of the disinterested directors, the decision that cleansed the transaction will itself be subject to scrutiny, but is typically protected by the BJR.)

☑   If the transaction has not been "cleansed," the transaction is "voidable" by the corporation, and the director(s) who violated their fiduciary duty of loyalty may be subject to damages.

Some typical situations that create conflicts of interest include:

☑   Self-dealing: this situation arises when a fiduciary for the corporation enters into a transaction with himself or herself or with an entity in which he or she (or a family member) has a substantial financial interest.

☑ Taking a *corporate opportunity*: this situation arises when a fiduciary for the corporation misappropriates an opportunity that belongs to the corporation. (See below for more details.)

☑ Stealing: this situation arises when a fiduciary of the corporation takes something of value such as money/assets from the corporation for himself or herself.

☑ Executive compensation: this situation arises when the executives whose compensation is at issue are also on the Board of Directors that votes to determine their compensation.

☑ The evaluation by the Board of Directors of whether, and how much information, to disclose to shareholders (particularly when the nature of the disclosure might impact the liability of all or some of the Board of Directors).

☑ Entrenchment: this situation arises when directors take steps to prevent others from removing them from their positions with the company for any reason.

☑ Situations in which a key player's personal financial interests are, at least potentially, in conflict with the financial interests of the corporation. (For example, if a Board member of corporation A, also owned stock in a competing company B and corporation A was preparing to take action which might capture market share from company B.)

Cleansing

A transaction is cleansed if:

☑ The transaction is **approved by a vote of a majority of the fully informed, disinterested directors.** (Note that a majority of the *disinterested* directors is not the same as a majority of the directors. If a Board of Directors is comprised of 15 individuals and 10 of them have a conflict, there would be only 5 disinterested directors, and a majority of the disinterested directors would be 3 of those 5. While this is the standard in Delaware, students should check the specific requirements in

the applicable statute since the exact requirements
may vary in different states.); or

☑ The transaction is **ratified by the informed
shareholders**. (Note that in some states there is no
specific requirement the shareholders be
"disinterested." Other states, like California, do
require the transaction be approved by the
"disinterested" shareholders.); or

☑ The transaction is **shown to have been
"intrinsically fair"** to the corporation. (In general,
"intrinsic" or "substantive" fairness relates to the
price and terms of the deal.) (Note that there is a
more expansive definition of "fairness," called "entire
fairness," which is applied in transactions involving
the merger or acquisition of the corporation and is
discussed below.)

ILLUSTRATIVE PROBLEM

PROBLEM 5.3

Benjamin, Justin, Rachel, Allison, Paul, Robert and Lexi form
the Board of Directors of Renegade, Inc., a Delaware corporation.
When Renegade, Inc. is looking for a new corporate headquarters,
Lexi suggests that they purchase an office building that she owns.
The transaction is approved by Benjamin, Justin, Rachel, Allison
and Paul; Robert votes no and Lexi abstains. Renegade purchases
this building for $12 million. Lexi makes $6 million on the deal that
she had disclosed to the Board in advance. The shareholders do not
vote on the transaction. If this transaction is challenged by a
shareholder, what is the likely result?

Analysis

Lexi has a conflict of interest so the transaction would be
evaluated under the duty of loyalty. The duty of loyalty provides
that in a conflict of interest, the transaction must by "cleansed"
either by a vote of a majority of the disinterested directors, by a vote
of the shareholders or by showing the transaction was substantively
fair. In this situation, it seems that out of seven directors of
Renegade, Inc., six were disinterested and five voted to approve the
transaction. Assuming that the five were fully informed (as it
appears they were given Lexi's disclosures), and that they were
truly disinterested and not related to or influenced by Lexi (and we
have no indication that the other directors were "interested" in any

way), then it appears that the transaction has been cleansed by a majority (five out of six) of the disinterested directors. Since the transaction was cleansed, there is no need to have a vote of the shareholders or to show fairness.

The decision by the disinterested directors to approve the transaction could be challenged as a violation of the duty of care. However, assuming that there was no illegality, fraud, egregious decision or waste, conflict of interest or bad faith and, assuming that the five directors who approved the transaction took reasonable steps to investigate the transaction and to inform themselves, then their approval would be protected by the Business Judgment Rule. Therefore, it seems unlikely that the challenge to the transaction will succeed.

THE CORPORATE OPPORTUNITY DOCTRINE

An area that arises under the duty of loyalty is the "Corporate Opportunity Doctrine." The Corporate Opportunity Doctrine is not a separate duty. Rather, it is a subset of the duty of loyalty. In fact, most issues that arise under this doctrine could be handled by a traditional duty of loyalty analysis. Instead, however, specific rules have developed to deal with these specific types of problems. The Corporate Opportunity Doctrine stands for the principal that **a fiduciary (an officer or director) of the corporation may not take, for personal gain, an opportunity like a business venture or a new opportunity or discovery, in which the firm has a property right, and use it for his or her own advantage without first offering it to the corporation.**

The Corporate Opportunity Doctrine generally applies to:

    ☑   A corporation's officers and Board members (but not its shareholders who do not have another position with the firm); and

    ☑   Certain other individuals who have a fiduciary (or fiduciary-like) relationship with the corporation (such as a lawyer or a consultant).

Note that agents have similar duties to their principals that would cover the corporation's employees as well, but under agency law, not corporate law.

Just what is a "Corporate Opportunity"?

In order to evaluate a problem involving a corporate opportunity, students must first be able to determine whether something qualifies as a corporate opportunity. This determination is often the most difficult (and most important) aspect of the entire analysis. If a corporate opportunity is not present, the doctrine does not apply, and the opportunity may be "taken" by the individual in question. However, if a corporate opportunity is present, the student must evaluate the fact pattern to determine whether the opportunity was "misappropriated" and, if so, whether there are any defenses.

There are several definitions of a corporate opportunity that have developed over the years. Most states use some type of **hybrid test** that includes a blend of tests. Almost all tests include some question of whether the opportunity is something that is consistent with the corporation's current, or anticipated future, business, and whether it is something that the corporation has the financial resources to pursue. An early definition of a corporate opportunity was something in which the corporation had an **interest**, an "**expectancy**" or a **necessity**.

☑ An "interest" is something in which the corporation has a preexisting contractual right.

☑ An "expectancy" is something to which the corporation does not necessarily have a legal right, but, given the other contractual dealings of the corporation, there is a reasonable expectancy that the opportunity would be offered to the corporation (e.g., a lease renewal).

☑ A "necessity" is something that the corporation needs in order to stay in business (e.g., certain raw materials necessary to manufacture a product).

LINE OF BUSINESS TEST AND FAIRNESS TEST

Because the above definitions were relatively narrow, an additional test developed known as the "**line of business**" test. The line of business test was articulated in the 1939 case of *Guth v. Loft* in which the court explained that a corporate opportunity would include activities "as to which . . . [the corporation] has fundamental knowledge, practical experience and ability to pursue, which, logically and naturally, . . . [are] adaptable to its business [taking into account the corporation's] . . . financial position, . . . reasonable needs and aspirations for expansion. . . ." *Guth v. Loft,* 5 A.2d 503, 514 (Del. 1939). The idea behind this test is that if the opportunity falls within the corporation's business or its prospective business, it should still be deemed to be a corporate opportunity. A corporate opportunity under this test includes not just where the business is and what it is doing right now, but where the firm is headed in the future. Most hybrid tests include the "line of business" concept and some aspect of the interest, expectancy, and necessity tests.

Some states (although not California or Delaware) employ a "fairness test" to evaluate whether something is a corporate opportunity. Under the fairness test, one would need to determine whether the officer or director taking the opportunity would violate *equitable standards of what is fair and equitable by corporate standards.*

COMMON DEFENSES

There are also a variety of defenses to a determination that something is a corporate opportunity. In other words, even if an opportunity would fall under one of the above "tests," it might still be found not to qualify as a corporate opportunity if a valid defense is present. As a result, someone who takes the opportunity would not be liable if they can show that the corporation was not able to take advantage of the opportunity, so it was not truly a "corporate opportunity."

One common defense is the **"incapacity" defense**. The incapacity defense would apply if a corporation were not able to take advantage of the opportunity. A corporation might be subject to this defense if it could not take advantage of the opportunity because of legal restrictions such as antitrust laws, contractual restrictions in a loan agreement, or if the corporation was in bankruptcy and thus subject to restrictions on its business dealings. A corporation might also not be able to take advantage of an opportunity because of practical restrictions—for example, if the corporation did not have the financial resources to purchase, or the skills to engage in, the opportunity; if the holder of the opportunity refused to deal with the corporation; or if the corporation lacked the skills to engage in the opportunity. The incapacity defense would also apply if a corporation's charter prohibited it from engaging in the activity involved in the opportunity.

There is also a defense called the **"source" defense**. This defense arises when an opportunity is presented to someone, not because of their corporate position, but because of their personal skills, attributes, or expertise. In such circumstances, an opportunity which otherwise might qualify as a corporate opportunity might be deemed not to be because the opportunity is determined to belong to the individual, not to the corporation.

REQUIREMENT OF OFFERING THE CORPORATE OPPORTUNITY TO THE CORPORATION

Any time a corporate opportunity exists, a person bound by the doctrine who wishes to take advantage of the opportunity must fully disclose the opportunity and his or her interest in the opportunity to the Board of Directors. The Board of Directors has what amounts to a right of first refusal on the opportunity. If the Board properly rejects the opportunity, following a full disclosure, the individual may take the opportunity for him or herself. Note that in order for a disclosure to be effective, one may not just casually inquire whether the firm is interested in the opportunity. The opportunity AND the person's interest in taking the opportunity must both be disclosed. If the Board does not properly reject the opportunity and the individual takes the opportunity, that "breach" might still be "cleansed" by disclosure to, and approval by, the shareholders or by showing that the transaction was fair.

DAMAGES

A violation of the corporate opportunity doctrine is subject to various equitable remedies such as constructive trust, so that the benefits that were received in violation of the doctrine are held "in trust" for the corporation. Of course, any violation may also be subject to damages.

CORPORATE OPPORTUNITY ANALYSIS

A corporate opportunity problem typically involves a situation in which a fiduciary of the corporation is presented with an "opportunity." These problems can be evaluated using the following analysis:

☑ First, a determination must be made as to whether the opportunity is a "corporate opportunity." (See analysis above.)

☑ If it is not, then there is no breach of fiduciary duty, regardless of the fiduciary's actions with respect to the opportunity.

☑ If it is a corporate opportunity, then one must examine the facts to determine if the opportunity was disclosed to the appropriate corporate authority, such as the Board of Directors.

☑ If the fiduciary does not *properly* disclose the opportunity, and then takes the opportunity for herself, then there is a breach of the duty of loyalty.

☑ If the fiduciary does *properly* disclose the opportunity, and the opportunity was properly rejected by the corporation, then there is no breach of fiduciary duty. Note that if full disclosure is made to the Board of Directors, and the Board votes to permit the fiduciary to take the opportunity, this creates a "safe harbor" for the individual (subject of course to the limits of the BJR). (There are cases in which courts have found that more informal disclosures to Board members or senior management have been sufficient, but, since they do not create a "safe harbor," those more informal disclosures might still be subject to review by a court.)

☑ If the corporation does not *properly* reject the opportunity, and then the fiduciary takes the opportunity for herself, then there is a breach of the duty of loyalty. (Note that like all breaches of the duty of loyalty, this breach could be "cleansed" by an informed vote of the shareholders or by showing fairness. However, that type of "cleansing" rarely occurs in the corporate opportunity context.)

Note that in the above analysis, liability is based upon taking the opportunity. There is not liability (at least under the corporate opportunity doctrine) for possessing or knowing about a corporate opportunity. However, one could imagine a situation in which failure to exercise an opportunity on behalf of the corporation, or failure to inform the corporation about a desirable opportunity, might constitute a violation of the duty of care or the duty of loyalty, depending upon the specific facts.

ILLUSTRATIVE PROBLEM

PROBLEM 5.4

Wendy is an officer and director of Carrot Company, Inc. ("CCI"). CCI distributes carrots and food products containing carrots to grocery stores throughout the U.S. One day when Wendy is at the supermarket looking at the different types of carrots available, a man named Bugs comes up to her and shows her a new invention, which is the best carrot peeler Wendy has ever seen. When Wendy tells Bugs that she works for CCI, Bugs asks Wendy if

CCI would be interested in buying the invention. Wendy explains that CCI would probably not be interested, but that she would be willing to form a company with Bugs to produce and distribute the invention. Wendy quits her job at CCI, starts a company with Bugs and makes millions of dollars. CCI finds out and sues Wendy for taking a CCI corporate opportunity. Would Wendy be liable?

Analysis

If the carrot peeler was a corporate opportunity that Wendy misappropriated without the informed consent of CCI, she will be liable. In evaluating the transaction, one of the most significant questions is whether or not the carrot peeler represented a "corporate opportunity." While there are various tests, depending on jurisdiction, we can ask if the carrot peeler represented an interest, expectancy or necessity. It is unlikely that CCI had an interest in the carrot peeler since there was no mention of a contractual right or that it was necessary for CCI's business because CCI's business does not seem to depend on the peeler. In addition, there is no mention of any expectancy that the carrot peeler be offered to CCI as would be the case with a lease extension. The next question is whether the carrot peeler was in CCI's current or prospective line of business. Although we do not have a substantial amount of information about CCI, we must still try to determine if the carrot peeler would fall within CCI's line of business. We should ask if the carrot peeler involved an opportunity within CCI's current, or anticipated future, business, and whether CCI had the resources to take advantage of it. One significant question would be whether CCI sells any other devices related to carrots or does it just sells food. If CCI sells other "carrot related" devices, the carrot peeler would clearly be in its line of business. If CCI does not sell any such devices, but had discussed and considered selling such devices if the opportunity arose, the carrot peeler still might be within the CCI line of business. If CCI is purely a food business and never had an interest in any device (carrot related or not), the carrot peeler might well be outside of CCI's line of business and would not have been a corporate opportunity. Note that if Bugs had approached Wendy at the office and desired to offer the carrot peeler to CCI, regardless of whether it fell within CCI's line of business, Wendy would have had an obligation to disclose the information about the offer to CCI.

Given how many companies engage in related lines of business, let's assume that CCI had sold some devices over the years, so the carrot peeler would be a within CCI's line of business. Even if the carrot peeler was within CCI's line of business, Wendy might still have some defenses that might show that this was not a corporate opportunity. One defense is the **"incapacity" defense**. The incapacity defense would apply if CCI was not able to take advantage of the opportunity even if CCI had been offered the opportunity. CCI might be subject to this defense if it did not have the financial resources to purchase the carrot peeler, if CCI's charter prohibited it from any activity other than the sale of carrots and food containing carrots, or if there were some antitrust prohibition against CCI moving into the carrot device market. In any event, there is no indication that any of these circumstances would apply to the facts in the hypothetical, so it is unlikely that the incapacity defense would apply here. Since there is no indication of financial problems, this defense seems unlikely to succeed. It is also unlikely that the "**source**" defense would apply in this situation. This defense occurs when an opportunity is presented to someone, not because of their corporate position, but because of their personal skills, attributes or expertise. In this instance, there is no indication that, other than being at the market, Bugs had any such reason to approach Wendy.

Once something is a corporate opportunity, one must determine whether the individual disclosed the opportunity to the corporation. In this instance, Wendy should have disclosed the opportunity to CCI's Board of Directors. If Wendy had made a full disclosure to CCI's directors, and a majority of the disinterested Board voted to allow Wendy to take the opportunity, Wendy would not have liability. (Note that the Board's decision would probably be protected by the BJR.) If the Board did not approve Wendy's appropriation of the opportunity and Wendy did not take the opportunity, she would not have liability for violating the corporate opportunity doctrine. However, in this instance, Wendy did not disclose the opportunity to the Board of Directors or to anyone else at CCI, and she did appropriate the opportunity, so she will have liability.

Remember that the corporate opportunity doctrine falls under the duty of loyalty. As in all duty of loyalty cases, even if a transaction is not cleansed, the defendant typically has the opportunity to show that the transaction was "fair" to the corporation. However, in the case of corporate opportunities, it is almost impossible to show that the appropriation was fair since the individual taking the opportunity rarely pays anything for it. It is unlikely that the defendant could then argue that paying nothing was a fair price for the opportunity.

DOMINANT SHAREHOLDERS

Typically, fiduciary duties do not apply to a corporation's shareholders. They usually apply only to a corporation's "fiduciaries," which include its directors, officers and agents. An "ordinary" shareholder of a corporation does not have duties to her fellow shareholders. She can vote in an irresponsible manner. She can vote selfishly for a transaction that will benefit her, even if she knows that it will be bad for the long-term interests of other shareholders.

However, this absence of responsibility changes if a shareholder is a "dominant" shareholder. Because a dominant shareholder has more influence over the corporation and over the Board of Directors, there are certain instances when dominant shareholders are bound by certain fiduciary duties. In these instances, only certain "duty of loyalty" transactions are implicated. The idea is that if a shareholder has a large enough ownership interest to "control" the Board of Directors, any transactions that involve that shareholder being treated in a different way than the other shareholders are suspect.

Suspect transactions involving a dominant shareholder are reviewed with the same scrutiny applied to other duty of loyalty issues. However, in the instance of a dominant shareholder, the Board is not allowed to "cleanse" the transaction, and even ratification by the disinterested shareholders just shifts the burden of proof. Ultimately, the question is whether the transaction was "intrinsically fair" (unless a merger is involved, in which case "entire" fairness—both fair procedures and fair price—is required). If there has been no shift of the burden of proof, the dominant shareholder must show that the transaction was intrinsically fair. If there has been a shift of the burden by ratification, the objecting shareholders must show that the transaction was NOT intrinsically fair.

The general rule is that:

☑ Shareholders acting as shareholders have no obligation to one another.

☑ However, there is an exception to this rule. A shareholder does have obligations when that shareholder has *so much stock* that he or she is considered to have control. In such cases, that shareholder has an obligation to "minority" shareholders in certain "duty of loyalty" transactions.

☑ When a dominant shareholder exists, one must ask whether the transaction in question involves a situation in which the dominant shareholder has a conflict or in which the dominant shareholder is receiving a benefit at the expense of the minority shareholders or that the minority shareholders do not receive.

☑   If so, if a fully informed, majority of the minority shareholders have not approved the transaction, the dominant shareholder will probably need to show that the transaction was fair to the corporation either through intrinsic fairness, or, in the case of a merger, entire fairness.

☑   If a fully informed majority of the minority shareholders has approved the transaction, then the transaction may still be challenged, but the burden shifts to the minority shareholders to show that the transaction was not fair to the corporation.

How much stock is required for someone to be a dominant shareholder?

Of course if a shareholder has over 50% of the corporation's stock, that shareholder is a dominant shareholder. However, 50% is not required. Frequently, a dominant shareholder may have as little as 25% or less. Ultimately, the question turns upon whether, given the nature of the corporation and the holdings of the other shareholders, the holdings of a particular shareholder are sufficient for that shareholder to exert control over the corporation. In other words, the assessment of shareholder "dominance" is context dependent. If one shareholder has 25%, that shareholder is not dominant if someone else has 75%. However, if one shareholder has 25% of the corporation's stock and all of the other shareholders each hold 1% (or less), the shareholder with 25% might very well be "dominant."

There are a few other points to remember. If more than one shareholder is acting in concert, their "group" may be considered a "dominant" shareholder. Also, there is an important exception to this rule: If the controlling shareholder (or "group") owns all of the outstanding stock of the corporation, the rule does not apply because there is no minority to be potentially injured by any of the dominant shareholder's actions. Remember, just because a dominant shareholder is present does NOT mean that the BJR does not apply. The BJR does not apply to a transaction involving a dominant shareholder only when the dominant shareholder has a conflict of interest. If a dominant shareholder benefits to the detriment of the minority shareholder(s), there is a conflict of interest. Thus, the BJR would not apply. However, rather than following a standard duty of loyalty analysis to evaluate a questionable transaction, a dominant shareholder analysis would apply.

Students should also be aware that a dominant shareholder may be an individual or an entity. If an entity is the dominant shareholder, the corporation in which it holds a dominant position is its subsidiary. Many dominant shareholder cases involve a situation in which there is a parent company that does not own 100% of the subsidiary, so the subsidiary is not "wholly owned." If the parent owns more than 50% of the subsidiary, the subsidiary is "majority controlled." If not, the subsidiary is "minority controlled." Either way, if the parent has control, it is a dominant or controlling shareholder and subject to the increased duties to the "minority" shareholders discussed in this section.

The following is a list of sample transactions that may or may NOT fall within the dominant shareholder analysis:

☑ **Large dividends**—The dominant shareholder causes the corporation to issue large dividends that will be distributed pro rata to all shareholders. Because both the minority and the majority would receive a proportionate share of the dividend, there is no dominant shareholder issue, and the appropriate test would be the BJR.

☑ **Failure to enforce a provision in a contract**—If the dominant shareholder has an interest in the other party to the contract, this action would be subject to a dominant shareholder analysis because the dominant shareholder, as a party with an interest in the contract, would be (at least potentially) receiving a benefit from the corporation that the minority shareholders would NOT be getting. Therefore, the appropriate test would be intrinsic fairness. On the other hand, if the dominant shareholder has no interest in the other party to the contract, there would be no conflict and the transaction would be subject to the BJR. (Note that in the test for intrinsic fairness, the dominant shareholder must prove that the price and terms of the transaction were not unfair to the minority shareholders.)

☑ Selling the company to an outside third party would be subject to the BJR.

☑ Selling the corporation to an entity in which the dominant shareholder has an interest is subject to the dominant shareholder analysis and a showing of fairness. Note that because the sale of the corporation is involved, the test would be "entire" fairness (which includes substantive fairness and procedural fairness) not just intrinsic fairness.

The bottom line is that most shareholders do not owe each other fiduciary duties in their capacity as shareholders. A dominant shareholder problem arises only when a dominant shareholder (or shareholder group) exists and that shareholder is receiving something of value that the other minority shareholders are not receiving. Students should look for a dominant shareholder who has a conflict of interest (AKA a duty of loyalty issue) as an indication that the foregoing analysis should be applied to the facts.

Other issues that might arise

Note that under Delaware law, ratification occurs when the Board of Directors or a committee of the Board, in good faith, authorizes the contract or transaction by the affirmative votes of a majority of the disinterested directors. However, in dominant shareholder cases, the Board is almost never disinterested. There is a theoretical possibility that in a cumulative voting situation, the Board of Directors could have members who were appointed by the minority shareholders and had neither a connection to the dominant shareholder nor were they subject to the dominant shareholder's influence. While it is unclear what would happen if there were truly disinterested directors who did approve the transaction, there is a strong argument that such approval would cleanse the transaction, subject only to the BJR and not to a showing of intrinsic fairness by the dominant shareholder.

"Entire fairness" versus "intrinsic fairness"

In most transactions in which a party must show fairness, the required showing is known as "intrinsic fairness." Intrinsic fairness involves the substance of the transaction. In other words, the question is whether the price and terms of the transaction were "fair" to the corporation. **"Entire fairness" involves the substance of the transaction as well as the process and procedure by which it was accomplished,** and both must be shown to be fair. Most transactions only involve intrinsic fairness. However, entire fairness arises in situations in which a dominant shareholder is involved AND the complained of transaction is a merger (or some other transaction upon which the shareholders are entitled to vote). In these transactions, because of the shareholders' right to have a say in the deal and because of the significance of the transaction, courts have required that the additional component of procedural fairness be present. The requirement of entire fairness is seen below in Chapter 10 in conjunction with the concept of "cash out" mergers in which a shareholder who is forced to sell their stock in the corporation has the right to be treated properly on a procedural basis as well as merely to receive a fair price for their stock.

ILLUSTRATIVE PROBLEMS

PROBLEM 5.5

Ken holds 82% of Red Rum Corp., a Delaware corporation. Bari owns 13%, Owen owns 3%, and Quinn owns 2%. The Board of Directors, of which Ken is the Chairman, decides to sell the most guarded (though far from the only) asset of the corporation, the Red Rum recipe, to a competitor, Blue Rum Corp., for $35 million. Ken really supports the sale since he is "getting on in years." The sale is approved by a majority of the Board. Owen sues Ken for breach of fiduciary duty, claiming that Ken is a dominant shareholder and that the transaction is unfair since it will eliminate Red Rum's one competitive advantage. How would this transaction be evaluated?

Analysis

The transaction would be evaluated using the BJR. Even though Ken is a dominant shareholder, there is no indication that the corporation is entering into a transaction in which Ken has a conflict of interest or in which Ken is getting something that the other shareholders are not. The $35 million proceeds would go to Red Rum. If Red Rum were to dissolve, the proceeds would be distributed (after paying creditors) to the shareholders in accordance with their percentage interests. Therefore, the fact that the other shareholders do not want to sell is not relevant. Control does have some advantages. There would be some check on the transaction. That "check," however, would be much less stringent than a dominant shareholder analysis. Under the BJR, the transaction would be allowed, unless Owen could show that the transaction involved either fraud, illegality, conflict of interest, bad faith, waste, an egregious or irrational decision, no decision or an uninformed decision. If Owen cannot show any of these, the transaction will be allowed, and neither Ken nor the Board of Directors will incur liability. In this particular transaction, assuming that the Board made an informed decision and there is a business reason for the sale, Owen will not be able to overcome the BJR.

PROBLEM 5.6

Assume the same facts as in problem 5.5 above, but instead of selling the Red Rum recipe to Blue Rum Corp., Red Rum enters into a new transaction with a corporation called Bottle It, Inc., to handle the production of Red Rum's product. Bottle It, Inc., charges a little more than the company that formerly handled bottling and production for Red Rum, but the Board of Directors thinks Bottle It, Inc., will do a better job. It also turns out that Bottle It, Inc., is owned by Ken and his sister Melanie. Now, Quinn sues Ken for damages. Does she have a case?

Analysis

Whether Quinn will prevail depends upon several factors. Since Ken owns 82% of Red Rum Corp., he is a dominant shareholder. In this instance, because Ken has a conflict of interest, the transaction will be subject to a dominant shareholder analysis. Since Ken owns part of Bottle It, Inc., and Red Rum has entered into a transaction with Bottle It, Inc., that transaction must be more closely evaluated. The transaction cannot be cleansed by the Board of Directors since the presumption is that Ken, as a dominant shareholder, controls the Board. The transaction could be submitted for approval to the fully informed shareholders. If the disinterested, fully informed shareholders do not vote on the transaction, or do not approve the transaction, Ken must show that the transaction meets the intrinsic fairness test. In other words, Ken must show that the terms of the deal with Bottle It, Inc. were fair and reasonable to Red Rum Corp. If Bari, who owns 13% of Red Rum Corporation, is a disinterested shareholder, is fully informed and votes to approve the transaction, the transaction would be "approved" by a majority of the disinterested shareholders. However, under the dominant shareholder analysis, the transaction is still not "cleansed" as it would be in a typical duty of loyalty case. Instead, the burden of proof shifts to Quinn, the plaintiff, to show that the transaction was unfair to Red Rum Corp. If Quinn cannot meet this burden, the transaction will stand, and Ken will not be liable. Note that because the transaction with Bottle It, Inc. does not involve a merger or sale of assets, intrinsic fairness is the applicable measure, not entire fairness.

FIDUCIARY DUTIES SUMMARIZED

As seen in the preceding materials there are several different tools and measurements that are used to assess a transaction or action by a corporation or its fiduciaries. In order to determine which assessment to use, one needs to determine what happened and who was involved. When evaluating such problems, students might want to ask some preliminary questions to aid them in evaluating the fact pattern. These questions include:

☑ Did the Board of Directors act, or did the situation involve a failure to act?

☑ Was a dominant shareholder involved in the transaction, and, if so, did the transaction involve a conflict of interest, or did that dominant shareholder receive something that the other shareholders did not receive or did not receive in proportion to their holdings in the corporation?

☑ If there was not a dominant shareholder involved (or a transaction which would trigger a dominant shareholder analysis), did a director or officer have a conflict of interest in the transaction?

☑ Was the transaction "cleansed"?

☑ Would the transaction qualify for protection of the BJR?

☑ Even if the transaction is not protected by the BJR, did it violate the duty of care?

☑ Even if a duty was violated, was the transaction "fair" to the corporation?

Once some of the preliminary issues have been determined, a fact pattern should be evaluated under the applicable analysis, summarized below.

Duty of care—

☑ If there was an informed vote of the Board of Directors and none of the BJR exceptions apply, then the BJR typically applies and the transaction is protected.

☑ If the BJR does not apply (see above), then there should still be an actual duty of care analysis (or duty of loyalty analysis if applicable).

☑ If there was a violation of the duty of care, the parties involved may still be protected if there was an informed shareholder vote or if the parties involved can show that the transaction was "fair" to the corporation. (In a duty of care claim fairness would be an affirmative defense, not a bar to the claim.)

Duty of loyalty for directors and officers—

☑ If there was a transaction involving a conflict of interest, but not a dominant shareholder, the conflict may have been cleansed by the fully informed approval of a majority of the disinterested directors. Such approval would eliminate the duty of loyalty claim.

☑ THEN, the disinterested majority's approval of the transaction would still be evaluated under the BJR and, if necessary, a duty of care analysis.

☑ If all of the directors are interested or if the transaction was not cleansed by the Board of Directors, then the transaction may still have been cleansed by a vote of the fully informed shareholders.

☑ If the transaction was approved by a majority of the disinterested shareholders, then there is no further analysis required.

☑ If the transaction was approved by a majority of the shareholders but in order to obtain the approval of a majority of the shareholders the votes of shareholders who are "interested" in the transaction were required, then there is a question as to whether the transaction was cleansed. (In California, the transaction would not be cleansed. In Delaware, it is unclear. The Corporations Code and case law of the relevant state should be reviewed to determine the requirement.)

☑ If the transaction was not cleansed by the shareholders or the directors, then the defendant has the burden of proving fairness.

Duty of loyalty for dominant shareholders—

☑ In situations in which there is a duty of loyalty problem involving a dominant shareholder, the transaction cannot be cleansed. (See note above about the possibility of cleansing IF one could show that there were truly disinterested directors on the Board, a majority of whom approved the transaction.)

☑ If there was a shareholder vote to ratify the transaction, then, although the transaction is still not cleansed, the burden of proof *might* shift to the plaintiff to show that the transaction was unfair.

☑   If a majority of disinterested shareholders voted to approve the transaction, then the burden shifts to the plaintiff to show unfairness.

☑   If a majority of disinterested shareholders did not vote to approve the transaction (or if there was no shareholder vote), then the burden is on the defendant to show fairness.

☑   If the transaction involved a merger (or some other significant transaction on which the shareholders would be entitled to vote), then the defendant needs to show *entire fairness* (substantive AND procedural fairness). Otherwise, the measure is *intrinsic fairness* (substantive fairness only).

CHAPTER 6

Shareholders and the Rights and Restrictions Associated with Ownership

While a great deal of a typical Business Associations course focuses on the internal structure and operation of the firm, there are several issues that arise relating to the rights, privileges and preferences of shareholders. Shareholders, unless they are also directors, officers or employees, are not involved in the management of the corporation. Therefore, there are not typically fiduciary duties associated with the role of shareholder. (While, as discussed in the previous chapter, there are such duties in the case of a dominant shareholder, these duties arise because of the dominant shareholder's potential ability to exert control over the corporation even without having a position on the Board of Directors.) Because shareholders do not typically exercise control in their shareholder role, their voting decisions are not regulated. (This means that most shareholders may vote on an uninformed, foolish, and even a selfish basis.) This lack of control also forms the rationale for shareholders' limited liability. However, in exchange, shareholders may not control the management of the corporation from their shareholder role. Consistent with this limited role, there are restrictions on the subject matter about which shareholders have input, and there are limits on the matters that are appropriate to submit to shareholders for a vote.

Shareholders vote on major transactions, elect Board members and may also vote on various resolutions that are typically not binding on the Board. A good way to understand this division is to remember that shareholders get to decide who will operate the corporation, but they may not operate the corporation themselves.

SHAREHOLDER OWNERSHIP RIGHTS

When an individual (or entity) owns any portion of a corporation, that ownership interest is represented in shares of stock. The stock of a corporation may be divided into as many

111

shares as the owner or owners desire. There may be one share of stock, representing the entire ownership (100%) of a corporation, or there may be millions of shares. When a corporation is formed, the Articles of Incorporation set forth how many shares are authorized and whether there is more than one "class" of stock. If there is only one class of stock, that class is typically known as "common" stock. Common stock typically has the right to vote AND the right to receive dividends, if any. Common stock also represents a claim on any assets remaining in the corporation once all creditors have been paid, and once any obligations, which might exist on other classes of stock, if any, have been satisfied. This right to claim that which is left is known as a "residual claim," and the shareholders holding such a right are known as **residual claimants.**"

The rights associated with a share of common stock usually fall into one of two categories:

☑   Economic rights; and

☑   Voting rights

Every corporation is required to have these rights present in its shares. While in most corporations the economic rights and voting rights both reside in the corporation's common stock, there is no requirement that these rights be present in the same class of stock.

SHAREHOLDER ECONOMIC RIGHTS

Regardless of how many shares (or classes) of stock a corporation has **authorized**, economic rights are determined based on how many shares are **issued and outstanding (i.e., shares that are actually owned by shareholders at any given point in time).** Assuming there are no other classes of stock in a particular corporation, the shareholders of the common stock may determine their percentage of the total rights by looking at the number of shares they hold compared to the total number of shares that are issued and outstanding. If a shareholder holds 10 shares, and there are a total of 200 shares issued and outstanding (all of the same class of shares), then that shareholder is entitled to receive 5% of the **dividends** paid to shareholders and 5% of any money that is paid to shareholders upon the liquidation of the corporation.

SHAREHOLDER VOTING RIGHTS

Shareholders do not manage the corporation. The Board of Directors is charged with the responsibility of management. However, shareholders vote to elect directors, and that power to elect directors is critical to the control over the corporation. Shareholders vote on other matters as well, such as whether to grant approval of certain significant transactions outside of the corporation's ordinary course of business that would involve a fundamental change to the corporation. Shareholders also have the power to vote on resolutions. These matters are discussed below.

Shareholders typically vote on the following matters:

- ☑ Election of directors;

- ☑ Fundamental changes to the corporation (such as merger, sale of all the assets, corporate dissolution and amending the Articles of Incorporation or the Bylaws); and

- ☑ Shareholder resolutions (Note that resolutions may take two different forms: (i) resolutions which are proposed by a corporation's management such as a resolution to ratify an option plan or an action taken by the Board of Directors; and (ii) resolutions which are proposed by the shareholders, requesting or advising that the Board take certain action).

HOW DO SHAREHOLDERS VOTE?

Shareholder voting can take place at any meeting of the shareholders. A shareholder usually may vote all of the shares owned by that shareholder on a particular matter. For example, if a shareholder has 100 shares, that shareholder's vote on a particular matter counts 100 times. If another shareholder has 200 shares, that shareholder's vote on a particular matter counts 200 times. If those were the only two shareholders, the shareholder with 200 shares would prevail on every vote (assuming that a majority vote was required to win). In other words, a shareholder's percentage ownership of a corporation matters to determine how much voting power that shareholder has and how much control that shareholder can exercise over the corporation. Percentage based voting is referred to as "*pro rata*," meaning that shareholders vote in proportion to their holdings. (Note that directors serving on the Board do NOT vote on a pro rata basis. Directors vote "*per capita*," or per person, so each Board member receives one vote.)

Typically a simple **majority** (greater than 50%) vote is required to take an action, and shareholders are entitled to one vote for each share they hold. However, sometimes a corporation's organizational documents, such as the Articles of Incorporation or the Bylaws, may provide for different voting structures or different numbers of affirmative votes required to approve certain matters. If a percentage greater than a simple majority is required to take some action that greater percentage is called a "**super majority**." Super majorities may be required for all votes or only for votes on specific matters, or not at all. It depends on the governing documents of the corporation.

Shareholders who hold stock on a certain date, known as the "**record date**," are entitled to vote in shareholder elections immediately following that date. The Board of Directors establishes the record date (typically a few weeks before a scheduled shareholder vote), and it determines which shareholders are entitled to vote at a particular shareholders meeting or on a particular proposal, even if they sell their shares after the record date but prior to the vote.

Cumulative Voting

Cumulative voting is an alternative to traditional voting and is used to give minority shareholders a greater opportunity to select a director to a corporation's Board. In a traditional voting structure, the majority shareholder (or shareholders) would be able to appoint all of the directors on the Board. With cumulative voting, shareholders are entitled to spread out their votes for several directors or to "accumulate" all their votes to select one or two directors, to maximize minority shareholders' impact and to increase the chance for a minority shareholder to elect a director to the Board. In some states, such as California, cumulative voting is required, except in publicly held corporations. In other states, this structure is optional. Cumulative voting works as illustrated in the following example:

ILLUSTRATIVE EXAMPLE

RJB Corporation has three shareholders, Rachel, Justin and Benjamin. Benjamin owns 30% of RJB, Justin owns 10% and Rachel owns 60%. RJB has three seats on its Board of Directors. Under traditional voting, Rachel would be able to select every Board member because she would have a majority vote and would prevail in each vote. However, in cumulative voting, each shareholder is allocated votes equal to their number of shares multiplied by the seats on the Board. So, if Rachel had 6 shares, she would receive 18 votes (3 Board seats times 6 shares); if Justin had 1 share, he would receive 3 votes; if Benjamin had 3 shares, he would receive 9 votes. Each shareholder could vote all of their votes for one director seat on the Board or spread their votes out over several seats.

Under cumulative voting, the three Board nominees who receive the highest total number of votes are elected to the Board.

Therefore, it should be apparent that, while Rachel has enough votes to elect two directors, she cannot divide her votes over three seats and win each seat. If Rachel allocates 9 votes to nominee A and 9 votes to nominee B, she will have no votes remaining to allocate to any other nominee. If she allocates fewer than 9 votes to any nominee, then that nominee will not have as many votes as Benjamin's nominee. Benjamin can allocate all 9 of his votes to one nominee (e.g., nominee C), and that nominee will be one of the top three vote recipients and, so, be elected to the Board. Through cumulative voting, a minority shareholder is not able to control the Board but is able to have representation on the Board. Note that Justin does not have sufficient votes to elect a nominee to the Board. Cumulative voting is not a guarantee that every shareholder will have representation. It is just an effort to increase representation. The greater the number of seats on the Board, the smaller percentage of stock ownership necessary to be able to elect someone to the Board with cumulative voting.

PROXIES

Often a shareholder is not able to attend a meeting but would still like to vote on a matter. In these instances, the shareholder may give a **proxy** to someone else to vote that shareholder's shares. A proxy is a written (or these days it might be an electronic) document that is given to another person, allowing (or instructing) that other person to vote on the shareholder's behalf. (In the corporate context a proxy refers to the right to vote a person's shares, but the term could apply to any vote.) The person who is given a proxy to vote is called the "**proxy holder**." Proxies may give the holder discretion or no discretion in that they may provide specific instructions on how the shares are to be voted, or they may leave the discretion of how to vote to the proxy holder. Proxies may also be revocable. In other words, if Adam gives his proxy to Lisa to vote at ABC Corporation's annual meeting, but Adam shows up at the meeting and wants to vote, he may revoke his proxy and vote his shares (provided that there is no agreement between the two that makes the proxy "**irrevocable**").

Proxies are often important because in order to have a meeting of the shareholders of a corporation a **quorum** is required. A quorum is a minimum number of people, voters or votes (in this case shareholders), that must be present at a meeting in order to make the proceedings at a meeting valid. Quorum requirements are usually established by statute but may be modified, subject to statutory limits, in a corporation's Bylaws. A typical quorum requirement for a shareholder vote would be fifty percent of the votes, plus one. So if a corporation has 5,000 shares issued and outstanding, 2,501 shares would be required to be represented at a meeting in order to have a quorum. Note that because shareholders vote based upon percentages, it is the number of shares that is relevant and not the number of shareholders. Because so few shareholders actually attend annual meetings (at least of large corporations), without the use of proxies, the corporation's shareholders would be unable to vote because the quorum requirements would not be met. Therefore, a corporation's management will often solicit proxies from its shareholders prior to a meeting in order to meet the quorum requirements and have a meeting at which a valid election may be conducted.

PROXY RULES

There are several rules governing the entire proxy process (the "**Proxy Rules**") which are addressed in Regulation 14A, adopted under the Securities Exchange Act of 1934 (the "1934 Act"). The Proxy Rules regulate the manner and means by which proxies may be obtained or solicited. In order to understand these rules one must understand the term "solicitation," which includes:

☑ Any request for a proxy;

☑ Any request to execute, not to execute, or to revoke a proxy; and

☑ Furnishing a form of proxy *or other communication*, reasonably calculated to result in the procurement, withholding, or revocation of a proxy. (Courts have found that even communications, which may "constitute a step in a chain of communications designed to accomplish such a result" may also constitute a "solicitation." *Long Island Lighting Co. v. Barbash*, 779 F.2d 793, 796 (2d Cir.1985)).

Prior to the time that any person makes a "solicitation," the person being solicited must first receive or have received a "proxy statement." Rule 14a–3 *et seq.* also regulates the form, content and filing requirements for proxy statements. These rules, which prohibit materially misleading statements, are intended, among other things, to provide for adequate disclosure to shareholders before their proxies are solicited.

There are also several exceptions to what constitutes a solicitation. These exceptions are important since only communications with shareholders that constitute "solicitations" under the Proxy Rules are regulated. Communications that are not "solicitations" are not subject to the Proxy Rules. Exceptions to "solicitations" include:

- ☑ Public statements or speeches or advertisements stating how a shareholder intends to vote and the reasoning behind that vote;

- ☑ Solicitations by someone (other than, among many other exceptions, an affiliate of the corporation or a party in interest) who does not intend to act on another's behalf;

- ☑ Any solicitation made to 10 or fewer persons, provided it is not made by the corporation; and

- ☑ Advice to any person with whom the person furnishing the advice (the "advisor") has a business relationship (provided that such advisor does not have certain other interests or undisclosed connections to the corporation that would amount to a conflict of interest).

PROXY FIGHTS

Sometimes different groups within a corporation will have different positions on how the shareholders should vote. In addition, there are sometimes challenges to the existing management (i.e., the Board of Directors) of a corporation, and situations may arise in which different, competing groups of potential directors are battling for control of a corporation. In those instances, the outcome will often depend on which group has collected the most proxies. For this reason, a battle to obtain control of a corporation through a vote of the shareholders is referred to as a "**proxy fight**."

Proxy fights are one way a group might attempt to take control of a company (as opposed to "tender offers" or "acquisitions," discussed below). Proxy fights often occur when a group that wants to gain control, known as the "**insurgent group**," tries to become elected to the Board and oust existing management, known as the "**incumbent directors**," by soliciting proxies from a large enough number of shareholders to elect its (the insurgent group's) own representatives to the Board of Directors. Of course, there are several rules that govern the process of soliciting and obtaining proxies for a corporate election. Many of these rules are set forth in Rule 14(a), promulgated under the 1934 Act. For example, **Rule 14a–7** provides that, when an insurgent group wants to contact shareholders and provide material related to the contested vote, EITHER:

☑ Management may mail the insurgent group's material to the shareholders directly and charge the group for the cost; OR

☑ Management can give the insurgent group a copy of the shareholder list and let the insurgent group distribute its own materials.

As one can imagine, management typically prefers to control contact with its shareholders, so there is often an additional dispute about providing an insurgent group with access to a shareholder list, which includes shareholder contact information.

RECOVERING COSTS ASSOCIATED WITH OBTAINING PROXIES IN A BATTLE FOR CONTROL

Once the proxy battle is over and one side has won and the other has lost, the parties often turn to the issue of getting their costs reimbursed. The rules might vary from state to state, but, in general, there are different rules that govern the reimbursement of costs for insurgents and for incumbents. When the incumbent directors expend money to defend their positions from an insurgent effort to oust them, as long as the expenses are *not excessive* and *not illegal*, there is typically no problem with the incumbent group reimbursing themselves once they are victorious. The rules for reimbursement of expenses are as follows:

☑ The corporation may NOT reimburse either party (the incumbents or the insurgents), UNLESS the dispute involves a **question of corporate policy**. The dispute cannot just involve an argument that one group is better than the other. Of course, because people are aware of this rule, most proxy battles are presented as matters involving "policy" disputes;

☑ The corporation may ONLY reimburse **reasonable and proper expenses** (Note that there is a relatively broad definition of "reasonable and proper," and different courts in different situations have found that it includes: disclosure statements; telephone solicitations; and in some cases, even in-person visits to corporate shareholders.);

☑ The corporation may reimburse the incumbents, whether they win or lose; and

☑ The corporation may reimburse insurgents **only** if they win and (if they do not want that reimbursement to be subject to attack) **only** if the corporation's shareholders ratify the reimbursement, after full disclosure.

SHAREHOLDER PROPOSALS

Rule 14a–8 allows qualifying shareholders to submit certain proposals to their fellow shareholders for a vote by having these proposals placed on the company's proxy statement to the shareholders and have the company bear the expenses. The biggest question that arises in this area (and therefore, the question most frequently asked of students) is what criteria need to be satisfied in order for a shareholder proposal to "qualify" to be included in the proxy statement. Realize that shareholders (even through a proposal) do not get to "control" the Board of Directors. The proposals must relate to certain areas over which the shareholders have control. In order to satisfy the requirement that a proposal be within an area which is a proper subject for action by the shareholders, most proposals are worded as recommendations (rather than mandates) and are nonbinding in nature.

There are both procedural and substantive requirements that must be met for a shareholder proposal to be included in a company's proxy materials. The procedural requirements include:

☑ In order to be eligible to submit a proposal, a shareholder must hold $2,000 in market value of the company's stock (or 1% of the company's voting stock), and the shareholder must have held it, continuously, for the 12 months preceding the proposal;

☑ A shareholder may not submit more than one proposal for each shareholders meeting;

☑ A proposal may not exceed 500 words;

☑ Most proposals must be submitted to the company at least 120 days before the company's proxy statement is to be released; and

☑ Either the shareholder or the shareholder's "qualified representative" must attend the meeting at which the proposal is to be considered.

The substantive requirements for a shareholder proposal include:

☑ The topic of the proposal must be a proper subject for actions by shareholders under state law of the state in which the corporation is organized;

☑ The proposal may not, if implemented, cause the company to violate any law;

☑ The proposal may not address a personal grievance or special interest, which is not applicable to the other shareholders;

☑ If the proposal relates to the company's operations, those operations must involve at least 5% of the company's assets, net earnings or gross sales, *OR* the operations must otherwise be "significantly related to the company's business." (Proposals will be included notwithstanding their failure to reach the specified economic threshold IF a significant relationship to the company's business is demonstrated on the face of the resolution or in the supporting material);

☑ The proposal must not violate the Proxy Rules (such as those prohibiting material misleading statements);

☑ The proposal cannot be beyond the company's power to implement (such as a vote requiring the world to adopt a universal currency);

☑ The proposal may not address management functions, such as the company's <u>ordinary</u> business operations;

☑ The proposal may not relate to specific amounts of cash or stock dividends; and

☑ The proposal may not directly conflict with one of the company's own proposals that is being submitted at the same meeting.

☑ In addition, if the proposal was previously submitted within the last 5 years and did not receive the required percentage of votes, it may be excluded by the company. (However, if more than 10% of the shareholders voted in favor of the previously submitted proposal, it will not be excluded on these grounds. If fewer than 10% of the shareholders voted in favor of the previously submitted proposal, the rules become more complex.)

THE DODD-FRANK ACT, DIRECTOR NOMINATIONS AND "SAY ON PAY"

Under the authority of the Dodd-Frank Act of 2010, the Securities and Exchange Commission (the "SEC") adopted rules that purported to provide shareholders with increased input about the directors elected to a company's Board. The rules were adopted to address the concern that shareholders of publicly traded companies do not have the right to nominate directors and typically could only vote on a "slate" of directors proposed by the Board of Directors. The SEC's new Rule 14a–11 of the 1934 Act applied to public companies and would have allowed certain shareholders (those who had owned at least 3% of the outstanding shares of that corporation for a continuous three-year period) to nominate a director for inclusion on the "slate" of directors using the corporation's proxy solicitation materials. The SEC placed limitations on the number of nominees that could be proposed by shareholders and any nominee had to meet certain standards of independence that apply to directors generally. However, Rule 14a–11 was vacated in *Bus. Roundtable and Chamber of Commerce of the United States of America v. S.E.C.*, 647 F.3d 1144, 396 U.S. App. D.C. 259 (D.C. Cir. 2011) because the court found that that the SEC "acted arbitrarily and capriciously here because it neglected its statutory responsibility to determine the likely economic consequences of *Rule 14a–11* and to connect those consequences to efficiency, competition, and capital formation." The court also noted that, when the SEC adopted Rule 14a–11, the SEC simultaneously amended *Rule 14a–8* to prevent companies from excluding from their proxy materials shareholder proposals to establish a procedure for shareholders to nominate directors. Since Rule 14a–8 was not challenged in the case, its status is unclear. Furthermore, efforts continue to enable shareholders to have a greater ability to nominate directors. It is unclear whether the SEC will revise and reissue rules or if other changes will take place or if these efforts will be successful.

The Dodd-Frank Act also resulted in the SEC's adoption of Rule 14a–21(a), which requires publicly held companies to provide shareholders with an advisory "say on pay" vote (at least once every three years) on the compensation of a company's senior executives. Section 14A(a)(1) of the 1934 Act and Rule 14a–21(a) adopted thereunder require that public companies must provide "a separate shareholder advisory vote in proxy statements to approve the compensation of their named executive officers . . ." Although such a vote is required every three years, and although the new rules also provide that public companies must have shareholders vote on how frequently the "say on pay" votes should occur and whether the vote should occur every year, every two years or every three years, most companies, thus far, have adopted an annual frequency for these votes. Note that these votes are "advisory" and are not binding on the company.

SHAREHOLDER INSPECTION RIGHTS

Shareholders also have rights to inspect corporate records. However, the rules typically provide that inspection rights are only afforded to shareholders who hold some minimum ownership stake in the corporation. For a variety of very legitimate reasons, shareholders may want to communicate directly with other shareholders and/or may need access to corporate records other than just shareholder lists. However, other concerns must be balanced against a legitimate interest in shareholder lists and corporate records.

The tension arises in that some shareholders want access to information for an improper purpose, and corporations have an interest in protecting certain information. Furthermore, shareholders do not want to be on mailing lists to receive solicitations to purchase products or services just because they happen to be shareholders in a corporation. For example, if Walter owns stock in a publicly traded company, which manufactures washing machines, and Sara wants to obtain the addresses of the corporation's shareholders merely for the purpose of trying to persuade those shareholders to invest in her new laundry detergent company, that is an improper purpose. However, if a shareholder in a corporation seeks to communicate with other shareholders to solicit support (consistent with the proxy rules) for a shareholder proposal, that would be a "proper" purpose.

The evaluation of these situations is further complicated by the fact that it is not merely the purpose of the shareholder that matters, but also the type of record to which the shareholder seeks access. In many states, including Delaware, depending upon the type of records being sought, the burden of proof will shift, requiring either that the corporation show an improper purpose or that the shareholder seeking access to records must show a proper purpose. If the shareholder wants to obtain a list of shareholder names, the burden of proof is on the corporation to show that the shareholder does NOT have a proper purpose. However, if the shareholder wants to obtain corporate records, the burden of proof is usually on the shareholder to show that he, she or it has a proper purpose.

While these situations might be heavily fact dependent, over the years, the following have been found to be instances involving a "proper purpose":

☑   An effort to gain control of the corporation (unless it is for a hostile or detrimental purpose to the corporation or its shareholders, rather than to current management);

- ☑ An effort to gain a shareholder list for someone else trying to gain control of the corporation;

- ☑ An effort to investigate alleged corporate mismanagement or malfeasance;

- ☑ An effort to gather information to assess the value of one's shares; and

- ☑ An effort to communicate with other shareholders in connection with a proxy fight or a shareholder proposal.

Examples of reasons for seeking access to corporate information that would be deemed to be an "improper" purpose would include information related to:

- ☑ Finding potential customers for a personal business venture;

- ☑ Persuading the corporation to adopt one's social or political concerns, irrespective of *any economic benefit to the shareholders of the corporation*;

- ☑ Instituting a **strike suit** (a suit without substantive basis, designed to obtain money or property from the corporation because the costs of litigation far exceed the costs of settlement) against the corporation;

- ☑ Seeking proprietary information such as trade secrets or other intellectual property; and

- ☑ Seeking information to aid a competitor of the corporation.

One court explained a denial of access to a shareholder by distinguishing between a proper purpose that involves *any economic benefit to the shareholders of the company* and an improper purpose that was to persuade the company to adopt the shareholder's social and political concerns. *State Ex Rel. Pillsbury v. Honeywell, Inc.*, 291 Minn. 322, 191 N.W.2d 406 (Minn. 1971). As explained above, shareholders do not have a right to inspect the corporate records for an improper purpose.

The bottom line is that shareholders should have a right to information because they are entitled to know about their investments and to be involved with their investments. However, this right is subject to certain limitations that require a proper purpose and are designed to prevent one shareholder, exercising his, her or its rights, from negatively impacting the corporation solely (or primarily) for personal reasons and to the detriment of the rights of the other shareholders.

ILLUSTRATIVE PROBLEMS

PROBLEM 6.1

Pete, Jennifer, Daniela, Ben and Jordan are shareholders in a public corporation called Palace Hotels, Inc. The Board of Directors of Palace Hotels, Inc. wants to open a huge resort in Las Vegas. Pete, Jennifer, Daniela, Ben and Jordan think this is a terrible idea that will harm the company. They launch a proxy fight to take control of Palace Hotels. The existing Board prepares detailed information about why Las Vegas is a great location for a resort and spends additional funds making their argument in person to some of Palace's major shareholders. After the vote, Pete, Jennifer, Daniela, Ben and Jordan gain control of Palace Hotels. Which of the groups may be reimbursed for their expenses?

Analysis

No party may be reimbursed unless the dispute involves a question of policy. Because the dispute involves whether to open a Las Vegas resort, the central issue is clearly one of corporate policy. The firm may reimburse the incumbents for their expenses incurred in the fight for control, provided that the expenses are reasonable and proper. (Since courts have been known to construe "reasonable expenses" broadly, it seems likely (at least without more information of impropriety) that the incumbents' expenses from preparing information and even from meeting with major shareholders, would be considered "reasonable.") Since Pete, Jennifer, Daniela, Ben and Jordan (the "insurgents") gained control of Palace Hotels, Inc., they also may be reimbursed for their reasonable and proper expenses. (Had the insurgents lost, they would not be entitled to reimbursement.) However, if Pete, Jennifer, Daniela, Ben and Jordan want to make certain that the reimbursement is not subject to attack, they would want the Palace Hotels, Inc. shareholders to ratify the reimbursement, following full disclosure, of course.

PROBLEM 6.2

Karen and Rio are shareholders in Martha's Cookie Corporation ("MCC"), a publicly traded Delaware corporation. Two months prior to the MCC annual meeting, Karen and Rio request access to a list of all MCC shareholders and a list of the secret ingredients used in the MCC cookies, alleging that MCC has been using inferior cookie ingredients and that the MCC business is suffering as a result. Will Karen and Rio be likely to obtain the materials sought if their purpose in requesting these materials is to show that the MCC management is doing a bad job of running MCC and should be replaced?

Analysis

The two requests would be evaluated under different standards. Both requests would require some evaluation as to whether Karen and Rio had a proper purpose in requesting the information. With respect to the MCC shareholder list, Karen and Rio's purpose of communicating with other shareholders about management failures is a proper purpose. Since in the case of a request by a shareholder for a shareholder list, the burden would be on MCC to show that the purpose was improper, and there is no indication of an improper purpose, Karen and Rio would most likely be entitled to obtain the MCC shareholder list.

The result would most likely be different with respect to the request for the list of secret ingredients. The list involves proprietary information, and Karen and Rio would not be entitled to such information merely by alleging that the list contained inferior ingredients. Furthermore, the burden would be on Karen and Rio to show that they had a proper purpose. And, although their stated purpose seems to be somewhat related to the request for information, that does not overcome the need for the corporation to protect its proprietary information. Note that if there were some evidence of wrongdoing by MCC management, Karen and Rio might be able to sue, and whether or not access to the recipe was appropriate could be determined by the courts. However, in the shareholder right to corporate information scenario, unless Karen and Rio could meet the burden of proof, the proprietary information would be protected.

PROBLEM 6.3

Pinocchio Inc. is in the process of being acquired by Monstro Corp. Prior to the acquisition, the Board of Directors of Pinocchio Inc. voted to give bonuses to a large number of mid-level employees, payable after the close of the acquisition and provided that those employees would work for the company until the acquisition was completed. The bonuses are contingent on the successful completion of the Monstro acquisition. Pinocchio Inc. calls a meeting of its shareholders to approve the merger. There are 10 million shares of Pinocchio Inc. issued and outstanding. The shares are held by 500 different shareholders. Although only 82 shareholders attend the meeting, 8.3 million shares vote to approve the acquisition. One shareholder, named Jay Cricket, objects to the bonuses and claims that the shareholders should have the right to vote on the bonuses as well. Mr. Cricket also claims that, because there were less than 251 shareholders at the meeting, there was no quorum and the vote approving the acquisition is not valid. Please evaluate Mr. Cricket's assertions.

Analysis

Unfortunately for Mr. Cricket, he will lose on both claims. The bonus payments to mid-level employees, even if announced in conjunction with an acquisition, are not subject to a separate shareholder vote since employee compensation involves ordinary management issues and are not a matter about which shareholders are entitled to vote. While the bonuses should have been disclosed in conjunction with the vote on the acquisition, shareholders would not be entitled to a separate vote on the bonuses themselves. If the shareholders did not want Pinocchio Inc. to pay the bonuses, they could have voted against the acquisition.

In addition, it seems that Mr. Cricket is confused about quorum requirements. Most quorum requirements mandate that 50% plus one of the *shares*, NOT of the *shareholders*, entitled to vote at a meeting, be present. Since there were a total of 10 million shares outstanding and 8.3 million shares voted to approve the acquisition, there were more than 50% plus one of the shares of Pinocchio Inc. represented either in person or by proxy. Therefore, a quorum was present, and the vote approving the merger is valid (at least as far as the quorum requirements are concerned).

CHAPTER 7

Issues of Control

As discussed above, corporations are often categorized by different features. One of the most common differentiators is whether a corporation's stock is publicly traded or privately held. The former are often referred to as "**public**" companies; the latter as "**closely held**" or "**close**" corporations. Although all corporations have a Board of Directors, officers, and shareholders, the distinction between public and closely held corporations relates to the number of shareholders and the market for the corporation's stock. In a public company, the stock is often owned by thousands of shareholders, most of whom do not know each other. The stock of the corporation (or at least one class of stock) has been registered with the SEC, and may be bought or sold on one of the public exchanges, such as the New York Stock Exchange or NASDAQ. A closely held corporation's stock is typically held by a relatively few number of shareholders. Its shares are not publicly traded and sales of stock take place in private transactions, typically requiring an exemption from the registration requirements of the 1933 Act (as defined below). Closely held corporations are also called "**private companies**" and often have shareholders who also serve on the Board of Directors and hold positions as officers as well.

While control can become an issue in all corporations, this issue is often different in closely held corporations. In public companies battles for control can take the form of proxy fights or tender offers. These battles, which typically take place on a large scale, are primarily related to the size of the company and the vast number and anonymity of the shareholders. In closely held corporations the struggle for control often focuses on a shareholder's ability to control votes, often through agreements or the structure of the business.

One reason why these issues are different in a closely held corporation is that the shareholders often serve on the Board of Directors and as the company's officers. Often control represents the ability to determine and pay salaries in these corporations. In addition, the employee/shareholders of these corporations will often prefer to receive salaries instead of dividends to avoid double taxation. Since there is no public market for the stock and often no (or limited) dividends, control provides an individual or a group of individuals with access to income from the "value" of the closely held corporation.

Remember that the Board of Directors selects the employee/officers and determines how much salary they will make. If a shareholder is not an employee, then that shareholder would only receive money through dividends. However, the Board of Directors determines how much, if any, dividends will be paid. Therefore, control of the Board of Directors results in the ability to control the payment of money to shareholders, whether those shareholders are hired as employees, and how much salary they will receive if hired. Of course, these decisions are limited by fiduciary duties, but they are also protected, in many instances, by the Business Judgment Rule. The individuals elected to the Board of Directors are usually determined by a majority of the shareholders. Therefore, if one shareholder owns a relatively small percentage of a corporation's stock and someone else owns a majority of the corporation's stock, the shareholder holding a minority of the shares does not have the ability (at least under ordinary voting rules) to require that he or she be elected to the Board. Because the Board of Directors makes the decisions, which govern the corporation, the minority shareholder cannot institute dividends or require that he or she be hired by the corporation.

It is against this backdrop that several devices relating to control have developed. However, in order to understand these devices, one must keep the preceding construct in mind to have a sense of the importance of control and the potential access to income (and other corporate resources) that is at stake, and the way control and devices to exercise control are moderated by fiduciary duties.

DEVICES FOR CONTROL

Most control devices are designed to provide a shareholder or a group of shareholders with sufficient votes to determine or to impact certain important decisions in a corporation. Some of the most common devices include:

- ☑ Voting Trusts;
- ☑ Vote Pooling Agreements;
- ☑ Shareholders Agreements; and
- ☑ Irrevocable Proxies.

It is important to remember that (in all but a very few exceptions allowed in certain limited instances in shareholder agreements) these control devices may only relate to the way that shareholders' votes are cast. Shareholders (except in some limited instances involving dominant shareholders) may vote in their own self-interest. However, while shareholders may act selfishly, directors may not act in their own self-interest. Directors must act in the best interest of all the shareholders—not just the shareholders that elected them. Because directors are bound by fiduciary duties to all of the shareholders, directors must be "free" to make their decisions based upon their good faith determination of what is best for the corporation and ALL of its shareholders. Using an agreement to restrict a director's vote violates this principle. **Therefore, shareholders may agree to exercise control to determine who will be directors, but not to determine how those directors will vote**.

A *Voting Trust* is a device whereby two or more shareholders place their shares in "trust." The trust has a trustee who is responsible for voting the shares. The trust is typically governed by a trust agreement, which determines how long the trust will last and how the shares will be voted. For example, the trust agreement may provide that the shares are voted in accordance with one person's determination, by a vote of the parties, by one person one year and another person the next year, or even by a flip of a coin. The advantage of a voting trust is that there is little question about enforcement since the trustee holds and votes the shares. Voting trusts also avoid the problems of deadlocks among shareholders. However, shareholders might be uncomfortable with turning over possession of their shares to a trustee and the loss of control that accompanies relinquishing possession. Also, there is often a limit (usually determined by state law) on the number of years for which a voting trust might exist. This limit is typically 10 years in most states, but may vary from state to state. Finally, it is important to remember that voting trusts relate to the election of directors to the corporation's Board, not to how those directors will vote. Director votes may not be controlled by a voting trust.

A *Vote Pooling Agreement* is a device that is similar to a voting trust. However, there is no trustee, and the shareholders do not typically relinquish control over their shares. A vote pooling agreement is an agreement between, or among, two or more shareholders that states that the parties' shares will be voted in a certain way, based upon some criteria. As in the case of a voting trust, the criteria in a vote pooling agreement can range from a vote among the parties to the agreement, to the determination of a "neutral" party, to the flip of a coin. Vote pooling agreements are very flexible and may be used in a variety of situations. For example, a vote pooling agreement:

☑   May cover all shareholder votes or only certain votes such as the election of directors;

☑   May be for an unlimited period of time or for a defined period;

☑   May cover a portion of a shareholder's shares or all of their shares (e.g. John will vote 60% of his shares pursuant to a vote pooling agreement with Sally, but he may vote the other 40% as he chooses); and

☑   May delegate control to an individual who has a relatively small ownership percentage.

There is no requirement that the person who controls the shares under a Vote Pooling Agreement and that person's relative percentage ownership in the corporation correlate. For example, a wealthy shareholder, Rich, might want to persuade a brilliant young law student, named Brill, to run a legal research corporation called "LRC." Brill agrees to run the corporation, but since Brill will only own a small percentage of LRC, Brill will only take the job if he can exercise voting control. Brill and Rich can enter into a vote pooling agreement that provides all of their shares in LRC will be voted as determined by Brill, provided that the shares will be cast to elect both Brill and Rich to LRC's Board of Directors.

Shareholder Agreements deal with a wide variety of matters relating to the corporation. Some of these matters might involve matters unrelated to control of the corporation, such as transferability restrictions or the corporation's rights to repurchase stock upon the occurrence of certain events. However, shareholder agreements might also be used to handle matters relating to voting and/or control. Note that a vote pooling agreement might also be called a "Shareholder Agreement." Typically, a shareholder agreement covers matters beyond those that would be handled in a vote pooling agreement, but a vote pooling agreement might be contained in a shareholder agreement, *even if it is not labeled as such*, and an agreement that deals only with vote pooling might be called a shareholder agreement. The name is less important than the substance of the agreement. Shareholder agreements might also address specific matters, such as who will be appointed to the Board of Directors or which groups will have the right to select certain seats on the corporation's Board of Directors. Sometimes, shareholder agreements will attempt to address matters beyond the realm of shareholders and more in the area of management, such as who will be selected as officers or what dividends will be paid. In general, such efforts are unenforceable. However, there are exceptions, which are discussed below.

Irrevocable Proxies are discussed above in a broader context. However, in the context of control, irrevocable proxies are used in a similar way to other voting arrangements with one important difference: a proxy is typically given to one entity or individual (who has an interest in the corporation) to enable that individual to have control. So, unlike a voting trust or a vote pooling agreement through which two or more people work together to exercise collective control, a proxy usually involves one (or more) shareholders handing over their votes to a third party to increase that person's control.

As mentioned above, a proxy is typically revocable. To make a proxy irrevocable, it must be "**coupled with an interest**." An "interest" may be a job with the corporation, a loan made to corporation, or some other interest in the firm. In the example above in which Brill will only take the job at LRC if he can exercise some control, it is possible that, instead of using a vote pooling agreement, Rich could have given Brill a proxy to vote Rich's shares in LRC. Brill's position at LRC would have satisfied that irrevocability requirement of an "interest." So, the proxy would have been coupled with an interest and could have been made irrevocable should the parties have chosen to add that feature. (Just because a proxy is coupled with an interest does not automatically make it irrevocable. The parties must intend for the proxy to be irrevocable and may only make it so if it is coupled with an interest.) The proxy may be "irrevocable" for as long as the interest lasts. In the above example, if Brill stops working for LRC, he would no longer have an interest in the corporation, and the proxy would become revocable by Rich.

LIMITS ON CONTROL ARRANGEMENTS

As mentioned above, the general rule is that shareholders may agree on how they will act as shareholders. They may, for example, agree to elect certain directors to the Board. However, shareholders may NOT agree on how those directors will vote as directors or what actions those individuals will take as directors. So, even if shareholders agreed that they would elect each other to the Board of Directors, they could not agree that, once they were on the Board, they would elect each other as officers. An agreement to elect one another as officers would not be enforceable since such decisions must be exercised consistent with a director's fiduciary duties to act in the best interests of the corporation and of ALL of its shareholders, not consistent with contractual obligations to certain shareholders.

However, there are some exceptions to this principle which would allow otherwise unenforceable agreements (or provisions in agreements) to be enforceable:

☑ Typically, shareholders may agree how they will vote on certain matters as directors (such as dividends or the election of officers) if **ALL** of the shareholders have entered into the agreement. This is sometimes known as a "**shareholder unanimity exception**."

☑ There are also cases *in some states* that hold that, even if all of the shareholders are not parties to the agreement, the agreement is still enforceable, **provided that** (a) the shares of the corporation are closely held; (b) none of the shareholders who were not parties to the agreement object; AND (c) the terms of the agreement are reasonable.

Students might ask who is trying to prevent the agreement from being enforced in the above scenarios. It is usually a party to the agreement who has had a change of heart and does not want to comply with the agreement. When one party sues for enforcement, the other party argues that the provision is void or unenforceable. The bottom line black letter law is:

☑ Shareholders can agree about how they will vote as shareholders.

☑ Shareholders CANNOT agree about how they will vote as directors (with fiduciary duties) <u>UNLESS:</u>

• The agreement is signed by ALL the shareholders; <u>OR</u>

• Perhaps (in some states, sometimes), when the minority shareholders (who have not agreed) do not or cannot object, AND the agreement is reasonable.

ILLUSTRATIVE PROBLEMS

PROBLEM 7.1

Sara owns 72% and Dan owns 28% of a business called Furniture Friends, Inc. ("FFI") that manufactures furniture. FFI is a corporation. Sara and Dan enter into a 15-year shareholder agreement to elect each other to the FFI Board of Directors, to elect each other as co-president, and to pay salaries of at least $100,000 each per year. After seven years, Sara and Dan have a fight. At the next annual meeting, Sara reneges on the agreement and elects Bill to the Board of Directors. Dan does not have enough votes to elect himself to the Board of Directors. The FFI Board does not appoint Dan as co-president. Instead, the Board elects Sara as the sole president. Dan sues to enforce the agreement. Assuming that Sara is paid a reasonable salary, what is the likely result?

Analysis

While in general, shareholders may agree on how they will vote as shareholders, they may not agree on how they will vote as directors. In the above problem, Sara and Dan could agree to elect each other to the Board of Directors, but, under the basic rule, they could not agree to make each other co-president and to pay $100,000 salaries. HOWEVER, this situation falls into one of the exceptions to this rule. Since there are no other shareholders in FFI, there is no one who would be hurt by Dan and Sara's agreement about how they would act as directors. Therefore, Dan and Sara's agreement would be enforceable. Furthermore, while most voting trust agreements are limited to 10 years, there is no such limit on shareholders agreements, so the length of the agreement would not impact its enforceability. Therefore, it is likely that Dan would prevail in his suit against Sara.

PROBLEM 7.2

Kai is the president of Ocean, Inc. When Kai became president, he obtained an irrevocable proxy to vote all the shares of Ocean, Inc.'s biggest shareholder, Wally Whaler, for as long as Kai is employed by Ocean, Inc. One day, Wally gets mad at Kai and attempts to revoke this proxy. If Kai objects, will Wally be able to revoke the proxy?

Analysis

The general rule is that proxies are revocable, unless the parties agreed to make a proxy irrevocable and the proxy is coupled with an interest. In this situation, the parties seem to have identified Kai's proxy as "irrevocable," and that proxy is indeed coupled with an interest (i.e., Kai's position as an employee of Ocean, Inc.). Therefore, as long as that interest remains, Wally may not revoke the proxy. If Kai ceased to be employed by Ocean, Inc., then the proxy would no longer be coupled with an interest (unless there were some other interest of which we are unaware), and it would be revocable by Wally.

PROBLEM 7.3

David, Mindy, Carly, Rocky and Jason are all shareholders in the Comedy Café Corporation ("CCC"), and each owns 12% of CCC. The five shareholders enter into a vote pooling agreement in which they agree to vote together to exercise control over CCC. As a result, each year the group is able to hold three of the five seats on the CCC Board of Directors. (CCC uses cumulative voting to elect directors.) One year, Carly, Rocky and Jason are serving on the CCC Board, and Jason is running for president. However, because Rocky is mad at Jason, Rocky votes for Wendy (who is aligned with a different group of shareholders). As a result of Rocky's vote, Wendy wins. David, Mindy, Jason and Carly are furious and want to sue Rocky for breaching their agreement. Will they prevail?

Analysis

David, Mindy, Carly, Rocky and Jason's vote pooling agreement may be used to govern how the parties to the agreement will vote as shareholders, but not as directors. This situation is an example of what may and what may not be covered by such an agreement. Rocky is not bound by the vote pooling agreement in his capacity as a director, and he may vote as he chooses. In fact, he has a fiduciary duty to all shareholders to vote in the best interests of the corporation. However, the following year, Rocky cannot prevent David, Mindy, Jason and Carly from picking someone from their group besides Rocky to sit on the CCC Board of Directors, and Rocky will still be bound to vote in accordance with the vote pooling agreement even if it means that he needs to vote for someone other than himself to serve on the Board.

ABUSE OF CONTROL

As discussed above, the general rule is that shareholders do not owe fiduciary duties to other shareholders. However, in certain situations where a dominant (or controlling) shareholder is present, there are some limits on this principal, resulting in some limits on dominant shareholders for actions that might be taken by those shareholders that involve self-dealing. In closely held corporations there are some additional issues that arise because of the potential for "**freeze outs**."

A freeze out occurs when the majority shareholder or block of shareholders earns a return at the expense of the other shareholders, often channeling corporate funds to the controlling shareholder block and depriving other shareholder(s) of the opportunity to share in funds paid out by the company. A freeze out involves a situation in which a minority shareholder is blocked from holding a paid position with the corporation, such as a position as an officer or an employee, by the majority shareholder (or a block of shareholders establishing a majority). A typical freeze out has the following features:

☑ The corporation does not pay dividends (or pays minimal dividends), so that none (or little) of the corporation's profits are distributed to its shareholders; and

☑ the only (or the vast majority of) corporate funds that are "paid out" are paid in the form of salary to those shareholders who are also employees; and

☑ the "frozen-out" shareholder is prevented from holding a paying position; then,

☑ as a result, the minority shareholder, or shareholders, do not receive any of these corporate funds distributed as "salary," and therefore, are unable to "profit" in any way from their investment in the corporation.

It is important to keep in mind that it is not just the actions or circumstances that are relevant in evaluating a "freeze out" situation; it is also the *intent* behind the actions and circumstances. The frozen-out shareholder must be able to show a breach of duty and that the majority group is diverting the profits of the corporation to themselves to the exclusion of the frozen-out shareholder and, therefore, depriving the frozen-out shareholder of his or her rightful return on his investment.

It is also important to remember that freeze outs are not always actionable. A shareholder who holds a minority (non-controlling) position in a corporation must know that being frozen out is a possibility. This possibility does not have to do with the shareholder's expectations about how he or she will be treated by the majority, just with the mathematical realities of the situations. The majority controls most (or all) of the corporation's decisions. To the extent those decisions are made by the corporation's Board of Directors, they are regulated by fiduciary duties. However, these duties do not encompass many of the situations in which a shareholder would be frozen out. We have already seen that a dominant or controlling shareholder (or even a group of shareholders acting in concert to control a corporation) is subject to a special fiduciary duty. This duty, essentially the duty of loyalty, prevents self-dealing so that the shareholder may not take the profits of the corporation for herself and deny those profits to the minority shareholder. On the other hand, this duty is subject to a fairness analysis. So, if a dominant shareholder pays herself a reasonable salary and does not pay dividends, it is often hard for the minority shareholder to show that such action is unfair. However, in the situation in which the dominant shareholder pays herself a salary well in excess of reasonable compensation, leaving no funds to distribute to the minority shareholder(s), it would be much easier to show that the duty of loyalty had been violated.

ILLUSTRATIVE PROBLEM

PROBLEM 7.4

A closely held Delaware corporation, New Tech, Inc., is developing a new sophisticated computer chip. New Tech, Inc. has four shareholders: Aaron, Betty, Carol, and Doug. Aaron, Betty and Carol have advanced degrees and work experience in computer science and/or engineering. Doug has no expertise whatsoever in this area. He watches television all day and only became a shareholder because his sister is married to Aaron, and Doug's sister convinced Aaron to let Doug invest in the corporation. Each shareholder invested $5,000 and owns 25% of New Tech, Inc. New Tech, Inc. has three directors: Aaron, Betty, and Carol. Aaron, Betty, and Carol are also the officers and employees of the firm. Aaron, Betty, and Carol are hard at work on developing a break-through product for New Tech, Inc. They also do some computer consulting work, which brings in a small amount of income. This income is used up each year paying the small (and entirely fair and reasonable) salaries of Aaron, Betty, and Carol. While all four shareholders had hoped within three years New Tech, Inc. would be making a large profit, the timeline has shifted (through no fault of Aaron, Betty, and Carol) to seven to ten years. Doug decides that he wants to work for New Tech, Inc. and earn a salary too. When Aaron, Betty and Carol refuse because Doug does not have any applicable skills, Doug claims that he has been wrongfully "frozen out." Will he prevail?

Analysis

In order to prevail, Doug will need to show that a fiduciary duty owed to him has been breached. Even though Doug's situation involves the same features listed above as characteristics of a freeze out, there has been no wrongdoing because Aaron, Betty and Carol have acted reasonably and *have not acted with the intent of depriving Doug of his rightful return on an investment while distributing that return to themselves.* Doug did not have a reasonable expectation of employment with New Tech, Inc. Aaron,

Betty and Carol are paying themselves small salaries, which, we have been told, are "entirely fair," and there are not excessive profits that are being distributed in the form of salary. Therefore, it is unlikely that Doug will be able to show that the other shareholders have breached a duty to him. So, it is unlikely that Doug will prevail.

However, if New Tech, Inc. finally sells its breakthrough product and makes millions of dollars, and Aaron, Betty and Carol pay themselves multi-million dollar salaries, leaving no money to distribute as dividends, then Doug's claim of wrongdoing against the other three shareholders would be substantially strengthened. This would be true because the "profits" of the company, which should go to increase the value of the entire company and therefore, the value of all the shareholders' investment(s), would instead be taken in the form of salary only by the shareholders who work for the company and therefore, improperly taken from the "frozen-out" shareholder, Doug.

FIDUCIARY DUTIES IN FREEZE OUTS

Freeze outs are handled differently in different jurisdictions. In Delaware, the fiduciary duty of a dominant shareholder is frequently applied to freeze out situations. As we have already seen, a controlling shareholder's actions are limited by the fiduciary duty of loyalty. These fiduciary duty limits prohibit controlling shareholders (or a group of shareholders acting together) from taking the benefits of ownership of the corporation for themselves. An action by a controlling shareholder to take money or other assets belonging to the corporation and distribute those assets to herself would be a conflict of interest and a violation of the duty of loyalty. (When evaluating a freeze out problem, students should be aware that most courts will treat a group of shareholders acting together (who *collectively* hold a dominant/controlling ownership position in the corporation) as a dominant shareholder.) It is important to remember that the directors of a corporation, even if they are also shareholders, always have fiduciary duties to ALL of the shareholders. Of course, minority shareholders know that they are in a non-controlling position and cannot force the other shareholder(s) to elect a minority shareholder to the Board of Directors or to hire him or her as an officer. On the other hand, a controlling shareholder often does have the power to be elected president of the corporation by other directors and paid a salary. Provided that the salary satisfies "fairness standards," it is unlikely that a minority shareholder could show a violation of any fiduciary duties.

Other jurisdictions, such as Massachusetts, apply a partnership-like analysis to **closely held** corporations. Courts in these jurisdictions often find that there are some fiduciary duties among shareholders in a closely held corporation reminiscent of certain duties seen in partnerships. In general, the courts in these jurisdictions have taken the position that **shareholders in closely held corporations owe each other a duty of good faith**. In the often cited Massachusetts case, *Wilkes v. Springside Nursing Home, Inc.*, 353 N.E.2d 657 (Mass. 1976), the court set up the following analysis for freeze out situations: In a freeze out, the majority or the controlling group must have a "legitimate business purpose" for its action and, even if there is a legitimate business purpose, the minority shareholder will still have the opportunity to show that the "same legitimate objective could have been achieved through an alternative course of action less harmful to the minority's interest." (*Id.* at 663.) Courts must then balance the legitimate business purpose against the minority shareholder's proposed alternative.

Ultimately, these different approaches will still result in a similar outcome in a substantial number of cases. In the Delaware approach, the restrictions on dominant shareholders and the fiduciary duties of directors will still prevent many of the actions which would be barred by the *Wilkes* approach, which applies a duty of good faith to shareholders. These cases are very dependent on the specific facts and often turn on whether "fair" salaries are being paid and whether the controlling group can show a legitimate business purpose. It is important to remember that neither every situation involving a minority shareholder who does not receive dividends or salary, nor every discharge of an at-will employee who is also a minority shareholder in a closely held corporation, is a breach of a fiduciary duty.

EMPLOYEE OR SHAREHOLDER

Many of these "freeze out" cases involve a shareholder's claim that he should be allowed to be an employee and receive a salary since that is the only way funds are distributed by the corporation. Often these cases will turn on an assessment of whether the individual is (a) a shareholder whose right to employment is a byproduct of his position as a shareholder or (b) an employee who happened to obtain shares as a result of employment. At-will employees who just happen to be shareholders do not usually have the fiduciary duties, discussed above, protecting their rights to employment. On the other hand, most employee/shareholder situations can often be avoided if there is an employment agreement present. In many such situations, courts will rely on the employment agreement to determine the rights of the employee/shareholder, rather than more abstract applications of fiduciary duties. In many situations, controlling shareholders have used employment agreements to their advantage to secure their rights to terminate the employment of an employee who is also a minority shareholder.

MINORITY SHAREHOLDER PROTECTION

A minority shareholder who is concerned about being frozen out has very limited options. In most closely held corporations there is little (and often no) market for shares in the corporation. Even in situations in which buyers might be interested in purchasing shares in a closely held corporation, few of those buyers would be willing to pay money for shares in a corporation held by someone who is already, or likely to be, frozen out. Shareholders facing this situation might be able to acquire some level of protection through agreement or through provisions placed in the corporation's governing documents. Some of the options for a minority shareholder facing a freeze out or concerned about protecting themselves against a freeze out might include:

- ☑ A shareholders agreement, protecting the minority shareholder's right to be on the Board of Directors and/or (if all the other shareholders agree) to be an officer;

- ☑ An employment agreement, assuring the minority shareholder of a certain position with the corporation and a salary;

- ☑ A buyout agreement (or a shareholders agreement containing buyout provisions), entitling the minority shareholder to force the company to buy his or her shares under certain circumstances, such as a freeze out;

- ☑ Statutory dissolution (sometimes, even minority shareholders have the right in a closely held corporation to force a dissolution) which would result in payment for the minority shareholder's interest in the dissolution process or in a settlement with the majority shareholder block; and/or

- ☑ Mandatory dividends (provisions requiring that certain dividends be paid might be included in the corporation's Articles of Incorporation).

TRANSFER OF CONTROL

Because control of a corporation has substantial value, purchasers of stock in a corporation who are acquiring control are often willing to pay more for that control. Control might enable someone to improve the company and extract more value. Control might let someone determine who will be on the Board of Directors and who will be the corporation's officers. It is important to note that "control" does not need to be 51%. Control is the percentage of stock sufficient to enable the holder of that stock to elect a controlling block of the corporation's Board of Directors. While there are several ways of acquiring control of a corporation, one of the easiest is to purchase a controlling block of stock in the corporation from another shareholder. When control is purchased, the amount which the purchaser pays in excess of the "market value" of the stock is known as a "**control premium**."

There have been several cases about control premiums and the sale of control that raise the issues of fairness to the other shareholders who are not receiving the control premium. However, the bottom line is that, absent looting of corporate assets, conversion of a corporate opportunity, fraud, or other acts of bad faith, a controlling shareholder is free to sell, and a purchaser is free to buy, that controlling interest at a premium. Note that unlike the sale of stock to acquire control, courts are generally unwilling to allow the sale of a corporate office or directorship. These situations are scrutinized more carefully since it is more likely that some improper motive or action is involved. One cannot generally "buy" a Board seat. The resulting rule is that a shareholder may sell control but not offices in a corporation. Note that if a purchaser acquires a majority interest in a corporation, some courts would allow the selling shareholders to facilitate the resignation of the existing Board to be replaced with the purchaser's nominees, rather than requiring the purchaser to wait for the expiration of the current directors' terms. This is not considered a "sale" of office as much as a sale of control and the "fruits" of that control.

ILLUSTRATIVE PROBLEM

PROBLEM 7.5

Chip owns 32% of Denim Duds, Inc. ("DDI"), a publicly traded clothing manufacturing company. Judy would like to have control of DDI, and she buys all of Chip's stock for $14/share even though the other shares of DDI are trading at $11/share. This represents a premium of $7.5 million to Chip. Jim is a DDI shareholder who is not happy about the deal. He sues Chip derivatively to recover the $7.5 million premium on behalf of DDI, with the purpose of sharing the premium with the other shareholders. What is the likely result?

Analysis

In general, control premiums are permitted. Here, there is no evidence of fraud, bad faith or looting of corporate assets. There is no indication that Chip has any obligation to the other shareholders. Therefore, he is free to transfer a controlling interest in DDI and to receive a premium (even a $7.5 million premium) for that transfer.

SHAREHOLDER ACTIONS

When a shareholder has a complaint regarding a corporation in which she holds stock, there are two types of actions that she may bring: a direct action or a derivative action.

Shareholder Direct Actions

In a direct action, the shareholder makes a claim in her own name against the corporation, or against a director or officer of the corporation, for a wrong that was done directly to her. In other words, the wrong must have impacted the shareholder directly. Direct actions are often brought as class actions if the wrong complained of effects many shareholders. In such instances, the shareholder sues as a representative of a "class" of similarly situated shareholders who have suffered from the same wrong. Such suits are still "direct." (A direct class action suit (under Federal law) would be governed by the provisions of Federal Rule of Civil Procedure 23.)

Examples of direct lawsuits include:

- ☑ A suit to compel the payment of dividends;

- ☑ A suit to enjoin an activity that is *ultra-vires*;

- ☑ A suit claiming security fraud;

- ☑ A suit brought to protect certain shareholder rights (such as preemptive rights or the right to vote on a matter);

- ☑ A suit in which a shareholder has been denied rights (for example redemption rights, or the right to inspect the corporation's books and records); and

☑   A suit involving a shareholder-employee who is fired
and forced to sell stock and is suing to recover his job
and/or stock.

Shareholder Derivative Actions

In a shareholder derivative action, the complained of wrong
has damaged the corporation and, as a result of the harm to the
corporation, negatively impacts the shareholder. In instances in
which the wrong has hurt the corporation and the corporation has
failed to act, the shareholder might be able to bring a suit
compelling the corporation to take action against the perpetrator of
the wrong. A derivative action is a suit in equity against the
corporation to force the corporation to sue a third party. When
bringing a derivative action, a shareholder actually brings two
suits. The shareholder simultaneously sues the corporation and the
party (which may be an officer, a director, or an outside third party)
against whom the shareholder is asserting the corporation has a
claim. The nature of a derivative suit is the shareholder suing to
force the corporation to take some action to address *some harm to
the corporation*.

Examples of a shareholder derivative lawsuit include:

☑   A claim that a director has violated his duty of care to
the corporation by making a bad deal with an outside
third party;

☑   A claim that an officer has misappropriated a
corporate opportunity (or committed some other duty
of loyalty violation), and the corporation has failed to
take action against her;

☑   A claim that a third party who has a contract with the
corporation has breached that contract and the Board
has failed to take action against that third party;

☑   A claim that senior management's salaries are
excessive; and

☑   A suit seeking to prevent management practices
which are calculated to prevent challenges to current
management.

There are several differences between a direct and derivative
suit. Because of such differences and the different rights and
requirements associated with each type of shareholder suit, parties
will often dispute which type of suit is appropriate. In order to
understand why the parties would care about which type of suit

(direct or derivative) was brought, it is important to understand some of the differences between them.

Differences in the posture of derivative suits and direct actions:

☑ Only shareholders can bring derivative suits (not creditors).

☑ Because a derivative lawsuit arises out of a "wrong" done to the corporation, any remedy or recovery goes to the corporation—not to the shareholder bringing the lawsuit.

☑ Because a direct lawsuit arises out of a "wrong" done to the shareholder, the shareholder bringing the direct lawsuit may collect damages.

☑ In a derivative lawsuit, the corporation is required to pay for the shareholder's attorney fees, PROVIDED that the shareholder is successful in the suit.

☑ There are many more procedural "hurdles" to meet in a derivative suit than there are in a direct suit.

There are additional requirements, which must be satisfied before a shareholder may bring a derivative lawsuit. These requirements vary from state to state. However, some of the basic requirements include:

☑ Contemporaneous Ownership. A shareholder seeking to bring a derivative lawsuit typically must have been a shareholder at the time of the injury claimed and at the time that the suit is brought. (Some states also require that the shareholder remain a shareholder through the court's decision. Other states allow for exceptions to this requirement if certain circumstances are shown (such as no similar action has been brought by other interested parties, the plaintiff acquired shares prior to any public disclosure, a showing that the suit could prevent a defendant from profiting from the willful breach of a fiduciary duty, and no unjust enrichment to the corporation).)

☑ In some states, a shareholder holding less than five percent of the corporation's outstanding stock is liable for the costs associated with bringing an unsuccessful derivative suit.

☑ In some states, shareholders must purchase a bond when bringing a derivative suit to cover the potential costs to the corporation of an unsuccessful suit. (Note that there is no bonding requirement in Delaware.)

Even if the above requirements have been met, there are additional obstacles (depending on the state) that a plaintiff will have to overcome in order to bring a derivate suit.

The Demand Requirement

Since the very nature of a derivative suit is that the claim belongs to the corporation, most states require that the shareholder approach the Board of Directors and demand that the Board pursue litigation before the shareholder is allowed to bring a derivate suit in the name of the corporation. However, if demand is made on the Board and the Board determines not to bring the suit, then that decision is usually protected by the Business Judgment Rule. As a result, plaintiffs usually seek to avoid making "demand" on the Board of Directors. In fact, there are clear circumstances in which the "Demand Requirement" is excused, and no demand need be made on the Board.

Demand is excused when asking the Board to bring a suit would be "futile." In order to determine when demand would be futile, one must examine the applicable case law. Each state will have slightly different standards. However, the basic concept should be the same. Typically, one must show that there is reasonable doubt that the majority of the directors are disinterested AND independent. (A director is **not** disinterested if he or she has a material financial interest in the challenged litigation. However, the mere fact that a majority of directors voted to approve the transaction and are named as defendants does not alone make them "interested.") Alternatively, the plaintiff could show that there is a reasonable doubt that the challenged transaction was a valid exercise of business judgment. (If the plaintiff can show that the transaction would not be subject to the protection of the business judgment rule (e.g. *conflict of interest, fraud, waste, procedural challenge*, etc.), then an exception to the demand requirement might apply.) Finally, demand is excused if the Board is not independent, typically because it is controlled by the individual who is the focus of the underlying suit. Be aware that the test of the futility of demand relates to the Board of Directors' ability to make an unbiased decision at the time the suit is brought. It does not evaluate the composition of the Board at the time of the action that is the subject of the suit. It evaluates the Board's ability to evaluate the lawsuit at the time it is being brought. As a result, if there has been significant change in the composition of the Board between the time of the alleged wrong and the time the complaint is brought, it might be difficult to satisfy this test.

In Delaware, demand is deemed "futile" if:

☑ A majority of the Board has a material financial or familial interest in the transaction;

☑ A majority of the Board is incapable of acting independently for some other reason such as domination or control (usually by an individual who is "interested"); or

☑ The underlying transaction is not the product of a valid exercise of business judgment. (Note that since the BJR is inapplicable where the Board did not exercise any business judgment (the "oversight" cases), some argue demand is automatically excused in oversight cases. It is not.)

If demand is NOT excused, then the Board (or a majority of disinterested directors) may dismiss the action, and that dismissal will typically be protected under the Business Judgment Rule. If demand is excused but the shareholder makes the demand anyway, then the futility argument is forfeited, and the Board then has the right to hear the demand and to dismiss the claim.

Special Litigation Committees

In recent years, corporations have appointed "special litigation committees" to evaluate derivative litigation. A special litigation committee is a committee of disinterested Board members and some outsiders that evaluate the lawsuit. The idea behind the "committee" is that, even if the Board is not in a position to evaluate the litigation from an unbiased perspective, it can still appoint a committee of unbiased members to evaluate whether the litigation is in the best interests of the corporation. Based upon the recommendation of the special litigation committee, the Board can still move to dismiss a derivative action, and, assuming that the special litigation committee is disinterested, that dismissal would be subject to the protection of the Business Judgment Rule.

A shareholder who is dissatisfied with the special litigation committee might be able to attack the special litigation committee's judgment on limited grounds. The shareholder might argue that the special litigation committee's judgment was not proper because:

☑ The decision was procedurally defective. (In other words, the special litigation committee used an improper or ineffective method to investigate the case.) Usually the special litigation committee's substantive interpretation is protected by the BJR.

☑ The special litigation committee failed to act independently, in good faith, and with a reasonable investigation. (This requirement means that even a determination by the special litigation committee that dismissal is appropriate may be attacked unless the corporation can show that the committee acted independently, with the requisite investigation, and in good faith. Cases have strictly construed the requirement that the special litigation committee have disinterested directors, and even a tangential connection between members of the special litigation committee and the other directors (such as working for a university that received substantial donations from the company which were approved by the Board) has been found sufficient to invalidate a recommendation of a special litigation committee.) Even this test will be construed differently in different states. Some states, such as New York, are more deferential to special litigation committees. Other states might require stricter scrutiny of the committee. For example, some states require that directors who have a financial interest in the transaction may not be involved even in the selection of the committee.

☑ A small number of states, including Delaware, have an additional requirement that the court exercise its own business judgment in evaluating the decision to dismiss.

DERIVATIVE LAWSUIT SUMMARY

Ultimately a typical derivative lawsuit might evolve as follows:

☑ Corporation ABC does something (allegedly) wrong and a shareholder (or group of shareholders) wants to sue the directors for breach of fiduciary duty to the corporation (not to the shareholder). Since the directors are not going to sue themselves, the shareholder needs to bring a derivative lawsuit.

☑ **First**, the shareholder must post a bond to cover costs in the event that the shareholder loses.

☑ **Second**, the shareholder must make a demand on the Board of Directors to pursue the litigation, **OR** show that a demand on the Board of Directors is excused (because it is futile to make a demand on the Board) by showing, for example, that a majority of the Board has an interest in the transaction in question or that the Board is controlled by someone with an interest in the transaction, or that a reasonable doubt exists about the exercise of sound business judgment with respect to the transaction in question.

☑ **Third**, if there is a special litigation committee, the special litigation committee has to agree with the shareholder and allow the shareholder to bring his case, OR if the special litigation committee votes to dismiss the lawsuit, then the shareholder will need to argue that the decision of the special litigation committee is invalid, either because the process for investigating the claim was flawed, the members of the committee were not "disinterested," or the committee's decision itself violated the BJR. If the shareholder does not prevail on any of the foregoing, in a limited number of states, the shareholder can hope that the court evaluating the matter will think that the suit nevertheless should proceed based on the court's independent business judgment.

☑ If the shareholder can overcome these obstacles, then the shareholder will be allowed to bring the derivative lawsuit.

ILLUSTRATIVE PROBLEMS

PROBLEM 7.6

Building Supplies, Corp. ("BS Corp.") was responsible for the construction of several buildings in downtown Mapleville. Because a few BS Corp. employees used faulty materials in constructing the buildings, a few of the BS Corp. buildings were badly damaged during an earthquake. The City of Mapleville sued BS Corp. for several million dollars and won. Subsequently, a BS Corp. shareholder, Piper, filed a derivative lawsuit against the directors of BS Corp. for failure (a) to take, or even to consider taking, action sufficient to oversee the BS Corp. employees and/or (b) to prevent the type of misconduct that resulted in the Mapleville wrongdoing. What type of suit could Piper bring and what potential procedural defenses might the BS Corp. directors present?

Analysis

Because the harm alleged is to BS Corp., not to Piper directly, the suit would have to be a derivative lawsuit. Before the suit could be brought, Piper would either need to make demand on the Board of Directors or show that demand was futile. Assuming the BS Corp. Board of Directors was comprised of the same individuals who had failed to prevent the wrongdoing, it is likely that Piper would succeed in asserting that demand would be futile. Because the failure to supervise would not be protected by the BJR AND the Board was comprised of the same individuals who allegedly failed to supervise, it is likely that demand would be excused. If, however, the Board had a number of new members who were not dominated or controlled by the others, or if the Board could show that it had no notice of the potential for impropriety and no duty to supervise, then futility would be more difficult to show. Even if Piper could show futility, the BS Corp. Board might still appoint a special litigation committee to evaluate the case. In a more permissive jurisdiction (like New York), if the special litigation committee recommends the claim be dismissed, then, assuming the committee was comprised of disinterested individuals who properly investigated the claim, the claim would probably be dismissed, subject to the BJR. In some jurisdictions, Piper might still prevail if she could show that the members of the special litigation committee were appointed by interested members of the Board of Directors. In a small number of jurisdictions, including Delaware, Piper might still prevail if the court reviewing the decision of the special litigation committee found that the decision to dismiss Piper's lawsuit was contrary to the court's opinion of good business judgment. In several jurisdictions, even if Piper prevailed in her effort to bring the derivative action, she would still be required to post a bond to cover BS Corp.'s costs of the suit if Piper were to ultimately lose the underlying substantive case against the Board of Directors for the Board's failure to prevent the Mapleville misconduct.

PROBLEM 7.7

Major Paper Corporation is a publicly traded company. It has over a billion dollars in assets. The president of Major Paper Corporation, Peg, decides that in order to secure future supplies for the corporation, Major Paper Corporation will spend over one hundred million dollars to purchase forest lands, strategizing that the trees on this land can be used to supply paper to a Major Paper Corporation for years to come. The deal is approved by Major Paper Corporation's Board of Directors. Once the deal is completed, Peg makes a big announcement to the industry about Major Paper Corporation's innovative steps to vertically integrate the industry. Three months later, groundbreaking environmental legislation is passed, covering most of the trees on the land that Major Paper Corporation purchased. In addition, there is a real estate bust, and the land loses additional value. By conservative measures, the land is worth 20% of what Major Paper Corporation paid for it. Angry Andy is a shareholder in Major Paper Corporation. Because of the losses from the transaction, Andy's stock in Major Paper Corporation has fallen substantially in value, and he wants to sue Peg. He also wants to sue the government for passing legislation which made his Major Paper Corporation stock lose so much value. What type of suit (or suits) may Andy bring?

Analysis

Andy is essentially claiming that Peg and the Board members who approved the deal have violated their duty of care to Major Paper Corporation. Even though the result of this alleged violation is a reduction in the value of Andy's stock in Major Paper Corporation, Andy's "injury" is a result of the corporation's losses. Peg did not directly reduce the value of Andy's shares. Peg (at least according to Andy) hurt Major Paper Corporation, and that injury made Andy's shares decrease in value. This situation is a classic derivative claim. If Andy wants to bring a suit against Peg and the Board, he must bring another derivative action, which would be subject to the obstacles and defenses detailed above. Furthermore, it is up to the corporation whether or not to sue the government about the legislation. Andy does not have the right to sue the government since the alleged harm was suffered by Major Paper Corporation. If the corporation does not sue the government, Andy must bring another derivative suit in his effort to compel Major Paper Corporation to sue the government. It is likely that it would be much more difficult for Andy to overcome the requirement for demand on the Board in such an action because it would be difficult to show the Board of Director's "interest" in not bringing a suit against the government.

CHAPTER 8

Securities Laws

T
he securities laws in the United States are detailed and
complex. In fact, there is an entire law school course focused
only on these laws. However, any class on business
associations should provide an introduction to these laws
and highlight certain securities rules and regulations since
securities represent and define the ownership structure of the a
corporation. Securities laws set forth parameters by which directors
and officers must conduct themselves when the corporation's
securities are involved. The basic areas of focus in a business
associations course often involve anti-fraud legislation in, or arising
under, the Securities Act of 1933 and the Securities Exchange Act of
1934 (referred to as the "1933 Act" and the "1934 Act", respectively).
A primary effort of these securities laws is to promote full disclosure
and prevent "fraud." In order for these laws to apply to a given
situation, a "security" must be involved. This might seem like a
simple matter. However, because the securities laws provide such
powerful tools, it becomes a critical question to determine when
they apply. As a result, there has been a lot of litigation over just
what constitutes a "security."

WHAT IS A SECURITY?

There are certain specific "instruments" such as shares of
stock, which are almost always considered to be securities.
However, there are other situations in which an instrument,
contract, scheme or structure needs to be evaluated to determine if
it indeed qualifies as a "security." In general, unless an instrument
is already considered to be a security (such as stock), the
circumstances surrounding the transaction must be evaluated. A
typical transaction involving a security is one in which an
investment is made with another person, or entity, from which the
investor expects to profit, based on the efforts of others.

Section 2(1) of the 1933 Act lists two broad categories of
instruments, which qualify as a security. There are specific
instruments that automatically (or almost automatically) qualify as

a security in one category and some general "catchall" definitions in the other category. Some of the specific instruments include:

☑ Stock;

☑ Notes;

☑ Bonds;

☑ Debentures;

☑ Options; and

☑ Voting Trust Certificates.

The general category definitions of a security include more general definitions categories such as:

☑ *Evidence of indebtedness*; and

☑ *Investment contracts.*

Finally, the securities definition in the 1933 Act includes any instrument that is "commonly known as a 'security.'" In addition, the case law "clarifies" that the items listed are considered securities under § 2(1) of the 1933 Act, *unless* context requires otherwise.

For example, Rita owns a restaurant called the Financial Food Zone ("FFZ"). For an additional dollar, added to the price of a customer's meal, FFZ will provide that customer with a laminated stock certificate to use as a souvenir placemat. Marvin orders a meal, pays an extra dollar and receives his laminated stock certificate placemat. Marvin has not purchased a "security" from FFZ. He has purchased a placemat, and even though "stock" is considered a security, in this situation the context of the FFZ restaurant would show that the laminated stock certificates are not "securities" as contemplated in the definition contained in § 2(1) of the 1933 Act.

When trying to identify if a scheme, contract or instrument qualifies as a "security," one might look for the presence of some the following features, which are characteristics of typical securities:

☑ The right to receive dividends contingent upon an apportionment of profits;

☑ Negotiability;

☑ The ability to be pledged or hypothecated;

☑ Voting rights that accompany an instrument and correspond to the number of "shares" owned; and/or

☑ The ability to appreciate in value.

In evaluating an instrument, context is important and could lead a court to find something is or is not a security. Often, when an instrument is not included on the list of specific instruments, someone will argue that it falls into one of the general categories, often the "investment contract" category. In order to evaluate whether something is an **investment contract**, there are four requirements that must be considered (known as the "*Howey* Test"):

☑ A contract, transaction, or scheme through which a person **invests money** (or any other consideration);

☑ The investment is made into a **common enterprise** (either with "horizontal commonality" in which the investment is made with others or, in some circuits but not all, with "vertical commonality" in which the investment is made with a promoter who is working to make money for the investor);

☑ With the **expectation of profits** (or some other financial benefits); and

☑ With the **profits to come "solely" from the efforts of others**. (This "efforts of others" clause is intended to include the requirement that the investor NOT participate in the operation of the investment opportunity. To expect profit (or financial benefit) based on the efforts of others means that the investor is depending upon the work, skill, expertise and/or efforts of people other than himself or herself to produce the profitable result. However, most courts interpret the word "solely" in this context, to mean "primarily.")

An example of an investment that is not a security might be an investment in a general partnership. Since all of the partners have the right to be involved in management, it is rare that a partnership interest would be considered a security, since the "profits from the efforts of others . . ." aspect of the test is not met. Conversely, an interest of a limited partner in a limited partnership often is a security since limited partners typically do not participate in management, and therefore, the requirements of the "*Howey* test" are usually met.

REGISTRATION

Various provisions of the securities laws apply to different types of transactions. (Often, several different provisions will apply to the same transaction.) One example of this is the regulation of securities registrations. In order for a security to be sold to the public, it must either be registered or have an exemption from registration. There are many exemptions to registration, and the many private offerings proceed under those exemptions. However, if no exemption is available, then the company (or individual) issuing the securities (aka the "**issuer**") must "register" the securities. When a company's stock is registered, the *company* is usually described as "publicly traded." However, what this really means is that at least one class of the company's *stock* is publicly traded. It is possible for a company to have some of its securities be publicly traded and others not.

Section 11 of the 1934 Act regulates registration statements and creates responsibilities for the following groups of people:

☑ Anyone who signs the registration statement;

☑ Officers of the issuer;

☑ Experts who assisted in the preparation of the registration statement; and

☑ Underwriters promoting the offering.

If you are the issuer, you have strict liability for anything misleading (whether because of an omission or misstatement) in the registration statement. However, others connected to the registration statement have a defense of **due diligence** (basically a negligence standard). That due diligence defense typically requires:

☑ Reading the registration statement; AND

☑ Investigating the registration statement to make sure that the statements and assertions contained in that statement are true. (Note, if something turned out to be false, in order to avoid liability, the defendant in question would need to show that he or she did not know that it was false and should not have known it was false.)

A registration statement may be divided into two portions: the "**expertised**" portion and the "**non-expertised**" portion. In the expertised portion, accountants and auditors (i.e., the "experts") have gone through the statement and confirmed the information. The experts must conduct a *reasonable investigation* and have reasonable grounds to believe, and in fact believe, that the statements in the expertised portion of the registration statement are true. Non-experts must only show that they had no reason to believe and, in fact, did not believe that the statements in the expertised portion were misleading.

With regard to the "non-expertised" portions, the experts (who presumably did not work on these portions) have no liability. The non-experts must conduct a *reasonable investigation* and have reasonable grounds to believe, and in fact believe, that the statements in this non-expertised portion of the registration statement are true. The standard of care applied to these tests is the care that a reasonable person would exercise if his money were at stake.

PRIVATE PLACEMENTS

If an issuer wants to raise money without registering, then that issuer must have an exemption from registration. Various characteristics of the offering will determine whether it is exempt from registration. These factors include:

☑ **Size of the offering**. How much money is being raised? Note, there are exemptions for certain offerings under $1 million and $5 million.

☑ **Number of units offered**. How many shares are available and what percentage of the company's total ownership (i.e. "the pie") does that constitute?

☑ **Manner of the offering**. How do people hear about the transaction? Rules restrict advertising to, and solicitations of, the general public.

☑ **Number of offerees**. How many people are offered the deal? The focus of this factor is NOT on how many people actually invest, but how many are offered the opportunity to invest. This must be a limited number. (Note: often, different offerees are treated differently. Some exemptions do not "count" certain sophisticated investors, known as "**accredited investors**," as part of the number of offerees. An individual accredited investor typically has a net worth, not including the investor's house, over $1 million or income over $200,000 for the prior few years. There are different standards for corporations seeking accredited investor status. It is also important to show that an offeree has had access to information from, and about, the issuer.)

If a transaction is "exempt," the process of raising money for the corporation conducting the exempt transaction is often referred to as a "private placement." Most private placements are conducted under Regulation D or Section 4(2) of the 1933 Act. While private placements are exempt from Section 11 of the 1933 Act, they are still subject to Section 10b–5 of the 1934 Act as well as to other provisions of the Securities Acts. In addition to satisfying federal law requirements, securities transactions must also meet the requirements of any state in which they are offered. These state rules are known as "blue sky" laws and may vary from state to state. (If a securities transaction takes place entirely within one state, it is often exempt from federal registration requirements under an "intrastate" exemption.)

Crowdfunding Exemption

A provision in the Jumpstart Our Business Startups (or "JOBS") Act legislation of 2012, created a "crowdfunding" exemption (which has been included in the 1933 Act as a new section 4(6)), allowing entrepreneurs and small businesses to raise up to $1 million from a large number of investors, even if those investors are not "accredited." The concept of crowdfunding which has been facilitated, if not created, by the Internet, is that many investors will put up a small amount of money to provide investment to a business or even an idea. Under this provision in the JOBS Act, companies could raise up to $1 million from investors in a 12-month period without registering the transaction with the SEC. The final crowdfunding rules adopted by the SEC pursuant to the JOBS Act, limit contributions made by individuals, aggregated across all crowdfunding offerings over a 12-month period, as follows:

☑ The greater of $2,000 or 5 percent of an investor's net worth or annual income, for investors whose net worth OR annual income is less than $100,000; or

☑ The lesser of 10 percent of an investor's net worth or annual income, for investors whose net worth AND annual income is greater than $100,000;

☑ The amount invested by any individual under this exemption during the 12-month period, may not exceed $100,000; and

☑ Any money raised through this exemption must be raised through a broker or funding portal. (There are many regulations (beyond the scope of this book) imposing requirements and limitations on funding portals. The term "funding portal" is defined by the SEC as any person acting as an intermediary in a transaction involving the offer or sale of securities for the account of others, solely pursuant to Section 4(6) of the 1933 Act, that "does not (1) offer investment advice or recommendations; (2) solicit purchases,

> sales, or offers to buy the securities offered or
> displayed on its website or portal; (3) compensate
> employees, agents, or other persons for such
> solicitation or based on the sale of securities displayed
> or referenced on its website or portal; (4) hold,
> manage, possess, or otherwise handle investor funds
> or securities; or (5) engage in such other activities as
> the Commission, by rule, determines appropriate.")

The crowdfunding legislation endeavors to make it easier for a
small company to raise money through Internet portals and social
media, without the overwhelming cost and burden of regulatory
compliance that would be present when raising millions of dollars
through more traditional avenues. However, students should be
aware that even transactions that raise capital through an
exemption to the securities laws requiring registration are still
subject to the requirements and investor protections of other
securities laws such as Rule 10b–5, discussed below.

RULE 10b–5

Rule 10b–5 is probably the most important (or at least the most
utilized) piece of antifraud securities legislation. Rule 10b–5 may be
used both by the SEC and by private individuals in pursuing fraud
claims. (Rule 10b–5 is also used to restrict insider trading actions as
will be seen below.) A critical aspect of Rule 10b–5 is that it creates
liability for anyone who makes a misleading representation or
omission that is connected to the purchase or sale of a security. This
is different from "insider trading." This liability arises when
someone buys or sells a security, even if they do not buy it from or
sell it to, the person who makes the misleading statement. Rule
10b–5 has also been used to create a private right of action in areas
in which Congress has been silent. In other words, this is not just a
provision that the SEC can use to pursue those who make
misrepresentations. This Rule can be used by individuals as well.

Section 10(b) of the Securities Exchange Act of 1934 provides
that:

> It shall be unlawful for any person, directly or indirectly,
> by the use of any means or instrumentality of interstate
> commerce or of the mails, or of any facility of any national
> securities exchange—. . .
>
> (b) To use or employ, in connection with the purchase or
> sale of any security registered on a national securities
> exchange or any security not so registered, . . . any
> manipulative or deceptive device or contrivance **in**

contravention of such rules and regulations as the Commission may prescribe as necessary or appropriate in the public interest or for the protection of investors. [emphasis added.]

Notice that this provision requires the SEC to make "rules and regulations" to which Section 10(b) will apply. In following this requirement the SEC adopted Rule 10b–5, which states:

It shall be unlawful for any person, directly or indirectly, by the use of any means or instrumentality of interstate commerce, or of the mails or of any facility of any national securities exchange,

(a) To employ any device, scheme, or artifice to defraud,

(b) To make any untrue statement of a material fact or to omit to state a material fact necessary in order to make the statements made, in the light of the circumstances under which they were made, not misleading, or

(c) To engage in any act, practice, or course of business which operates or would operate as a fraud or deceit upon any person, in connection with the purchase or sale of any security.

CLAIMS MADE UNDER RULE 10b–5

There are several requirements that must be met in order to bring a claim under Rule 10b–5. However, even before a "would-be" plaintiff might be able to make a substantive claim under 10b–5, that potential plaintiff would first need to meet certain basic "standing" requirements. Here are some of the features of which to be aware when evaluating whether Rule 10b–5 may apply to a situation:

☑ Section 10(b) has an **interstate commerce jurisdictional requirement**. This requirement means that the statute (Section 10(b)) only applies if the fraud involved use of a "means or instrumentality of interstate commerce, or of the mails, or of any facility of any national securities exchange." *Intrastate* activities are not regulated by Section 10(b). So, if none of these interstate activities occur, there may be fraud, but Rule 10b–5 will not apply. For example, if Bob and Mary are on a walk in the park, and Bob tells a lie to Mary in order to get her to invest in his local candy store business, and Mary then gave Bob $1,000 to invest in his local candy store business, there might be liability under state law, but, unless there are additional facts involving interstate commerce, there would not be 10b–5 liability.

☑ Even if the facts meet the jurisdictional requirements, the plaintiff must show that the **activity involves a "security"**. (See above discussion about the definition of a security.) For example, if a defendant tells lies to get a tomato farmer to sell him tomatoes so the defendant can corner the tomato market, there is no 10b–5 violation since tomatoes are not securities. Note that Rule 10b–5 applies to ANY security, not just securities in a public corporation; it applies to closely-held corporations (even though they are private companies generally not subject to the 1934 Act) as well as transactions in government securities.

☑ Even if the facts meet the jurisdictional requirements and the "security" requirement, the activity **must involve a purchase or sale of securities**. If an individual or the corporation makes a false or misleading statement, BUT there is no associated purchase or sale of stock arising out of that false or misleading statement, there is no liability. For example, if the plaintiff decides *not* to sell or *not* to buy because of a misrepresentation or an omission, he may be damaged, but he does not have a claim under 10b–5.

How connected does the fraud have to be with the purchase or sale? The fraud need only *touch and concern* the transaction. While there is not a well-established definition of "touch and concern," even a tenuous connection between the "fraud" and the transaction will probably suffice.

Once the jurisdictional requirements have been met and there is a purchase or sale of a security, in order to show a violation of 10b–5, one still must satisfy the statutory requirement by showing that the defendant: (a) employed a device, scheme, or artifice to defraud; **AND** (b) either (i) made an untrue statement of a material fact, or (ii) omitted or failed to state a material fact necessary in order to make the statements made, in light of the circumstances under which they were made, not misleading; **OR** (c) engaged in "any act, practice or course of business which would operate[d] or would operate as a fraud or deceit upon any person," all in connection with that purchase or sale of a security.

In order to satisfy these statutory requirements, there are five elements that must be met. (Admittedly, some of these requirements overlap a bit):

☑   **Untrue statement or omission;**

☑   **Scienter (intent);**

☑   **Materiality;**

☑   **Reliance; AND**

☑   **Causation** (proximate cause or "loss causation").

In understanding how to evaluate a Rule 10b–5 claim, it is useful to have a concrete example to see how the facts would apply to each of the requirements. The following example about Corporation DK will be used to illustrate the application of the 10b–5 elements to a fact pattern:

ILLUSTRATIVE EXAMPLE

Corporation DK is a publicly traded corporation that produces high-sugar breakfast cereals for kids. The president of Corporation DK, Fred Filling, in an interview with a national television station about the impact of a recession on Corporation DK, says (knowing that it is not true) that "kids always want our cereal even if times are tough. We have determined that Corporation DK's earnings will not be impacted by the current economic downturn." Pam hears the statement, believes it and, in reliance on it, later that day logs into her internet brokerage account, and buys stock in Corporation DK, which is traded on the New York Stock Exchange. Once the news comes out that Corporation DK's stock has in fact been impacted by the economic downturn, the stock price falls, and Pam sells her corporation DK stock losing a great deal of money. In addition, Pam's daughter Emily, who has been eating the cereal for several months, goes to the dentist and has five cavities. Pam wants to know if she has a claim against Corporation DK for a violation of Rule 10b–5.

Analysis of 10b–5 Requirements

Since Pam heard the interview on a national broadcast, used the internet and bought stock (which is a security) on a national exchange, the interstate jurisdiction requirement is satisfied, as are the requirements of a purchase or sale of a security. In order for there to be liability under 10b–5, Pam must also show:

Untrue statement or omission

The defendant had to make a false or misleading statement or omit information, which made a statement false or misleading. In the example above, Pam would need to show that Fred's statement about the impact of the downturn was false or misleading. (As the president of Corporation DK, Fred is Corporation DK's agent, so Fred's statement is attributed to DK.) In situations in which liability is based on the omission of a material fact rather than a misrepresentation, then there can only be liability if there was a duty to disclose that fact.

Scienter (intent or knowledge of wrongdoing)

The defendant must have acted with an intent to deceive, manipulate, or defraud; negligence alone does NOT suffice (although some courts will allow "deliberate recklessness"). This standard is different than "fraud" because the intent relates to the representation and not to the transaction itself. Pam would need to show that Fred's statement was meant to deceive or manipulate the public. (If Fred made the statement without any regard as to whether or not it was true, that conduct might suffice as well in some circuits.) Since the facts reveal that Fred **knew** the statement was false, it is likely that this element would be satisfied.

Materiality

The defendant's misrepresentation or omission must have been material, meaning a reasonable investor would likely consider the misstatement or omission to be important in deciding whether to buy or sell. (Note that this standard is about the *reasonable investor*—not the eccentric investor.) In the above example, Fred's statement is material if a reasonable investor would consider it to be important. Since the corporation's ability to avoid the impact of an economic downturn could have a substantial effect on corporate earnings and stock price, it is likely that the statement would be considered to be material.

Materiality of a Contingent Event

Sometimes, a determination must be made about whether something that *might* happen is material. For example, if a corporation is performing secret work in order to discover a blockbuster drug, that potential discovery is a contingent event, which might or might not happen. In order to evaluate a contingent event, students should use a probability/magnitude test (sometimes called "**the *Basic* Test**" from a significant case outlining the test). In this test, one must evaluate the probability that an event will happen and the importance of the event, if it does happen. There are four possible results when looking at the probability and magnitude of an event occurring:

1.   A contingent event could have both a high probability of occurring and a high magnitude (i.e. significance or importance) if it does occur. If so, it is material.

2.   Conversely, a contingent event could have both a low probability of occurring and a low magnitude if it does occur. If so, it would not be material.

3.   Even an event that has a high probability of occurring but a low magnitude if it does occur, is still not material, since it is unlikely that something of little importance or significance would impact a company's stock price.

4.   The most difficult situation to evaluate involves a contingent event that has a low to moderate probability of occurring and high magnitude if it does. In fact, this scenario is what most of the materiality cases, involving a contingent event, center upon. Whether a contingent event in this category is "material" is ultimately a question of fact, and students should evaluate the possibility that a statement or omission that fits this profile could be either material or not material for purposes of determining liability under Rule 10b–5 liability. (Note that a merger is almost always high magnitude because of the impact that it has on a company's stock and on the value of the company. Even the low probability of a merger actually occurring might not be sufficient to prevent a determination of materiality.)

Reliance

If a plaintiff brings a private action, there must also be a showing that he or she actually AND justifiably relied on the defendant's misrepresentation. (Sometimes reliance is referred to as "transaction causation.") In the above example, since Pam actually heard Fred's statement and bought Corporation DK's stock following Fred's interview, it is likely that she will be able to show that she relied on that statement in her purchase of stock and that, since Fred was the president of Corporation DK and gave the statement in the context of a serious interview, Pam's reliance was justified. However, if the Corporation could somehow show that Pam had planned to buy Corporation DK's stock under any circumstances and/or that Fred's statement had no impact on

Pam's decision to purchase the stock, then the reliance requirement would not be satisfied, and Pam's 10b–5 claim would be defeated.

Reliance on Omissions

There are some situations in which the company or an officer of the company has a duty to speak but did not. If an event of large significance occurs, a company would typically have the obligation to disclose that event. The company's failure to disclose that event would be considered an omission. For example, if Fred had discovered that Corporation DK's cereal production plants had significant problems and the company was only going to be able to manufacture (and therefore sell) half as much cereal as it typically would in the current year, that information would be material and would have to have been disclosed. Failure to disclose it would have been a material omission. However, how does a plaintiff show that he or she "relied" on something that was not said? The answer is that, given the duty to disclose, a person is entitled to rely that appropriate disclosures will be made. In effect, they can rely on silence as a "statement" that there is no material information *that the company is required to disclose*, which has not been disclosed. Therefore, in the case of an omission, reliance is presumed, but this is a rebuttable presumption.

Fraud-on-the-Market

There are several cases involving affirmative misrepresentations (usually involving a large group of people), in which the plaintiffs cannot show that they each relied on the misstatement. It is around this situation that the doctrine of "fraud-on-the-market" has arisen. The **fraud-on-the-market theory** was developed as a way to show how a large group of people could have relied on a misstatement. The fraud-on-the-market theory creates a rebuttable presumption that, even if the plaintiff did not hear the misstatement, there was still reliance and, thus, the case can proceed. This theory creates **a presumption that the investor relied on the integrity of the market price, and so the investor does not even need to have seen or heard the misrepresentation to satisfy the reliance element. Fraud-on-the-market is invoked when there is a *public affirmative misrepresentation* AND *the market is an efficient market* (e.g. the stock market).** Fraud-on-the-market

ONLY works when there is an efficient market. It does NOT apply in private transactions. Behind the fraud-on-the-market theory is the concept that BECAUSE a large number of sophisticated analysts at a large number of firms read, evaluate public statements about a corporation, and make substantial decisions for their firms to buy or sell stock based on statements, those purchases or sales (because collectively, they are so large) affect the price of the stock. As a result, any misrepresentation is priced into the market and thus affects the price at which the unsophisticated investor buys and sells stock, even if that unsophisticated investor did not hear/read/rely on the actual misrepresentation. The practical impact of this theory is often to eliminate the reliance requirement in these cases. If the defendant wanted to avoid liability, the defendant would need to rebut the theory by showing that the misrepresentation did NOT affect the market price. Fraud-on-the-market relies on the notion that information is taken into account by the market, and the market operates efficiently given that information.

Defendants may rebut the applicability of the fraud-on-the-market theory to a particular transaction by showing that:

☑ The misrepresentation did NOT affect market price;

☑ The defendants issued corrective statements, which were also priced into the market;

☑ The plaintiffs would have bought or sold anyway, even with full disclosure (for example, if a plaintiff had to sell his stock because he had other financial problems); or

☑ The defendant did not rely on the integrity of the market.

Note that not all states recognize fraud-on-the-market as a valid legal theory that will take the place of reliance.

Causation

Causation is also known as "proximate cause" or "loss causation." To satisfy this requirement, it is not enough to show that the misrepresentation caused the transaction (see reliance above); the plaintiff also needs to show that the misrepresentation or omission caused the *loss* itself. In fact the plaintiff making a securities fraud clam must do more than merely allege that the price of the security in question was inflated because of the misrepresentation. The plaintiff must allege and prove the traditional elements of causation and loss.

In the example above, Pam would need to show that Fred's misstatement caused Corporation DK's stock to go up before Pam bought it and that, when the truth came out, Corporation DK's stock fell because of the discovery of the false statement. In order to defeat the element of causation, defendants such as Corporation DK might attempt to argue that the market didn't believe the interview, and that any movement in the stock price was caused by market factors or any factors other than Fred's interview.

An example of a loss that would not have been caused by the misrepresentation would be if Corporation DK's stock fell by 50% when Fred's lie was discovered, BUT, on the same day the entire stock market crashed 35%. Even if Corporation DK could not defeat Pam's 10b–5 claim, Corporation DK could probably show that the misrepresentation was not responsible for the 35% drop attributable to the market decline, but instead, was responsible for the 15% difference between 35% and 50%.

(Note that there are two "causation" concepts, which are frequently confused: transaction causation and loss causation. Transaction causation (i.e. the misrepresentation caused the plaintiff to engage in the transaction) is almost identical to reliance, and it is NOT the type of causation discussed in this section. Loss causation (i.e. that the misrepresentation caused the loss) is what is meant by the causation element.)

DAMAGES IN A 10b–5 CLAIM

Assuming the elements of a 10b–5 claim are satisfied, the defendant is liable for damages. (Note that in the example above, Corporation DK is going to be liable even though the statement was made by Fred, the president, because the president of a corporation is an agent for the corporation and, as seen in Chapter 1, a principal (i.e. DK corporation) is liable for the wrongful conduct its agents commit within the scope of the agency.).

Damages in a 10b–5 action may take the form of (a) "out of pocket" damages (which would involve a determination of the difference between the price actually paid or received and the price that should have been paid without the 10b–5 violation); (b) restitution (also known as "disgorgement," which would involve the defendant turning over the profit derived from the fraud to the plaintiff); (c) rescission (which could involve the return of the price paid or the securities sold by the plaintiff, or the difference between the original sale price and the subsequent sale price by the defendant); (d) benefit of the bargain damages (which might only arise in limited circumstances in which there is a difference between the value received and the value promised, which may be established with reasonable certainty); and (e) punitive damages in extreme cases. Any measure of damages might also include consequential damages under circumstances provided they can be shown with sufficient certainty. Neither punitive damages nor statutory penalties are available under Rule 10b–5 in a private cause of action (at least in the vast majority of cases brought), but plaintiffs bringing state law claims may be entitled to seek punitive damages under many states' laws. (Note that the plaintiff must also have standing and be able to show injury/damages.) In addition, the SEC may seek to impose monetary penalties (and various forms of bars and suspensions) on those who violate the Federal securities laws.

In a claim made under Rule 10b–5 for out-of-pocket damages, the plaintiffs are entitled to receive the difference between the price of the stock and its value on the *date of the transaction*, if the truth were known, measured by what a reasonable investor would have paid if she had known the facts. In the above example, if Pam could show that she paid $50,000 for the Corporation DK stock, but, if the truth were known about the negative effect that the economic downturn was having on Corporation DK, the price would have been $30,000, then Pam would be entitled to recover $20,000. This calculation would still apply whether Pam ultimately sold her Corporation DK stock for only $25,000 or $35,000. In other words, the calculation of damages is based upon the loss (*or the decrease in profits*) caused by the misstatement, not the purchase price minus the sale price.

CLAIMS NOT COVERED BY RULE 10b–5

Rule 10b–5 is NOT about correcting every wrong; it is about full disclosure. Once a full and fair disclosure is made, the fairness of the transaction is a not an issue under federal law. In such instances the appropriate remedy must be sought under state law. For example, inadequate compensation paid for a person's stock does NOT create a 10b–5 claim, *provided that person was provided with full disclosure relating to the inadequacy of the compensation*.

Furthermore, in order to support a claim under Rule 10b–5 the disclosure at issue must touch and concern the purchase or sale of stock. So, in the above example, if Pam's daughter Emily has five cavities that were caused by Corporation DK's over-sugared cereal. Even if Pam could show (a) that Corporation DK intentionally made false or misleading statements about the cereal and how it would not affect tooth decay; (b) that the statements were material; (c) that Pam relied on those statements; and (d) that the false statements caused Pam to feed the cereal to Emily which caused the five cavities, Pam would still not have a claim under 10b–5. Pam would not have a claim because cereal is not a security and her purchase of the cereal, even based upon a misstatement, does not constitute a violation of Rule 10b–5 by Corporation DK. Pam may have many other claims against Corporation DK such as a claim for false advertising or product liability. However, those claims do not arise under corporate law, so they are not considered here. **The question under a Rule 10b–5 claim is not whether a wrong has been committed; it is whether a wrong has been committed which satisfies the elements of the 10b–5 statute.** Students should also be aware that this analysis would not be changed by the fact that Pam also bought stock in Corporation DK. The purchase of stock is a separate transaction and does not impact the analysis of Pam's claim for damage to Emily's teeth. Note that if Corporation DK did lie about the harmful effects of its cereal, and that lie impacted the stock price, then those shareholders who bought or sold the stock might have a 10b–5 claim if they could show that the lie about the cereal caused damage in connection with the purchase or sale of Corporation DK's stock.

ILLUSTRATIVE PROBLEMS

PROBLEM 8.1

Locks Corporation is a major pharmaceutical firm that has one of its small divisions working on a cure for baldness. Research shows that the cure works on bald monkeys, but there haven't been any human tests. So, Locks has not yet applied for FDA approval. Is this information "material"?

Analysis

The discovery of a cure for baldness represents a contingent event. When evaluating the materiality of a contingent event, the *Basic* test is usually applied. That test examines both the magnitude and the probability of a specific event. The discovery of a cure for baldness would represent a significant and important event for Locks Corporation. Therefore, the magnitude of the event is high. However, it is unclear whether the probability is high based on the information given. Unless we have more information about the industry, it is impossible to know whether something that works on monkeys is likely to work on humans, and no human trials have been undertaken. From an outsider's perspective, one might suggest that the probability of success is "moderate." Given these circumstances, one might argue that the information about the success in tests on bald monkeys is material and should be disclosed since it is probably information, which a reasonable investor would want to know in making a decision about the purchase or sale of stock in Locks Corporation. Note that in a question in which the materiality of the success in the test on monkeys was an issue, students should argue both for and against materiality and then make a determination. In such a question, a continuing analysis would involve a statement like "If the information is material. . . ."

PROBLEM 8.2

QRS, Inc. purchases all of the assets of Beta, Inc., a wholly owned subsidiary of XYZ, Inc. Six months after the transaction, QRS discovers information about an important labor dispute relating to Beta, Inc., which it feels that XYZ should have disclosed. QRS sues XYZ for violation of Rule 10b–5, claiming that XYZ's failure to disclose was a material omission. XYZ moves for dismissal. What is the likely outcome?

Analysis

It is likely that the suit will be dismissed. Rule 10b–5 only applies to transactions involving the purchase or sale of securities. The purchase of assets is not a purchase of securities. Assets are not an "instrument" under section 2(1) of the 1933 Act. This investment does not qualify as an investment contract, and finally the investment does not meet the *Howey* test. The *Howey* test requires that an investment be made in a common enterprise with the expectation of profits to come solely from the effort of others. Here, while money was invested and there probably was an expectation of profits, there was no "common enterprise," and QRS was dependent upon its own efforts, not the efforts of XYZ. As a result, the QRS purchase does not qualify as a securities transaction, so there would be no recourse under Rule 10b–5. If QRS believes that it can show there was fraud in the transaction or a breach of the Asset Purchase Contract, then it might have a claim (or claims) under state law.

SARBANES-OXLEY

The Sarbanes-Oxley Act of 2002 ("SOX") was an effort to increase disclosure by, and oversight of, publicly traded companies in the wake of the Enron scandal. While SOX is filled with regulations, there are only a few that often arise in the introductory study of business organizations. One example includes the requirement that a publicly traded company's president or CEO as well as its Chief Financial Officer (aka Treasurer) must sign its financial statements, verifying that these officers have each reviewed the statements, the statements are accurate, and that the signatory takes personal responsibility for what is in the statements. Another SOX requirement is that public companies may not make personal loans to their officers or directors and must adopt a "code of ethics" for their respective CEOs and various financial officers.

SOX also places additional responsibilities on attorneys who are aware of their clients' violations of securities laws or fiduciary duty transgressions. SOX requires that attorneys who represent publicly held companies "report evidence of a material violation of the securities laws or breach of fiduciary duty or similar violation by the company or any agent thereof . . ." to the company's chief legal officer or CEO. If proper action is not taken in response to such a report, the attorney is then required to refer the matter to a higher authority within the company (such as the company's audit committee). These SOX regulations are not difficult, but they are numerous. Familiarity with a few of the areas in which issues might arise that are addressed in SOX will enable students to present an additional dimension to an analysis of a problem in which such an issue might arise.

CHAPTER 9

Insider Trading

The prohibition of insider trading of securities involves the concept that those with access to nonpublic information should not have an advantage over those from whom they buy, or to whom they sell, securities. There is a fair amount of debate over whether this restriction makes sense from an economic policy perspective. However, such policy debates are beyond the focus of this book. This chapter will focus on some of the significant restrictions on the purchase or sale of securities by a person who is in possession of material nonpublic information. Before examining these restrictions, it is important to note that the insider trading prohibitions do NOT create a blanket prohibition on such trading. The key to understanding insider trading is understanding that the law only goes so far in restricting trading on "inside" information. Students should not focus on whether the law prohibits trades while in possession of inside information, but WHEN the law prohibits such trades.

STATE LAWS REGULATING INSIDER TRADING

Prior to the passage of the 1933 Act and the 1934 Act, insider trading was regulated by state securities laws. Although Federal securities laws have not "preempted" this area, the state laws are not frequently used, and their development has not been significant. One reason for the lack of use of state securities laws with respect to insider trading is that these laws **primarily regulate face-to-face transactions**. Since most stock transactions take place over an exchange with an unknown person, there are few incidents when these state laws would apply. It is also important to remember that state securities laws (and for that matter Federal securities laws) involve a specialized area that focuses on wrongdoing involved in a specific type of transaction. The securities laws developed because of the difficulty in proving a fraud claim and the importance of public confidence in the securities markets. Even though there was already a cause of action to address "fraud," lawmakers felt that it was important to have "stricter" regulations of the securities markets. However, in instances of true deception and wrongdoing, plaintiffs will often have a state law claim for fraud in addition to any claim they might possess arising out of a violation of the securities laws.

Among states there is a wide range of positions taken in the cases involving insider trading. There are three different "standards" or "rules":

☑ **Majority Rule.** This rule takes the position that, except in instances involving fraud, officers and directors of a corporation may trade in the corporation's stock without disclosing material information. (*Note that while this rule is still called the "majority rule," it is no longer the rule in a majority of states, although it is still the law in several states.*)

☑ **Special Circumstances Rule.** This rule makes certain exceptions to the majority rule, taking the position that a corporation's officers or directors have a duty to disclose information before they trade with *shareholders of the corporation* when certain "special circumstances" are present such as when:

- The information is highly material;

- The officer or director conceals his or her identity or engages in some other act of fraud or deceit; or

- The officer or director is trading with an especially vulnerable person such as an elderly widow with no understanding of financial matters.

☑ **Minority Rule.** This rule (sometimes known as the "Kansas rule") takes the position that the corporation's officer and directors (i.e., the insiders) do have a duty to disclose material information whenever buying from a shareholder, at least in face-to-face transactions.

When faced with a question involving a *face-to-face transaction*, in addition to analyzing any applicable Federal securities laws, students should analyze the applicability of any state law, and, if the particular rule that applies in the jurisdiction is not given, students should evaluate the facts under each of the three rules listed above. In any such analysis students should recognize that the state law rules are based on the duties of "insiders" to the shareholders. There are many law professors (but not all) who would assert that these restrictions, to the extent they apply, would only apply to an insider's purchase from an existing shareholder, not an insider's sale of stock to someone who was not a shareholder at the time of the transaction. This distinction does not apply to suits brought under the Federal securities laws.

State Law Claims for Trades on National Exchanges

It is worth mentioning that there are state law cases that deal with transactions that take place on national exchanges and are not face-to-face. However, in the vast majority of these cases, state courts have not found a breach of duty on the part of the insider and, therefore, have not found liability. There are a few cases that suggest that under certain special circumstances there might be liability for the insider for such trades. So, even in these cases, students should probably raise the issue of "possible" liability under special circumstances and, of course, the potential for liability if actual fraud can be shown.

Derivative State Law Claims

Finally, it is important to note that these cases involve direct suits against officers and directors. There have been cases in which a shareholder brought a derivative suit against a director and officer for trading in the corporation's stock based on nonpublic information. One such suit required the defendants to disgorge the profits made on these sales to the corporation (*Diamond v. Oreamuno*, 248 N.E.2d 910 (N.Y. 1969)). However, several jurisdictions would find that allowing such a recovery in all such cases is too broad, and require that the insider's action have been contrary to the corporation's interests or harm the corporation in some way before a derivative suit to disgorge profits would be allowed to succeed. For example, if the insider were to purchase stock in a company that he knew the corporation was intending to acquire and his purchases of that stock raised the price the corporation had to pay, there would be a harm to the corporation AND a breach of the insider's duty. The corporation would have a claim against the insider, and, if the corporation refused to bring that claim, it could probably be brought in a derivative action.

RULE 10b–5 AND INSIDER TRADING

The vast majority of current insider trading restrictions arise under Rule 10b–5. However, these restrictions are analyzed under a slightly different approach than the Rule 10b–5 analysis in the preceding chapter. Insider trading involves a very specific trade under 10b–5 in which someone "deceives" by omission. The "omission" is that the person is in possession of material, nonpublic information, which, if known, would impact the price of the security. The securities laws try to prevent these situations by restricting the ability of someone in possession of such information to use it to profit from trading. However, one of the most important facts to understand about the insider trading laws is that these laws do NOT prohibit the use of all nonpublic information. Originally, the law did look like it was going to restrict the use of all inside information. This approach (sometimes characterized as a blanket duty to "**disclose or abstain**" from trading while in possession of material nonpublic information) was developed in *In the Matter of Cady, Roberts & Co.*, 40 S.E.C. 907 (1961) and *Securities and Exchange Commission v. Texas Gulf Sulphur Co.*, 401 F.2d 833 (2nd Cir. 1968). Because of the importance of these cases in forming the basis of the modern insider trading doctrine, they are still included in many casebooks. However, their blanket restrictions do not represent the current law in the area.

As the case law evolved, the Supreme Court limited restrictions on the use of nonpublic information to certain situations, primarily those in which the **use of the nonpublic information could be traced to a breach of some fiduciary duty**. Often law students (and courts) find these rules confusing. The result of these rules leaves some uses of "inside" information actionable, and other uses not actionable. Therefore, it is important to understand the structure, so that the issues may be properly evaluated.

The restrictions arising under Rule 10b–5 prohibit "insiders" at a company from trading in the company's stock if those insiders are in possession of material, nonpublic information. Under traditional insider trading, there needs to be a breach of the duty of loyalty by the insider (or temporary insider). An insider is someone who, by virtue of his or her position with the company, has a duty (or temporary fiduciary duties) to the company's shareholders. Whether there was a breach of that duty is measured by whether the insider received a personal benefit. This is the only breach (or personal benefit) that matters for traditional insider trading under Rule 10b–5. This benefit is typically a financial benefit that is gained by trading in the company's securities. However, the gain could also arise from a sale of the information to others. Absent a fiduciary duty to the shareholders, there is **NO** violation of Rule 10b–5 for trading on inside information.

It is important to understand that insiders (and constructive insiders, defined below) actually have a duty to disclose or abstain, meaning that, unless they disclose the information to the public, they must refrain from trading in the corporation's stock while they are in possession of material, nonpublic information. Note that insiders are not prevented from *possessing* material, nonpublic information; they just may not trade on that information. If they want to trade in the corporation's stock, then they must disclose the information. However, in the real world, the rule really becomes "abstain" since most corporate officers and directors are prevented from disclosure by their other duties to the corporation.

In order to evaluate an insider trading problem, there are several determinations, which should be made about the factual circumstances involved in the problem. Students should evaluate:

☑ Whether the information in the possession of the person involved in the trade is "material," nonpublic information;

☑ How did the person involved come to have the information;

☑ What did that person do with the information; AND

☑ Was there a breach of duty involved in the use OR the dissemination of that information?

Note that there is no requirement of reliance or causation in insider trading cases, just scienter and materiality. Insider trading problems fall into two categories: Traditional Insider Trading and Misappropriation. Furthermore, within each of these categories, there can be liability for someone who trades on the information AND for those who "tip," or provide the information to others, and for the recipients of those tips. This aspect of the law is known as tipper/tippee liability. The basic analysis of a traditional insider trading problem under Rule 10b–5 would involve the following:

☑ Did the defendant have possession of nonpublic information?

☑ If not, then there is no insider trading claim. However, if the defendant did have possession of nonpublic information, was that information "material"?

☑ If not, then there is no claim. However, if the defendant had possession of both material and nonpublic information, the next step is to determine if that person was either in a position with the company as:

a) An **"insider,"** meaning were he or she was an officer, director or a major shareholder (a typical measure of a major shareholder is a person who holds 10% or more of the company's stock); **OR**

b)   A "**constructive insider**." A constructive insider is someone like an accountant, underwriter, lawyer, or consultant, who has a special relationship of trust and confidence to the company, whose position provides access to confidential information, and the company has a reasonable expectation that the person will treat the information as confidential, AND the person does, in fact have an obligation to keep that information confidential by virtue of their position.

☑   If the defendant is neither an insider nor a constructive insider, then that person will not have liability under a traditional insider trading analysis, even if that person trades on inside information. However, that person might still have liability under a misappropriation analysis OR a tipper/tippee analysis. (See below.)

☑   If the above analysis reveals that the defendant was an insider (or constructive insider) in possession of material, nonpublic information, then one must determine if the "insider" traded, using that material, nonpublic information. If they did, they are subject to liability for those trades under Rule 10b–5.

Possession of Information Does Not Always Equate to Trading on Information

One limit on civil claims for insider trading is that when someone trades *while in possession* of material, nonpublic information, it merely raises a strong inference that the person traded on that information. BUT the insider can rebut the inference by demonstrating that he or she did not use the information in making the trading decision.

For example, Bob is a senior vice president at Epsilon, Inc. who is aware of material, nonpublic information which, when released, will cause the Epsilon stock price to fall. However, Bob's mortgage is due, and he has no other liquid assets. If Bob sells Epsilon, Inc. stock to pay his mortgage AND he can prove that he had to sell and the sale of the stock was unrelated to the inside information in his possession, then Bob should not be liable for violating the insider trading provisions of Rule 10b–5. In criminal cases the protections for a defendant are even stronger. In criminal cases, many courts will NOT even allow the inference equating possession with use of material, nonpublic information, and require that the government PROVE that the defendant *used* the information in the trade.

Limits on Traditional Insider Trading

It is important to be aware that traditional insider trading only covers actions that start with the breach of duty of an insider (or constructive insider). This limitation means that there are many situations in which people might trade on material, nonpublic information that would not constitute a violation of Rule 10b–5. For example, the traditional insider trading doctrine would not apply if an insider at Company A used nonpublic, material information about a new Company A product (which would impact Company B) to trade in the stock of Company B, because the Company A insider does not owe any duty to the Company B shareholders. While Company A insider's behavior might be regulated by other rules or regulations, the action is not a violation of the traditional insider trading rules.

TIPPER-TIPPEE LIABILITY

There are, of course, several ways to profit from inside information. The above analysis involves a typical situation in which an insider actually trades on that information. However, individuals might also share inside information with others. The dissemination of inside (material, nonpublic) information also has consequences. The insider trading rules limit the dissemination of material, nonpublic information ("**tipping**") by someone in possession of that information (the "**tipper**") and prohibit the use of that information by the recipient (the "**tippee**"). However, tipper/tippee liability must also be based upon a breach of duty and, with regard to the tippee, knowledge of that breach of duty.

Under this regime of liability, an insider (or constructive insider) is only liable for tipping if he or she violated a fiduciary duty by providing the tip. In this analysis the law is only interested in the duty of loyalty. The law measures whether the duty of loyalty was violated by asking if the insider (or constructive insider) received a "**personal benefit**" by providing the information to another person (i.e., tipping).

A tippee's liability is based completely on the tipper's liability. If the tipper has no liability, then the tippee cannot have liability. The tippee can "inherit" the tipper's fiduciary duty to the shareholders of the corporation not to trade on material, nonpublic information ONLY when the tipper tips in violation of a fiduciary duty, AND ONLY if the tippee knows or should know that the tip was a breach of the tipper's duty. (Note that knowledge that the tipper breached a duty means knowledge about the facts that would lead a court to determine a duty had been breached. For example, if an insider provides a tip in exchange for money, the tippee only needs to know that the insider tipped for money, not that tipping for money constitutes a breach of a fiduciary duty. This is a situation in which ignorance of the facts might be a defense; ignorance of the law is not.)

This existence of tipper/tippee liability requires that, even after following the traditional insider trading analysis to evaluate trades made by an insider, students analyzing an insider trading problem must go on to follow another line of analysis, regardless of whether or not the defendant entered into a personal trade, in order to determine if the insider also has "tipper" liability. Furthermore, any tippee who knowingly receives material, nonpublic information arising out of an insider's breach of duty can also be liable as a tipper, if that individual passes that information along to others in exchange for a personal benefit. Note that an individual may be liable BOTH as a tipper AND as a tippee.

Tipper Liability

A Tipper is liable if he or she:

☑ Discloses material, nonpublic information to others (i.e., Did he or she "tip" anyone?); AND

☑ That disclosure is made in breach of a fiduciary duty of loyalty (or in the case of a tippee, turned tipper, with the knowledge that the information was obtained as a result of a breach of a fiduciary duty of loyalty). In either instance, the question is the same: Did the tipper obtain a personal benefit by engaging in the "tipping"? The existence of a breach is measured by whether the tipper personally benefited, directly or indirectly, from the disclosure. A personal benefit is broadly defined. It can include any consideration, such as a monetary benefit, a *quid pro quo* (e.g., a tip in exchange for a tip), an enhanced reputation, or even a "gift" (Note that a personal benefit is NOT the desire to do public good.); AND

☑ Someone trades on that information. (Note that a tipper is liable if anyone along the chain of information dissemination trades on the information, not just the tipper's direct tippee.)

The tipper is not liable if no "personal benefit" is received or if no one trades on the information.

Tippee Liability

A tippee is liable if he or she:

☑   Receives material, nonpublic information which was disclosed in breach of a fiduciary duty by an insider (for the personal benefit of that insider) at the company whose stock is being (or will be) traded; AND

☑   The tippee knew or should have known that the tipper was breaching a duty by providing the information (remember that the breach of duty is measured by whether the tipper received a benefit); AND

☑   The tippee trades on that information; OR

☑   Provides the information to others (i.e., tips and becomes a tipper), receives a personal benefit for the tip, and someone trades on that information.

Tippees are not liable under traditional insider trading, unless the tipper has breached a duty. Tippees that do not trade do not become liable, UNLESS they become "tippers" and acquire tipper liability.

This analysis may be carried forward to a chain of subsequent tippees. In each instance, in order to measure if a tipper is liable, we must ask if that tipper knew or should have known about the insider's (or constructive insider's) breach of duty AND whether the subsequent tipper received a personal benefit. If so, then the subsequent tipper is also liable for trades made on any inside information he or she provides. In order to determine if the subsequent tippee is liable, we must ask:

☑   Whether the subsequent tippee knew or should have known about the original insider's breach of duty. Each subsequent tippee in the chain will be liable if he or she knew or should have known that the insider breached a duty. It is not relevant to the subsequent tippee's liability if other tippers along the way received a personal benefit.

☑   Even if the subsequent tippee knew or should have known about the original insider's (or constructive insider's) breach of duty, we must still ask if a trade, using the insider's information was ever made.

☑   If a trade has been made, and the above requirements are satisfied, then there is liability; if no trade has been made, then there is no liability.

When looking at tipping cases for traditional insider trading, it is important to remember that all liability originates with the insider's (or constructive insider's) breach of duty. If there is no breach of duty, there can be no liability. For example, Ivan is an insider at Delta Corp., and Ivan gives Roger a report, which he tells Roger is highly classified "inside" information because he wants to give Roger a "gift." However, unbeknownst to Roger, the information is not confidential. It was disclosed in an SEC filing three days earlier. Even if Roger believes that Ivan is violating the insider trading prohibitions of Rule 10b–5, and even if Roger trades on the information AND sells the information to others, claiming that it is "inside information," Roger cannot violate Rule 10b–5, because Ivan did not breach a duty. In other words, there is no Rule 10b–5 liability for an "attempt" to violate Rule 10b–5.

Additional Points About Tipper/Tippee Liability

A tipper may protect its tippees from liability by not telling the tippee the source of the information. If the tippee does not know (and has no reason to know) the source of the information, the tippee cannot know, or have reason to know, of the breach. Of course the tipper would still be liable, but the tippee would not be. One might also note that if the tippee truly did not know the source of the information, the information might not be material. In general, a person may trade on information he or she overhears. (Without a personal benefit to the person disclosing the information, there is no breach of duty.) However, if by overhearing the inside information, the person realizes (or should realize) that he or she is overhearing a breach of duty, then they may not trade on the information.

MISAPPROPRIATION

Misappropriation as a theory of liability developed over time. Prior to the *O'Hagan* case, (*United States v. O'Hagan*, 521 U.S. 642 (1997)) in order to find liability, one needed to show that the defendant breached a duty (or in the case of tippee liability, that the information arose out of a breach of duty) *to the company in whose stock the defendant had traded.* The **misappropriation theory broadens liability to include those who breach a duty to the source of the information**. Instead of asking about a breach of fiduciary duty to the company, the misappropriation theory asks about **fiduciary duties to the source of the information** and about whether the defendant breached (or knew about a breach of) a duty arising out of a relationship of trust and confidence ("RETAC") to the source of the information.

Even if a defendant does not have liability under traditional insider trading analysis 10b–5 outlined above, students should still perform an analysis under the misappropriation theory to determine if there is liability under a misappropriation insider trading analysis.

The questions asked to evaluate a violation of the misappropriation theory are very similar to those asked to evaluate a violation under traditional insider trading. In misappropriation, one is still looking for a breach of duty, and in the tipper/tippee analysis under the misappropriation theory, one still asks whether the tippee knew (or should he have known) about the breach of duty, which is still measured by whether the person breaching the duty received a personal benefit. However, misappropriation is trickier because it is not just about the insider's conduct. In evaluating whether there might be misappropriation liability, one needs to ask if anyone along the chain of information dissemination breached a fiduciary duty or a duty arising out of a RETAC. If a tippee knows, or should know, about a prior breach in the chain of that duty, then the tippee can be held liable for his or her trades.

The rule under misappropriation theory is that **a person commits fraud in a securities transaction when he or she "misappropriates" material, nonpublic information in breach of a duty (typically a duty of trust and confidence) owed to the source of the information, AND does not disclose his intentions to trade to the source of the information, AND trades on that information.** Note that the breach of duty is NOT a fiduciary duty owed to the company whose stock is traded; rather, it is a breach of **duty owed to the source of the information.**

Students are often puzzled by the misappropriation doctrine's requirement that disclosure be made to the source of the information. The requirement arose because the Supreme Court needed to find some fraud or "deception" connected with a breach of duty, in order to justify the expansion of the application of Rule 10b–5 to misappropriation cases that would not be covered by traditional insider trading. Since the defendant in most misappropriation cases does not have a duty to the person with whom she trades, the Court based liability on a breach of a duty to the source of the information. However, Rule 10b–5 also requires some fraud or deception. The Court took the position that this fraud or deception occurs when the "misappropriator" deceives the source of the information by letting the source believe the information will be treated as confidential. However, if this deception is a key requirement for the misappropriation doctrine to apply, then disclosure eliminates the deception. This requirement could produce odd results that would allow an individual (who was not a company "insider") to misappropriate information, tell the source that she was going to trade on that information, and then trade on the information, without liability under Rule 10b–5. The response is that although the "misappropriator" might incur liability under a variety of other legal theories, the disclosure eliminates the "deception" required for Rule 10b–5 to apply.

The basic assessment of an insider trading problem under Rule 10b–5 involving the misappropriation theory would involve the following analysis:

☑   **Did the defendant have possession of nonpublic information?**

☑   If not, then there is no 10b–5 insider trading claim under the misappropriation doctrine (or any other theory). If the defendant did have possession of nonpublic information, **was that information "material"?**

☑   If the defendant was in possession of material, nonpublic information, the next step is to determine how the defendant acquired that information. **Did that person acquire the information under a fiduciary relationship or a relationship of trust and confidence with the source of the information in which there are fiduciary (or fiduciary-like) duties?** (Several relationships might constitute fiduciary relationships or RETACs, including: employer/employee, attorney/client, doctor/patient, principal/agent, trustee/beneficiary, family members, etc.)

☑   Assuming there was a duty to the source of the information and/or a fiduciary relationship or RETAC, **was the information within the scope of that duty?** (Be aware that many people (and some judges) (unintentionally) skip this question in the analysis.)

☑   If the answer to any of the preceding questions is no, then the person is not liable under the misappropriation theory under Rule 10b–5. However, that person may still have liability under other rules or regulations.

☑ On the other hand, if the defendant did owe a specific duty to the source of the information, AND the information was within the scope of that duty and/or a relationship of trust and confidence, then the final step is to determine if the "defendant" traded using the material, nonpublic information without disclosing *their intention to trade to the source of the information*. If they did, they are subject to liability for their personal trades under Rule 10b–5.

More on Relationships of Trust and Confidence

One important aspect to note is that the duty to the source of the information may arise out of a traditional fiduciary relationship OR out of a relationship of trust and confidence (RETAC) similar in nature to those characterized by traditional fiduciary duties. In other words, the analysis involves asking if there was a breach of a fiduciary duty or a similar duty arising out of a RETAC. In an effort to expand the reach of the misappropriation doctrine, the SEC adopted Rule 10b5–2, which provides a non-exhaustive list of examples of relationships of trust and confidence for the purpose of misappropriation. Rule 10b5–2 provides that a duty of trust and confidence exists in the following circumstances:

☑ Whenever a person agrees to maintain information in confidence;

☑ Whenever the person communicating the material, nonpublic information and the person to whom it is communicated have **a history, pattern, or practice of sharing confidences**, such that the recipient of the information knows or reasonably should know that the person communicating the material, nonpublic information expects that the recipient will maintain its confidentiality; OR

☑ Whenever a person receives or obtains material nonpublic **information from his or her spouse, parent, child, or sibling** (provided however, that the person receiving or obtaining the information may demonstrate that no duty of trust and confidence existed with respect to the information, by establishing that he or she neither knew, nor reasonably should have known, that the person who was the source of the information expected that he or she would keep the information confidential, because of the parties' history, pattern, or practice of sharing and maintaining confidences, and because there was no agreement or understanding to maintain the confidentiality of the information).

MISAPPROPRIATION AND TIPPER-TIPPEE LIABILITY

The tipper/tippee analysis under the misappropriation theory is very similar to tipper/tippee analysis under traditional insider trading. However, there are distinctions in the analysis to account for the fact that the breach of duty under misappropriation arises out of a RETAC and disclosure must be made to the source of the information. There is one other important distinction which can complicate tipper/tippee liability under the misappropriation doctrine: in traditional insider trading, if there is no breach of duty by the insider, there can be no violation by the tippee, but under misappropriation, a breach of duty can arise at any point in the chain of information dissemination. So, students must look for any RETAC in which a duty of confidentiality has been violated as information passes along a chain of tippers and tippees.

As with traditional insider trading, even after following the above analysis and evaluating trades made by someone who has misappropriated information, students analyzing an insider trading problem must go on to follow another line of analysis, regardless of whether or not the defendant entered into a personal trade, to determine if the misappropriator also has "tipper" liability. Just as in a traditional insider trading tipper/tippee analysis, any tippee who knowingly receives material, nonpublic information, arising out of a misappropriator's breach of duty, can be liable as a tipper if they pass that information along to others in exchange for a personal benefit. Note that as under traditional insider trading, an individual may be liable BOTH as a tipper AND as a tippee.

An analysis of tipper/tippee liability under the misappropriation theory would be as follows:

Tipper Liability Under Misappropriation

A Tipper is liable if:

☑ The tipper is in possession of material, nonpublic information; AND

☑ That material, nonpublic information was acquired either:

- by the tipper through a fiduciary relationship or a similar relationship of trust and confidence (RETAC) with the source of the information, in which there are fiduciary (or fiduciary-like) duties; or

- by the tipper as a result of someone else violating a fiduciary duty arising out of a fiduciary relationship or RETAC with the source of the information, AND the tipper knew or had reason to know of that violation of duty; AND

☑ The tipper discloses the material, nonpublic information to others (i.e., Does he or she "tip" anyone?) and, as a result, receives a personal benefit (Under misappropriation, the existence of a breach is still measured by whether the tipper personally benefited, directly or indirectly, from the disclosure); AND

☑ The tipper did not disclose his or her intention to disclose the information to the source of the information; AND

☑ Someone who receives the information provided by the tipper trades on that information. (Note that a tipper is liable if anyone along the chain of information dissemination trades on the information, not just the tipper's direct tippee.)

Tippee Liability Under Misappropriation

The tippee is liable under the misappropriation theory if he or she:

☑ Receives material, nonpublic information from someone else; AND

☑ That information is provided (directly or indirectly) by someone (who could be any tipper in a chain of tippers), violating a fiduciary (or fiduciary-like) duty arising out of a fiduciary relationship or RETAC with the source of the information; AND

☑ The tippee knows or should have known that someone (meaning any tipper in the chain) was breaching a duty to the source of the information by providing the information; AND

☑ The tippee trades on that information; OR

☑   Provides the information to others (i.e., tips and becomes a tipper), receives a personal benefit for the tip, and someone trades on that information (i.e., becomes a tipper).

As in traditional insider trading, tippees who do not trade do not become liable, UNLESS they become a "tipper" and acquire tipper liability.

As mentioned above, because there can be several relationships of trust and confidence along a chain, there can be several points where a duty is breached. Therefore, it is possible, though unlikely, that unlike traditional insider trading, a duty may be resuscitated if anyone in the tipper/tippee chain has a relationship of trust and confidence with the person providing them with the information.

RULE 10b–5 SUMMARY

It is important to remember that Rule 10b–5 does not prohibit a person from trading on material, nonpublic information. Rule 10b–5 prevents a person from trading on material, nonpublic information when that person has a duty to the shareholders with whom he or she is trading or when that person has a duty to the source of that information that is violated by using it to trade. In order to make these restrictions effective, Rule 10b–5 implements a structure of tipper/tippee liability to restrict the use of any such information that is disseminated in a breach of these duties.

There are many areas that are not covered by Rule 10b–5. For example, a stock analyst (with no connection to Company Y or Company W) who realizes based upon in-depth research (which did not include any tips from insiders) that Company Y's stock is about to shoot up is free to purchase stock in Company Y. If the analyst were to similarly discover that Company W's stock was about to crash, he could sell that stock. In either instance, there should not be consequences under Rule 10b–5. Rule 10b–5 is based upon protecting certain information (i.e., information that might affect a company's stock price) that arises in fiduciary relationships or other similar relationships of trust and confidence. The fact that some conduct, which might be deemed undesirable, is not covered merely reflects compromises in the developments of the various insider trading doctrines. As mentioned above, it is easier to learn the rules of insider trading to determine which situations are covered than it is to distill a consistent governing principal to apply.

RULE 14e–3 AND INSIDER TRADING RELATING TO TENDER OFFERS

In an effort to prevent substantial trading on inside information relating to tender offers, the SEC adopted Rule 14e–3. A tender offer (which is discussed more thoroughly in the next chapter) involves a company, or individual, making an offer to acquire the stock of another company directly from the shareholders. In other words, the acquiring group makes an offer to buy shares directly from the shareholders of a "target" company who, if they decide to accept that offer, will then "tender" their shares to that acquiring group. Because the acquiring group typically wants to create an incentive for the shareholders to tender their shares, the purchase price offered by the acquiring group is typically well above the market price of the shares. Therefore, if someone were to know about the tender offer before it was made public, that person could buy the stock and profit from the increase in the stock price that almost always occurs when the tender offer is made public.

Prior to the adoption of Rule 14e–3, those in the acquiring group might tell others about their plans to make a tender offer to the shareholders of a particular company. The recipients of this material, nonpublic information would not be "insiders" of the target company, so they would owe no fiduciary duty to the shareholders of that company. Therefore, there would be no restrictions in traditional insider trading which would prevent them from trading in the target company's stock. Furthermore, even if the misappropriation doctrine applied at the time, the recipients of the information would not be bound by any duty not to use the information, since the source of the information, the acquiring group, typically was happy to have the recipients trade in the stock. As a result, there would be no prohibition on these types of trades of inside information. However, it would create an imbalance in dissemination of information within the market and hurt the perception that the market was a "level playing field."

Rule 14e–3 creates liability if a person trades while in possession of material, nonpublic information *relating to a tender offer* that was acquired from the person or entity making the offer (the "Offeror") once the Offeror has taken "substantial" steps toward making the offer. Although there are some limited exceptions to the Rule, Rule 14e–3 generally creates liability under the following conditions:

☑   A person (the "recipient") is in possession of information relating to a tender offer being made by someone other than the recipient; and

☑   The information is material; and

☑   The recipient of the information knows or has reason to know that the information is nonpublic information which came directly or indirectly from the Offeror, the target company (i.e., the issuer of the securities sought by the Offeror), or an officer, director, agent, employee or constructive insider of the Offeror or the target company; and

☑   The recipient of that information purchases or sells (or causes to be purchased or sold) securities of the target company or the Offeror at any time prior to the public announcement of the tender offer, without first disclosing the information (along with its source) to the person with whom the recipient is trading; **if, and only if . . .**

☑   **The Offeror has commenced or has taken substantial steps toward commencement of a bid for the target company (e.g., passage of a resolution about the tender offer by the Offeror's Board of Directors, formulation of a tender offer plan, arrangement of financing to pay for all or a portion of the tender offer, preparing tender offer documents/materials).**

It is important to note the there is no breach of duty required for liability under Rule 14e–3. If someone meets the above test and trades, they are liable. There is no need for separate standards for tippees under the Rule, since the standard is the same. There is also tipper liability under Rule 14e–3 for any person who meets the above criteria and communicates this information to others, if it is reasonably foreseeable that they (the others) will proceed to violate the Rule. However, there is a defense for a tipper who acts in good faith and communicates information about the tender offer to the Offeror or to appropriate agents of the Offeror or to the target company or to appropriate agents of the target company. There is an exemption under Rule 14e–3 for the Offeror and for any party (i.e., a shareholder of the target company) who tenders shares in conjunction with the tender offer. So, Rule 14e–3 would not prevent the Offeror from trading in shares of the target company, even before the tender offer was announced.

ILLUSTRATIVE PROBLEM

PROBLEM 9.1

One night at a fancy restaurant, John is using the bathroom when in walks Manny Mogul and Tom Tender. Tom and Manny do not notice John, but John recognizes them and knows that Tom is well known for his aggressive takeover business and Manny is an exceptionally wealthy businessman. Tom is trying to convince Manny to put up money to back Tom's tender offer for Target Corp., a publicly traded company. Tom says to Manny, "We have had the plan for weeks, the paperwork is done, and most of the financing is in place. If you will just agree to invest $10 million in the deal, we can commence the tender offer for Target Corp. early next week. If you don't think the deal will be successful, just read the latest report from Fancy Pants, Inc., where we both sit on the Board of Directors. Remember that you didn't want to do that deal either. We made a lot of money together on our investment in Fancy Pants, Inc., several years back, and we are still making money. Fancy Pants, Inc., is about to announce record earnings again." Manny says, "You always find the best deals. I will put up the rest of the financing for your tender offer for Target Corp." The next day John buys 1,000 shares of Target Corp. and 5,000 shares of Fancy Pants, Inc., which is also publicly traded. When the tender offer is announced, John makes a large profit on his Target Corp. stock. When Fancy Pants, Inc.'s earnings are publicly announced, John makes even more money on that investment. If the SEC discovers John's investments and all of the facts are known, will John have any liability for violation of the federal securities laws?

Analysis

Because he received information from Tom, John is a "tippee" of Tom, albeit an unwitting one. (The fact that John did not ask for the information, and Tom did not intend for Tom to hear the information, does not change Tom's status as a tippee.) There is only liability for a tippee under traditional insider trading prohibitions under Rule 10b–5 if there is a breach of duty by an insider or a constructive insider. Therefore, even though John was in possession of material, nonpublic information, he would not have liability under traditional insider trading under Rule 10b–5 since Tom did not breach a duty in telling Manny about the tender offer or about the Fancy Pants, Inc. earnings. Since Tom was seeking financing from Manny, their discussion about the tender offer for Target Corp. was perfectly appropriate. In fact the discussion probably made Manny a "constructive insider." Furthermore, since

Tom and Manny are both directors at Fancy Pants, Inc., there is nothing wrong with (i.e., no breach of duty arises out of) their discussion about information to which they both had access as directors. Finally, since neither Tom nor Manny received a personal benefit by "disclosing" the information to John (they did not even realize John was listening), there was no breach of duty by that disclosure either. Therefore, since there was no breach of duty by an insider or a constructive insider, there can be no violation by John of Rule 10b–5 under traditional insider trading.

Similarly, John will have no liability under the misappropriation doctrine. Since John did not have a fiduciary relationship or a relationship of trust and confidence with Tom or Manny, John had no duties, fiduciary or otherwise, to Tom or Manny (the sources of the information). Also, as discussed above, since neither Tom nor Manny violated any duty by discussing the information, John's use of the information did not violate the misappropriation doctrine.

However, under Rule 14e–3, John will have liability for his purchase of Target Corp.'s stock. This Rule requires no violation of duty. John was in possession of material, nonpublic information, which he received from the person/company making the tender offer (in this case Tom). John traded in the stock of Target Corp. before the tender offer was announced, and there is no indication that John made any disclosure of the information to the person from whom he bought the Target Corp. shares. Finally, it appears that Tom had taken the requisite substantial steps toward commencement of his bid for Target Corp. Tom had a plan, the preparation of materials/documents seems to have been completed and, with Manny's commitment in the bathroom, Tom had arranged for all of the financing. Since these substantial steps toward commencement of the offer had been completed, it seems that John would be liable for trades he made in Target Corp.'s stock, using the information he learned in the bathroom, prior to the time the tender offer was made.

On the other hand, John would not have liability under Rule 14e–3 for any trades he made in the stock of Fancy Pants, Inc. Since the information about Fancy Pants, Inc. did not relate to a pending tender offer, Rule 14e–3 would not apply. Furthermore, since the facts do not seem to implicate any action which is prohibited under the insider trading rules, it appears that John will not have liability under these rules for his trades (or profits) in the stock of Fancy Pants, Inc.

SHORT SWING PROFITS, SECTION 16(b)

When Section 16(b) of the 1934 act was enacted by Congress, it was not clear that Section 10(b) was going to apply to insider trading. Section 16(b) was intended to recapture any profits made by a corporation's "insiders" within a six-month period of time. Because the rule only applies to profits that arise within a six-month period of time, this rule is also referred to as covering "short swing profits." The rule, except in very unusual circumstances, requires virtually no analysis. It either applies to a situation or it doesn't. However, because the rule is so rigid, it does produce some odd results. It captures many "innocent" trades that, if some analysis were applied, would be unlikely to raise any issue and does not capture many trades that one might seek to prevent. To the extent students struggle with section 16(b), it is in their desire to analyze the result and not apply the rule "blindly." However, that is truly what is required here.

Section 16(b) applies to any insider at a "registered" company, who buys or sells equity securities in that company within a six-month period. It does not matter whether the insider purchases first and then sells or sells first and then subsequently buys. Any profit that the insider makes in such a transaction must be paid to the company. The rules of section 16(b) are listed below. Section 16(b):

☑ **Applies to all "insiders." An insider is considered to be an officer, director or a shareholder holding more than 10% of the corporation's equity securities.** Section 16(b) applies to someone who was an officer or a director of the corporation *either* at the time of the purchase *OR* at the time of the sale. However, it only applies to shareholders who beneficially (directly or indirectly) hold more than 10% of the corporation's equity securities *both* at the time of the purchase *AND* at the time of the sale in question;

☑ **Applies only to companies that are required to register under the 1934 Act.** Companies with more than $10 million in assets and more than 500 shareholders of record are required to register with the SEC ("Reporting Companies") and are subject to certain reporting and other requirements. Section 16(b) does not apply to closely held corporations;

☑ **Only covers transactions in a company's stock or convertible debt;**

☑ **Enables a company to recover any profit made by an insider within a six-month period.** (In evaluating the profit, the insider does not get to identify specific shares that were bought and sold. Any transaction in a company's securities may be matched with any other transaction in those securities that occurred within a six-month window to determine the maximum profit (with the exception of transactions made by shareholders (who were not also officers or directors) when they were not holders of 10% or more of the company's equity securities). That maximum profit is what is recoverable from the insider); and

☑ **Allows a shareholder of the company to sue derivatively** on behalf of a company to recover the profit if the company does not bring or diligently prosecute a 16(b) claim.

Section 16(b) does not include provisions relating to any tipping liability; there is no evaluation of whether a duty was breached, and there is no misappropriation. Note, however, that it would be possible for an insider to violate both section 16(b) and Rule 10b–5 with the same transaction. In evaluating a transaction subject to section 16(b), the percentage of stock owned by the officer or director is irrelevant. The percentage of stock owned is only relevant to determine if someone is a 10% shareholder.

Ten Percent Shareholders

The rules about 10% shareholders are fairly straightforward. However, they do occasionally cause confusion. There have been cases that evaluated which transactions "count" under section 16(b) with respect to a 10% shareholder, but the law is now settled with regard to this issue. The only transactions that matter for purposes of section 16(b) are transactions that take place when a person IS (already) a 10% shareholder. In other words, the transaction in which a person becomes a 10% (or greater) shareholder is not included when evaluating if someone has violated section 16(b) OR in evaluating the profit made. This means that a transaction by a 9% shareholder who buys 30% of the company is not counted for determining liability under section 16(b). A transaction by an 11% shareholder is counted. However, if the 11% shareholder sells 1.1% of her stock, reducing her holdings to 9.9% and then a few days later sells an additional 5% of her stock, the second transaction in which 5% was sold, is not included in any section 16(b) evaluation of violation or calculation of profits. This rigid construct can produce odd results where form triumphs over substance. However, that is the nature of section 16(b).

Notwithstanding this rigidity, there are a few extreme situations (often involving mergers) in which the application of section 16(b) would produce such an inappropriate result that courts have decided not to apply the rule in situations which are "unorthodox." *See Kern County Land Co. v. Occidental Petroleum Corp.*, 411 U.S. 582 (1973). In the *Kern* case, the Court determined that section 16(b) would not apply in situations in which:

☑ The purchase or sale of equity securities is involuntary (for example required by a preexisting contractual arrangement); and

☑ The specific facts of the situation do not create the possibility of "speculative abuse of inside information." (An example of this might be a situation that existed in the *Kern* case, in which the 10% shareholder, because it was at odds with the company, was extremely unlikely to, and did not, have access to any confidential information or input regarding the timing of the transaction.)

Students should be advised that these exceptions are relatively strictly construed and rarely apply in practice, but may arise slightly more frequently on law school exams.

The strict construct of section 16(b) does make it easy to avoid its application. For example, if an insider owns stock for six months and one day sells a substantial portion of that stock without a matching purchase, section 16(b) does not apply. As mentioned above, if a 10% shareholder reduces her holdings to just below 10%, then subsequent transactions will not be used for matching purposes, even if the purpose behind the action was to avoid the applicability of section 16(b).

One of the best ways to understand section 16(b) is to see it applied in examples.

ILLUSTRATIVE PROBLEMS

PROBLEM 9.2

Don is a director of Short Swing, Inc., a publicly traded company. Don owns 100 shares of Short Swing, Inc. stock, which he has owned for many years. On January 1, 2010, Don sells his 100 shares of Short Swing, Inc. stock for $30 per share, for a total of $3,000. The price of Short Swing, Inc. stock then drops, and on

March 13, 2010, Don purchases 300 shares of Short Swing, Inc. stock at $10 per share, also for a total of $3,000. When asked about the transaction, Don does not think he is liable. Since he sold for $3,000 and bought for $3,000, Don claims he did not profit. In addition, he says his holdings in Short Swing, Inc. are much less than 10%. Is Don correct?

Analysis

Don is not correct. Since Don is a director, it is irrelevant how much Short Swing, Inc. stock he held. As long as Don was a director EITHER at the time he sold OR at the time he bought and the purchase and sale of Short Swing, Inc. stock was made within a six-month window, he is liable. In addition, the calculation of how much profit was made is based on a per share basis, not an overall basis, as Don asserts. In evaluating a transaction under section 16(b), sales and purchases must be matched. It does not matter if the purchase or the sale came first, only that the sale and the purchase took place within 6 months of each other. In the above problem, Don sold 100 shares on January 1st and bought 300 shares on March 13th of the same year. There was a purchase and a sale that took place within a six-month period. Note that only 100 of the 300 shares bought are used for matching since there were only 100 shares sold. Since the 100 matching shares were purchased for $10 per share for a total of $1000, and Don sold 100 shares for a total of $3,000, Don will be liable to Short Swing, Inc. for his entire $2,000 profit.

PROBLEM 9.3

Assume the same facts as in the above problem 9.2. However, in addition, Don sells the 300 shares he bought on March 13, 2010 for $50 per share on May 5, 2010 for a total of $15,000. Now there are sales of a total of 400 shares and purchases of 300 shares within a six month period, so which are the proper sales to match?

Analysis

The transactions are matched to create the maximum profit. Therefore, because the transaction in which Don sold 100 shares on January 1, 2010 was at a price of $30 per share, which is less than $50 per share, the January 1st transaction would not be included. The 300 shares sold on May 5th would be matched with the 300 shares bought on March 13th. Don's profit would be $12,000, which would need to be disgorged to Short Swing, Inc.

PROBLEM 9.4

Olive is an officer of Short Swing, Inc., a publicly traded company. On June 1, 2010 Olive buys 100 shares of Short Swing, Inc. for $50 per share. That month the price falls, and Olive gets nervous. So, on July 1, 2010, Olive sells her 100 shares at $40 per share for a loss of $1000. The price of Short Swing, Inc. stock continues to fall, and Olive thinks it will not go any lower. So, on August 1, 2010, Olive buys another 100 shares at $30 per share. Unfortunately, for Olive, the price of Short Swing, Inc. stock falls even further, and on September 1, 2010, Olive sells the second 100 shares at $20 per share for another $1000 loss and decides that stock ownership is just not for her. Does Olive have any liability under section 16(b)?

Analysis

Unfortunately for Olive, she does have liability. This is one of the unusual (and perhaps unfair) applications of section 16(b). Even though Olive made a purchase followed by a sale and another purchase followed by another sale, her sales are grouped differently for analysis under section 16(b). Section 16(b) looks to calculate the maximum profit by matching any purchase and any sale within a six-month period. So, under that analysis, we would match Olive's purchase of 100 shares on August 1, 2010 for $30 per share with her sale of 100 shares for $40 per share on July 1, 2010. Under this calculation, Olive has a "gain" of $1000, which must be disgorged to Short Swing, Inc. The other transactions of June 1, 2010 and September 1, 2010 would produce a loss, so they would not result in any additional liability under section 16(b). This problem is a good example of how the form of the rule prevails over the substance. When applying section 16(b) students should not look for the fair result. The correct application of section 16(b) is the result that produces the maximum profit.

PROBLEM 9.5

Sam, who is neither an officer nor a director of Delta Corp., is a shareholder of Delta Corp., a publicly traded company. Delta Corp. has 100,000 shares of common stock issued and outstanding, and Sam owns 9,900 of those shares. On January 1, 2010, Sam purchases an additional 1,000 shares of Delta Corp. for $20 per share. On February 1, 2010 Sam sells 4,900 of his shares of Delta Corp. for $40 per share, leaving him with 6,000 shares. On March 1, 2010 Sam buys another 10,000 shares of Delta Corp. for $45 per share, and on April 1, 2010 Sam buys 2,000 shares of Delta Corp. for $35 per share. Does Sam have any liability under section 16(b)?

Analysis

Sam does seem to have some liability but only for a few of the transactions. The only transactions that are relevant for determining Sam's liability are those that took place while he was a holder of more than 10% of Delta Corp.'s stock. Since Delta Corp. has 100,000 shares outstanding, a shareholder would need to hold more than 10,000 shares to be viewed as an "insider" for purposes of section 16(b). Therefore, the transaction that took place on January 1st is not counted because, although the transaction made Sam a 10% shareholder, he only owned 9,900 shares of Delta Corp. *at the time of the purchase* (which is less than 10% of Delta Corp.'s stock). The February 1st transaction in which Sam sold 4,900 shares, took place when Sam was a 10% shareholder. So, that transaction is included in an evaluation of potential liability for purposes of section 16(b). The March 1st transaction is not included because, even though he was purchasing more than 10% of the Delta Corp., Sam only held 6,000 shares *at the time of the transaction*, which is below the requisite 10%. Finally, the April 1st transaction in which Sam buys 2,000 shares of Delta Corp. is included in an evaluation since he was a holder of more than 10% of the company's stock at the time of the transaction. So, there is only one purchase transaction (April 1st) and one sale transaction (February 1st) that took place within a six-month period that can be "matched." The 2,000 shares purchased on April 1, 2010 for $35 per share can be matched with just 2,000 of the 4,900 shares sold two months earlier on February 1, 2010 at $40 per share. In those matched transactions involving 2,000 shares, Sam purchased 2,000 shares for a total $70,000 and sold 2,000 shares for a total of $80,000, for a profit of $10,000. It does not matter that the sale transaction preceded the purchase transaction. Under section 16(b), Sam must disgorge his $10,000 profit to Delta Corp.

CHAPTER 10

Mergers and Acquisitions

While there is a separate law school course involving mergers and acquisitions, most business associations courses introduce the subject. This is true because many of the fundamental issues studied in business associations arise in the context of a merger or an acquisition. In addition, there are some variations in how certain fiduciary duty principles are applied in the context of a merger or an acquisition, which are necessary to grasp in order to complete one's introduction to the subject matter.

Much of this area involves learning the vocabulary and the associated concepts. A **merger** occurs when two companies come together to form one company. If one of the two original companies survives then the process is called a **merger**. If the combination results in a new company, then the process is called a "**consolidation**." Mergers and consolidations are accomplished through a statutory process in which the firms formally merge or consolidate through state law filings. There are also other structures that may be used when firms combine. Each structure will have its own advantages and disadvantages. There are three basic ways that companies may combine:

- ☑ **Statutory Merger:** a statutory merger involves a combination in accordance with applicable state law;

- ☑ **Sale of Assets:** an asset sale occurs when one company purchases all (or substantially all) of the assets of another; and

- ☑ **Sale of Stock:** a stock sale involves the purchase of the stock of one company by another entity or individual.

Technically, only a statutory merger is actually a "merger" or a "consolidation," and a sale of stock or assets is actually an "**acquisition**." However, often the technical definition of merger is not used, and the general term "merger" is used to describe any combination of firms. There are a variety of ways to structure mergers/acquisitions, and the structure is almost always determined by the underlying tax issues. While the specific tax issues are the focus of a course in corporate taxation, it is important to be aware of their importance. In all the above combinations there is an exchange of ownership for value. There are three categories of value that may be utilized (alone or in combination) to facilitate this exchange:

☑ Stock;

☑ Assets; and

☑ Cash.

In the most basic of mergers one company is identified as the "Acquirer" while the other is identified as the "Target." Even when the companies merging are of relatively equal size, it is useful to use these terms to understand the mechanics of how a merger takes place. In a simple merger or consolidation, there is only one company at the end of the process. In contrast, even in a simple sale of stock (e.g., when Corporation A purchases all of the outstanding stock of Corporation B), there are often two companies that remain following the sale. In a typical transaction, the Acquirer would "pay" the Target (or the Target's shareholders) either in cash or stock (or a combination of cash and stock) in exchange for assets or stock, depending upon the nature of the transaction. (Note that in some mergers a portion of the consideration might also include a promise to pay money (i.e., cash) in the future in the form of a promissory note or some other "debt" instrument.) In each of the three transactions students will want to ask:

☑ Do the shareholders get to vote on the transaction? (Note that the Board of Directors always gets to vote because the Board must approve the transaction.)

☑ Are dissenting shareholders (the shareholders who are against the transaction) entitled to "appraisal rights" (which are explained below)?

☑ How are liabilities of the Target treated?

☑ What are the tax consequences of the transaction? (Not addressed in these materials.)

Voting

In general, the management of a company would prefer to avoid shareholder votes because these votes can use up corporate time and resources. However, of greater concern is that the shareholders might vote "no" or less than a sufficient number of shareholders would fail to vote "yes." (Remember, there are rules about quorums and percentage of votes required.) If the transaction requires shareholder approval and does not receive it, the transaction cannot move forward. A shareholder vote is almost always required of the Target's shareholders in a merger, consolidation or acquisition. This is because the transaction usually represents a fundamental transaction for the Target company, and shareholders have the right to have a voice in such transactions. However, a more difficult question is whether the merger or sale requires a vote of the Acquirer's shareholders.

Appraisal Rights

Appraisal rights entitle shareholders of some corporations involved in a merger or consolidation (and in some states corporations involved in the sale of stock or substantially all of their assets) to certain rights if they "dissent" from the transaction. These dissenting shareholders are entitled to receive a different amount of compensation for the transaction, determined by a court. Rather than receive the consideration which they would have received in the transaction, shareholders who exercise their appraisal rights are entitled to have the "fair value" of their interest in the firm determined by a court (using an appraisal method which often includes financial analysts and/or investment bankers), and receive that amount instead. The "fair value" determined by appraisal could be more or less than the consideration paid in the transaction. However, if too large a number of shareholders seek appraisal of their interests, often the transaction will not proceed. If the transaction does proceed, many shareholders who originally voted against the merger might still prefer to accept the merger consideration rather than seeking to pursue their appraisal right because the litigation is often expensive, and it can take a substantial period of time to receive the "fair value," during which time the dissenting shareholder's stock is typically not liquid. Delaware and several other states do not provide an appraisal remedy if the shares involved are publicly traded since, at least in theory, those shares may be sold for fair value on the open market before the deal is finalized.

Statutory Merger

In a statutory merger two firms combine to form one firm:

- ☑ In either a merger or a consolidation, the new company holds **both** the assets and the liabilities of both firms.

- ☑ The transaction must be approved by the shareholders of both companies.

☑ Shareholders who do not approve the transaction (dissenters) are typically (with some exceptions) entitled to appraisal rights, unless both companies are publicly traded.

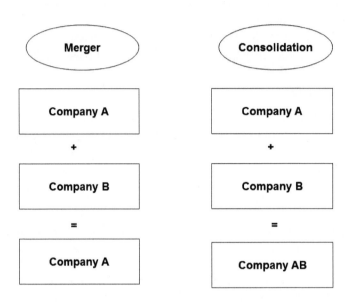

In traditional mergers the two companies negotiate the relative percentage ownership that each respective company's shareholders will hold in the new firm. Typically, the consideration paid to the Target's (in the illustration, Company B's) shareholders is stock in the surviving firm. However, it is permissible to pay the shareholders with other consideration. In a merger/consolidation the consideration passes to the Target's shareholders, provided they are not dissenting and opting to exercise their appraisal rights.

Sale of Assets

In a sale of assets, the Acquirer corporation gives the Target corporation either stock or cash (or some combination of cash and stock) in exchange for the Target corporation's assets. (See illustration, below.)

Following the sale, the Target usually has few or no assets, other than the consideration paid by the Acquirer. In a sale of assets, the Target must usually make its creditors aware of the sale so that the creditors may make a claim against the consideration being paid for the Target's assets. Once the Target's creditors have been paid and the Target has received the balance of the consideration paid by the Acquirer, the Target may then issue a liquidating dividend to its shareholders. If the liquidating dividend is cash, then the Target shareholders take the cash and are done. If any of the consideration paid by the Acquirer corporation was paid in stock of the Acquirer, then the Target shareholders will receive that stock when the Target is liquidated and become shareholders in Acquirer corporation. (See illustration, below.) A sale of assets can be a more complicated process than a statutory merger (especially if the Target has a substantial number of assets) because, among other requirements, a sale of assets will require the transfer of ownership of each specific asset of the Target being sold, and the title to different assets (such as real property versus personal property versus intellectual property) will all have different mechanisms of transfer.

In a sale of assets, the shareholders of the Target corporation are entitled to vote on a sale of all or substantially all the assets. (There might be some debate as to what constitutes "substantially all" of the assets, but generally sales in excess of 75% of the assets will qualify.) In Delaware, the shareholders of the **Acquirer** corporation are not entitled to vote, but some other states do allow shareholders in the Acquirer corporation to vote on transactions involving the sale of assets. Dissenting shareholders in the **Target** corporation are not entitled to appraisal rights in Delaware, but some states do provide Target company shareholders in a sale of assets transaction with appraisal rights. Dissenting shareholders in the Acquirer corporation are not entitled to appraisal rights. In addition, at least in theory, the Acquiring corporation will obtain the Target corporation's assets but not its liabilities. However, students should be aware that there are more rules creating successor liability which might come in to play, making it more difficult, but not impossible to avoid prior liabilities.

Sale of Assets

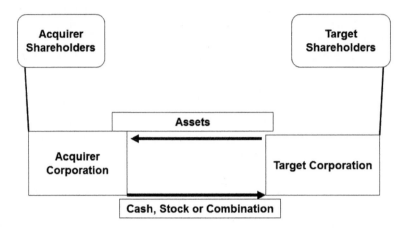

Sale of Assets: After Transaction (when Target shareholders given stock)

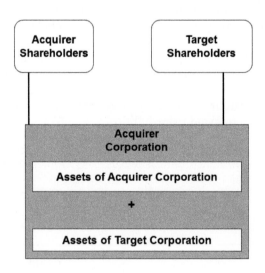

Sale of Stock

A sale of stock is very similar to a sale of assets. However, in a sale of stock, the Target corporation provides stock instead of assets. As a result, the Target corporation winds up as a subsidiary of the Acquirer corporation, so there are two "surviving" corporations instead of one. (See illustration, below.)

Sale of Stock: After Transaction
(when Target shareholders given stock)

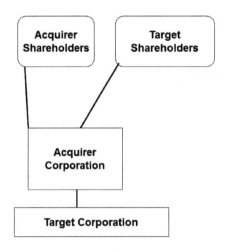

Typically, in a sale of stock the consideration from the Acquirer is paid to the Target's shareholders in exchange for their ownership interest in the Target. Like a sale of assets, the Target corporation's shareholders will be entitled to vote and have appraisal rights, and the Acquirer corporation's shareholders will only have these rights in a few states. However, the treatment of the liabilities of the Target corporation is different in a sale of stock than it is in a sale of assets. Because the Target corporation survives, so do its liabilities. However, those liabilities will likely be limited to the assets of the Target corporation. So, unless a creditor can pierce the corporate veil of the Target corporation or make a claim of some improper distribution to the Acquirer corporation, there should be some protection for the Acquirer corporation from the liabilities of Target corporation.

Triangular Mergers

The above forms are just the building blocks. Firms often enter into more complex transactions for a variety of reasons. One hybrid form is known as the triangular merger (or a reverse triangular merger). In this structure, the Acquiring corporation firm forms a subsidiary. The subsidiary is funded with cash and/or stock that will serve as the consideration for the ultimate merger. Then the subsidiary is merged with the Target. The Target becomes a subsidiary of the Acquirer and the shareholders of the Target corporation get stock and/or cash. If the Target corporation's shareholders receive some of the Acquirer's stock as part of the transaction, then they become shareholders in the Acquirer. When this structure is used, if the subsidiary of the Acquirer corporation survives, then it is called a "Triangular Merger." If the Target Corporation survives, then it is called a "Reverse Triangular Merger." (See illustration, below.)

Reverse Triangular Merger

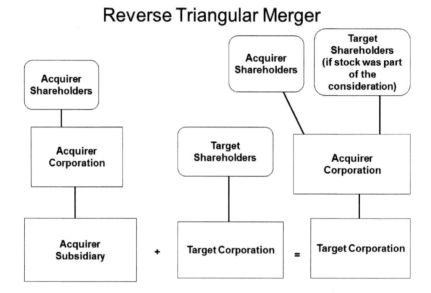

Triangular mergers represent an effort to capture the benefits of both a statutory merger and a sale of stock. Since the Acquirer corporation is typically the sole shareholder of its subsidiary, the Acquirer corporation's Board of Directors makes all decisions about the merger. The Acquirer corporation's shareholders neither vote nor receive appraisal rights since they are one step removed from the transaction. Of course, the Target corporation's shareholders still get to vote and receive appraisal rights, as (and if) provided by applicable state law. With regard to liability, as in a sale of stock, the Target corporation remains a wholly owned subsidiary of the Acquirer corporation. As a result, unless the Acquirer subsequently merges the Target subsidiary into the Acquirer, any liabilities of the Target would not become liabilities of the Acquirer, unless a creditor can pierce the Target corporation's corporate veil or make a claim of some improper distribution to the Acquirer corporation.

THE *DE FACTO* MERGER DOCTRINE

One of the big debates that can arise over the form of a business combination is about how much the form should matter. Shareholders are often angry and frustrated when a company manipulates the form of the transaction to avoid a shareholder vote or to avoid appraisal rights. The **de facto merger doctrine** involves focusing on the substance of the transaction, rather than the form. The doctrine is applied when a company manipulates the form of a transaction to avoid a result which would have applied had the transaction been accomplished in a more traditional manner (i.e., a merger). Under the *de facto* merger doctrine, if the transaction has the substantive effect of a merger, then the shareholders of the companies involved in the transaction are entitled to the same statutory protections they would have received had there been a merger. The doctrine essentially stands for the principle that when a shareholder is faced with a transaction that "so fundamentally change[s] the corporate character of [a corporation] . . . and the interest of the plaintiff as a shareholder therein, that to refuse him the rights and remedies of a dissenting shareholder would in reality force him to give up his stock in one corporation and against his will accept shares in another. . . ." (*Farris v. Glen Alden Corp.*, 143 A.2d 25, 29 (Pa. 1958).)

Delaware and a majority of jurisdictions do not recognize the *de facto* merger doctrine. Their logic is generally that states have different processes to achieve the same results and, as long as the process used is legal, courts should not recast the transactions as that would only increase uncertainty and litigation. (*See Hariton v. Arco Electronics, Inc.*, 188 A.2d 123 (Del. 1963).) However, most law professors still teach the de facto merger doctrine because it poses interesting questions about form and substance, and it is a good way to teach about mergers. Thus, students should be familiar with the concept.

Freeze Out Mergers

Freeze out mergers (also sometimes called "cash out mergers") are a process by which, in some states, a majority shareholder (or shareholders) may force the minority shareholders to sell their stock in a merger with (or acquisition by) an entity owned by the majority shareholder(s), enabling the majority shareholder(s) to acquire 100% control of the company. These transactions are often used following a tender offer to eliminate shareholders who did not tender their shares, but a freeze out merger is also used when a controlling shareholder or group of shareholders wants to own all of the company. Sometimes these transactions are also the final stage in a process known as "taking the company private" since they can result in a publicly traded company becoming a closely held, "private" company. These transactions are usually structured as triangular mergers in which the controlling shareholder creates a subsidiary, and the subsidiary enters into a statutory merger with the Target company in which the acquiring shareholder has a controlling interest.

These transactions, of course, involve a conflict of interest. However, the standard for reviewing a merger transaction, involving a controlling shareholder with a conflict of interest, is "entire fairness" (discussed above in Chapter 5). The entire fairness standard requires that the transaction must be accomplished by both a fair process and at a fair price. This standard means that as long as the majority shareholder effectuates the freeze out merger at a fair price and by a fair process, then the merger may proceed. Factors that courts might consider in evaluating whether a freeze out merger meets the test of entire fairness might include determining:

☑ Whether an independent committee was appointed to negotiate on behalf of the minority shareholders;

☑ Whether that committee was, in fact, independent, and whether there is evidence that it had true bargaining power;

☑ Whether the price paid to the minority shareholders reflected the value of the minority shareholders' stock as a percentage of the value of the entire firm or whether it was based upon a "minority discount";

☑ Whether a thorough and complete "fairness opinion" was prepared; and

☑ Whether the transaction was approved by a majority of the minority shareholders.

Delaware courts no longer require that the controlling shareholder present a business purpose for the merger. However, some states such as Massachusetts might, and a business purpose for the transaction might be useful in supporting the "fairness" argument. Note that if an independent committee of directors or an informed majority of the minority shareholders approves the transaction, the burden of proof will shift from the majority shareholder to the shareholders fighting the transaction to show that the transaction was unfair (although the standard is still entire fairness). Be aware that different states have different requirements for cash out mergers. For example, New York requires the approval of a super majority of the shareholders, and California will only allow a majority shareholder to "cash out" the minority in a "short form merger" in which the majority shareholder must own at least 90% of the corporation, and the transaction must be approved by the California Commissioner of Corporations.

Statutory Short Form Mergers

A statutory short form merger is a device that is authorized by state law. In many states (such as California as mentioned above) a majority shareholder (or group of shareholders) may perform a **cash out merger without shareholder approval,** provided the majority shareholder holds a certain significant percentage of the corporation's outstanding stock. The exact requirements (including the exact percentage required) are determined by state law, but 90% is the required percentage in Delaware and California and represents a typical requirement.

Short form mergers are often used following tender offers to eliminate any remaining minority shareholders. Because the process is simpler and easier than a (non-short form) cash-out merger, the goal of many tender offers (in which 100% ownership is desired) is to acquire a percentage of the corporation sufficient to complete a statutory short form merger.

HOSTILE ACQUISITIONS

A merger or a negotiated acquisition is a consensual processes. Both firms' Board of Directors must agree in order for the transaction to proceed. However, there are situations in which one firm or individual wants to acquire another, and the Board of Directors of the Target firm does not want to be acquired or does not want to be acquired by that particular person or firm. In these instances, the would-be acquirer can take other steps than those outlined above to acquire the firm. The process of excluding a Target's Board from the Acquirer's efforts to acquire control of a company is generally referred to as a "hostile takeover" attempt. Though these processes, to varying degrees, may be utilized in "friendly" circumstances as well, there are three main approaches that might be used to circumvent the Target's Board of Directors:

☑ **Tender Offers:** a tender offers involves a public offer, usually made to all the shareholders of the Target corporation, in which the Offeror offers to buy all, or a certain percentage of, the Target's shares at a specific price.

☑ **Direct Share Purchases:** direct purchases involve direct purchases of stock by the potential acquirer in the public markets or through privately negotiated transactions with a limited number of shareholders.

☑ **Proxy Contests:** as discussed above, proxy contests involve a battle for control of the Target's Board of Directors through the shareholder voting process.

TAKEOVERS

The final portion of most Business Organizations courses involves hostile takeovers. This is true not only because a number of interesting concepts are involved in these transactions, but also because these transactions integrate many of the principles of corporate structure, securities law and fiduciary duty studied throughout a typical course.

A hostile takeover involves an effort to acquire sufficient shares to control the Board of Directors (often through a tender offer), and then replacing the Board of Directors with the Acquirer's own slate of directors. This process is often followed by some form of statutory merger of the acquired Target entity into an entity controlled by the Acquirer and may or may not involve cashing out the remaining shareholders.

There are many rules governing tender offers. We have already seen Rule 14e–3 with respect to insider trading based on information about a tender offer, but there are many more. The most significant rules arise out of the Williams Act (1968), which amended the 1934 Act to add provisions relating to tender offers. These provisions are found in Sections 13(d), 13(e), 14(d) and 14(e) of the 1934 Act. Some of the significant provisions included in Section 13(d) of the 1934 Act include requirements that a person disclose:

☑ When that person acquires (directly or indirectly) more than 5% of a registered company's shares;

☑ Whether that person's intended purpose in acquiring those shares is to acquire control and/or to sell, liquidate or make a fundamental change to the Target company;

☑ The identity of the person acquiring the shares;

☑ The number of shares that are beneficially owned; and

☑ Any contracts, arrangements, or understandings that person has with anyone else with respect to any securities of the Target company.

Any person who commences a tender offer (often called the "Bidder") in an effort to acquire more than five percent of a company, must comply with the extensive rules and regulations arising under sections 14(d) and 14(e) of the 1934 Act. Bidders must provide a great deal of information which must include full and fair disclosure of all aspects of the tender offer, including all of the disclosures required under section 13(d), with respect to the tender offer. There are also specific ways in which a tender offer must be delivered to the Target company's shareholders. The Bidder must also make a public announcement that includes the Bidder's identity, the Target's identity, the amount of shares sought and the price at which the Bidder is offering to buy those shares. When this disclosure is provided, the Target company is required to respond.

DEFENSIVE TACTICS

Often companies try to resist a hostile takeover through a variety of tactics. These approaches will have different consequences and results. A brief summary of some of the more well-known (and colorful) terms and tactics is included below:

☑ **Greenmail**—Greenmail involves a payment made to a potential acquirer to incentivize them to leave the company alone. It usually occurs when a person has started to acquire a significant portion of shares in a Target company and the Target buys those shares back from the Acquirer for a price above the shares' market value. (Note that the IRS now taxes greenmail at a rate of 50% of the gain received.)

☑ **White Knight**—A white knight is a company that is sought by a Target company to avoid being acquired by in a "hostile" takeover. In a typical scenario, the Target company attempts to make a deal with the white knight which will rescue (i.e., acquire) the Target company, and, in theory, be better for the Target, than being acquired by the hostile Bidder.

☑ **Poison Pill**—A poison pill is, perhaps, one of the most familiar names used in takeover defenses. While there are several different forms of poison pills, the concept involves creating a device that multiplies the rights of shareholders (but not of the would-be Acquirer), so that a person who did acquire the company would find that the increased shareholder "rights" made the takeover so expensive that it would not be feasible. The idea is that an acquirer could not "swallow" the Target company without taking the poison pill, and the pill would destroy the acquisition. (There is a substantial amount of data and explanations of poison pills available, but an in depth discussion and specific examples are beyond the scope of this book.)

☑ **Share Repurchases**—Sometimes a company will offer to repurchase its own shares at a premium to thwart a hostile offer. This approach, as well as the use of poison pills, is often called a **scorched Earth policy** because it often involves damaging or weakening the Target company to make it unappealing to the Bidder.

☑ **Staggered Board**—Sometimes a company will create a staggered Board of Directors (also known as "classified Board") with a large number of directors whose terms expire in different years. For example, a company might have its directors serve for 3-year terms and only re-elect 1/3 of the Board each year. This type of structure would mean that it could take several years for a hostile Bidder, even if successful, to elect new directors to replace the existing directors.

☑ **Shark Repellent**—Shark repellent is a term that may be used to describe defensive measures which are typically adopted through a company's Articles or Bylaws which make it more difficult to acquire a company without the Board of Director's consent.

☑ **Golden Parachutes**—A golden parachute is an extremely lucrative termination package for a company's senior executives, which typically is activated if the executive is terminated or otherwise loses his or her position with the company. These devices are used in other contexts as well, but may also be used to create a disincentive to acquire the Target company.

☑ **Pac-man Defense**—The "Pac-man" defense is a strategy in which the Target company launches a hostile takeover on the Bidder in an effort to acquire control of the Bidder, rather than let the Bidder acquire control of the Target.

Fiduciary Duties in Takeover Defenses

One of the fundamental issues that arises with regard to all defenses to, and rejections of, unwanted takeovers is determining the duties of the Target company's directors. While earlier chapters have already examined fiduciary duties in the day-to-day operations of a corporation, the tests to evaluate whether fiduciary duties have been met are different in the context of a hostile takeover. This different approach arises out of two important distinctions. The first is that these transactions involve a fundamental change to the corporation and often represent the potential end of the corporation's existence. The second distinction is that most hostile takeovers represent a threat to the positions of the Target company's senior officers and directors, so their decisions are somewhat suspect and are not afforded the same deference as might occur in a typical application of the Business Judgment Rule.

In order to evaluate the actions taken by the Board of Directors in the face of a hostile takeover transaction, one must examine both the specific actions taken and the Board's motivation for taking those actions. When a company takes any defensive measures to fight off or to reject a hostile acquisition, the first level of analysis is to determine whether the company's Board of Directors is comprised of "inside" directors or "outside" directors. Inside directors are directors who are also officers of the company. Because they will lose their jobs if the hostile takeover succeeds, they have a conflict of interest. Therefore, inside directors' actions are subject to scrutiny under the duty of loyalty, not the duty of care. If a defensive action is taken by inside directors, or if their votes are necessary to approve an action, then it must be cleansed by a majority of the disinterested directors or by the shareholders after full disclosure. If the action is not cleansed, then it must be determined to be "fair" to the corporation, otherwise the directors supporting the action may be found to have violated their fiduciary duties and the transaction may be voidable and/or result in liability for those directors approving the action.

Outside directors, those who are neither employees of the Target company nor dependent on their positions with the Target company for their livelihood, are not viewed as having a conflict. However, there is still some additional scrutiny placed on their actions for the reasons stated above. In circumstances in which there are outside directors on the Board of Directors, even if there are also inside directors, the actions of the Board of Directors are typically evaluated under a measure known as the "*Unocal*" test, which was developed in the case *Unocal Corp. v. Mesa Petroleum Co.*, 493 A.2d 946 (Del. 1985). The **Unocal test** dictates that, when evaluating the actions of the Board of Directors in taking action against a takeover, there are two elements, or "prongs," which must be satisfied:

☑ The Board must show that it acted in good faith and, after reasonable investigation, **concluded that a danger existed to corporate policy and effectiveness**; AND

☑ The **action taken by the Board must have been reasonable in relation to the threat posed.** (The response must have been proportionate.)

Note that this test represents a shift from the Business Judgment Rule in that the burden is on the Board to show there was a "**threat**." In evaluating these prongs, students should be aware that a broad range of categories and constituencies may be considered in determining whether a danger exists to "corporate policy and effectiveness," which may include inadequacy of the price, the nature or timing of the offer, and the risk that the acquisition will not be consummated. The Unocal case also allowed for the possibility of evaluating the impact on groups other than shareholders, such as employees, customers, and creditors. However, students should be careful in this area. The impact on other groups may be a consideration, but not at the expense of the welfare of the company's shareholders. Threats that impact the shareholders will still have more "weight" than those that only impact other groups. The **proportionality requirement** prong of the test also has some flexibility since proportionality can be subjective.

Later cases have "clarified" that, while the defensive measures taken may not be "preclusive" or "coercive," the actions taken may be within a "range of reasonableness," which some believe means that courts will defer to any "reasonable" judgment of the Board. (*See Unitrin, Inc. v. American General Corp.*, 651 A.2d 1361 (Del. Supr. 1995).) In evaluating a problem using the *Unocal* Test, students should discuss whether the measure taken was reasonable or within the range of reasonableness. (Although many commentators have asserted that the results of the Unocal test are quite similar to the results one would get if applying the BJR, students should be careful to apply the Unocal test to evaluate defensive measures taken by a company's Board, and not to confuse their analysis by including references to the BJR.)

THE *REVLON* RULE

The Unocal test is used to evaluate defensive measures taken by a Board of Directors to fight a hostile acquisition attempt. However, there is one additional test that is used in circumstances when the Board is no longer taking action to preserve the company. In many hostile takeover situations, the Target company attempts to find a "White Knight," a company by which the Target company would prefer to be acquired. In these instances, the Target company often makes a deal with the White Knight to thwart the efforts of the hostile Bidder. However, in these instances courts have held that such actions are no longer "defensive" and are subject to a different level of scrutiny. This level of scrutiny is known as the **Revlon** Rule since it arose out of a case called *Revlon, Inc. v. MacAndrews & Forbes Holdings, Inc.*, 506 A.2d 173 (Del. 1986). The *Revlon* Rule (as enhanced by subsequent cases) dictates that:

☑ As long as a Target company is fighting off a takeover, then the *Unocal* test is the proper test to evaluate its actions; BUT

☑ As soon as the Target's Board is aware that a breakup of the firm is imminent; OR that

☑ A change in control is imminent (even if a break up of the firm is not); THEN

☑ The Board of Director's sole responsibility is to maximize the "value" that is received by the shareholders in the transaction.

Note that the measure is "value" to the shareholders. This does not always mean the highest dollar value. Many different (albeit reasonable) measures of value may be taken into account. This means that the Board has the ability to evaluate different offers and to select one that truly provides better value to the shareholders, rather than just selecting the highest bid from a mediocre company. However, the obligation is still to maximize shareholder value, and the Board may not make a deal with a White Knight instead of a hostile Bidder if the deal with the White Knight fails to maximize shareholder value.

Students should also be aware that under cases decided after *Revlon*, if the ownership of the Target company is being transferred from a company with many different shareholders to another with many different shareholders, then the *Revlon* Rule might not apply, and instead the *Unocal* test would. However, if "control" is being sold (meaning the ownership is being transferred from many different shareholders to one dominant shareholder), then the

Revlon rule applies, and the Board must maximize value to the shareholders. A change in control involves a shift in the ownership of the corporation from a "fluid aggregation" of dispersed shareholders to a unified entity or group.

ILLUSTRATIVE PROBLEMS

PROBLEM 10.1

Super Star Sales, Inc. ("SSS"), a publicly traded company, is trying to fight off a hostile tender offer by Takeover Team Corporation ("TTC") for $50 per share for a total of $2 billion in cash. After some investigation, SSS confirms its fears that TTC is known for breaking up companies and selling off their assets. SSS is concerned that the price of the tender offer is too low, and that if the takeover occurs, SSS employees and customers will suffer. In order to fight the takeover attempt, SSS tells its shareholders that SSS will repurchase up to 30% of the shares of SSS for $70 a share if, and only if, an outside group acquires 50% of the outstanding shares of SSS. The strategy prevents TTC from acquiring SSS, but TTC sues the Board for a breach of fiduciary duty. How would the Board's defensive maneuver be evaluated?

Analysis

Since this transaction involves a potential takeover of the company, the actions taken by the Board would face a higher level of scrutiny than the Business Judgment Rule. If there were only inside directors on the Board (who might lose their jobs in the takeover), the transaction might be evaluated under a duty of loyalty analysis. However, assuming there were outside directors on the Board, the transaction would be evaluated under the Unocal test. The Unocal test involves a two-pronged approach. The first prong involves the question of whether the Board acted in good faith. In this context, "good faith" means that, after conducting a reasonable investigation, the Board of Directors concluded (in good faith) that a danger existed to corporate policy and effectiveness. In this instance, the SSS Board identified threats to the SSS shareholders, employees and customers. Each of these constituents may be considered in evaluating whether a "threat" exists. Since there is no evidence that these concerns were raised in bad faith, and the Board seems to have investigated TTC, it appears that the first prong of the test was satisfied. The second prong involves the question of whether the corporation's response to the identified threat was proportionate to the threat. While this prong has a subjective element, it seems that the "self-tender" of $70 a share was calculated to defeat the threat and did not destroy the corporation. Furthermore, the response was neither preclusive (in that all shareholders could participate) nor "coercive" (in that the terms were clear, and shareholders were not "penalized" for not participating). So, it seems that SSS's actions were reasonable and certainly fell within a range of reasonableness, meeting the proportionality prong as well. Therefore, the requirements of the Unocal test seem to have been met, and the Board will likely prevail in the challenge to its actions. Finally, it should be noted that there is no suggestion of a pending sale of SSS or change in control that would have triggered the Revlon Rule.

PROBLEM 10.2

Use the same facts of the previous problem. However, assume the SSS offer to repurchase its own shares is no longer in place, and TTC still wants to acquire SSS. The CEO of TTC, Amy, tells SSS it will raise its offer to $75 per share for the SSS shares. The SSS Board hates the idea of selling the company to TTC, who it knows will break up and sell SSS. So, SSS approaches a "white knight" in the form of a company called Galaxy Good Guys, Inc. ("GGG"). SSS arranges a deal for GGG to buy SSS for the same price as was being offered by TTC ($75 per share). GGG plans to sell a division of SSS and borrow against some of the SSS assets to pay for the acquisition. The SSS Board quickly approves the deal without allowing TTC to make a counter offer. SSS then offers GGG a $500 million break-up fee so that TTC could no longer afford to buy SSS if SSS were to pay that fee. TTC, which already owns some SSS shares, files an action, alleging that the SSS Board has breached its duty to its shareholders, and seeking to force SSS and GGG to eliminate the breakup fee so TTC can continue to bid on SSS. What is the likely outcome?

Analysis

While a Board of Directors has a somewhat broad ability to adopt defensive measures under the Unocal Test and to consider "threats" to a broader number of constituencies, that all changes once the company is "up for sale." Once the breakup of the firm (or a change in control) is imminent, the Revlon Rule applies and the Board is required to maximize value to the shareholders. When SSS accepted the GGG deal, the SSS Board was no longer fighting a takeover, they were accepting a sale. In that sale, the existing shareholders of SSS would be, for the most part, selling all of their interest in SSS, and GGG would control the company. In addition, the financing of the deal by either GGG or TTC represents a break-up (at least in part) of SSS. Therefore, the SSS Board is obligated to negotiate a deal to get the best value for the SSS shareholders. By offering GGG a huge break-up fee, one sixth of the total deal price, the SSS Board is effectively stopping TTC from bidding on the company. In effect, the break-up fee prevents a bidding contest in which the acquisition price might go even higher. The question under the Revlon Rule is not whether the defensive measure is reasonable and proportionate. The question is whether it maximizes shareholder value. In this case, especially given the substantial size of the fee, it seems that the SSS Board's action limits or even reduces shareholder value. So, it is likely that a court would find that the SSS Board breached its duty and violated the Revlon Rule and, therefore, the breakup fee provision would not be allowed.

CHAPTER 11

Alternative Organizations

There are other structures which should be evaluated in the context of Business Associations. While it is not practical to provide an in depth analysis of each alternative organization in this book, the following is intended to provide a brief introduction to some of the more prominent features of these organizations.

S CORPORATIONS

An S-corporation is a corporation that has special tax status. It has the same form as a C-corporation and is typically governed by the same state corporate laws. However, unlike a C-corporation, which is taxed on its earnings and may face the issue of "double taxation" when it issues a dividend to its shareholders, an S-corporation is a **pass through entity**. This "pass through" status means that, rather than the entity paying income tax, its owners pay tax on their proportionate share of the earnings of the entity, and the entity is not taxed for dividends distributed to its shareholders. (This eliminates double taxation.) In exchange for this special status, the S-corporation is subject to certain restrictions. Some of the more significant restrictions on S-corporations are as listed below.

S-corporations:

- ☑ May not have more than 100 shareholders;

- ☑ Must have shareholders that are individuals (or estates, non-profits or certain trusts). Partnerships, LLCs, other entities and other corporations may not be S-corporation shareholders;

- ☑ May not have any shareholders who are "non-resident aliens"; and

- ☑ May only have one class of stock.

Other than these and a few other limitations imposed by the IRS, and various state laws, the state and Federal corporate laws governing S-corporations are the same as those governing C-corporations. Directors, officers and dominant shareholders of all corporations (S and C) are subject to fiduciary duties; Securities laws apply to transactions in the corporation's stock; plaintiffs may make arguments about piercing the corporate veil, and rules about control and voting are applicable. Since an S-corporation is often a less complex entity, there may be fewer opportunities for some of the rules and restrictions to come into play. (For example, S-corporations are not publicly held.) However, the same basic rules still apply.

LIMITED LIABILITY COMPANIES

The structure of an LLC combines the limited liability of a corporation with the flexibility of a partnership. While an in depth analysis of the LLC is beyond the scope of this book, it is important to understand some basic features of the LLC. The owners of an LLC are referred to as "Members." The person, or people, who operate the LLC, are called the "Manager(s)." An LLC may be "member managed" or "manager managed." An LLC is formed by filing Articles of Organization with the Secretary of State's office in the state in which the LLC organizer(s) wish to form the entity. An LLC is governed by both the statutory rules of the state and an "Operating Agreement". In most instances, the Operating Agreement will dictate how the LLC is governed, and the state's LLC statute will fill in any gaps not addressed in the Operating Agreement. As is the situation with partnerships, the statutory rules are known as the "default" rules. The default rules will also put limitations on just how far an Operating Agreement can alter the statutory framework. For example, most states will not allow the Operating Agreement to provide for a blanket waiver of all fiduciary duties of a manager. LLCs are typically not required to follow as many formalities as corporations. For example, unless required in the Operating Agreement, there is no requirement that the members of an LLC hold regular meetings.

The most significant features of an LLC are:

☑   Limited liability;

☑   Flow-through (also known as "pass through") taxation;

☑   The ability of owners to participate in management without risking personal liability;

☑   Flexibility in the ability to allocate profits and losses to members;

☑ Flexibility and choices in the entity's management structure (centralized or decentralized); and

☑ Partnership-like fiduciary duties.

Member Managed

In a member managed LLC, the entity has more of the "feel" of a partnership. The owners are engaged in the daily operation of the business as agents of the LLC. They will vote on matters related to governance and will have responsibilities consistent with the organization's Operating Agreement. States are split on whether the default rules for member voting should be pro rata (by percentage) as in a corporation or "per capita" (one vote per person) as in a partnership. In any event the voting rights of the members are typically set forth and determined in the Operating Agreement. In a member managed LLC, the members have fiduciary duties to the LLC and to each other, similar to the duties owed among partners in a partnership. Each member has the apparent authority to bind the LLC in transactions in the ordinary course of business, unless the member lacks the actual authority to act AND the person with whom the member was dealing had actual knowledge that the member lacked authority.

Manager Managed

In a manager managed LLC, the operation of the entity is handled by a "manager". The manager may be one person or several people. Although members often fill the role of manager, there is no requirement that a manager also be a member. The scope of the manager's responsibility may be set forth in the Operating Agreement. So, the manager may have a great deal of power over the entity or very limited power. Managers owe fiduciary duties to the LLC and to its members. Managers also have the apparent authority to bind the LLC in transactions in the ordinary course of business, unless the manager had no actual authority AND the person with whom the manager was dealing had actual knowledge that the manager lacked authority. Members (who are not also managers) of a manager managed LLC do not have the apparent authority to bind the LLC.

Taxation

LLCs are typically taxed like partnerships and follow partnership accounting. The profits and losses of an LLC are "passed through" to the members who are responsible for paying tax on the profits and will be able to report the losses (and typically take deductions for those losses) on their respective personal income tax returns. The LLC does not pay its own taxes. (Note however, that many states impose small fees and taxes on the LLC itself.) The IRS does allow an LLC to elect to be taxed as a corporation. However, this option is rarely selected since partnership taxation is one of the significant benefits of an LLC.

Liability of Members

In general, the owners of an LLC have limited liability and are not personally liable for the debts and obligations of the business. However, it is possible to "pierce" the LLC veil. The good news is that the standard for piercing the LLC veil is typically the same as the standard for piercing the corporate veil: a unity of interest (or disregard for the entity's separate existence) and some type of "fraud-like conduct" or injustice. The difference in LLC cases is that LLCs are required to follow fewer formalities. Therefore, an LLC does not violate the unity of interest test by not having formal meetings or failing to keep minutes (as can happen with a corporation), unless the Operating Agreement requires meetings. (Most Operating Agreements don't require meetings because they do not want to establish a basis for veil piercing down the road.) A member and an LLC may still violate the unity of interest test by co-mingling funds, by not keeping separate financial records or bank accounts, by failing to respect the separate existence of the LLC or by undercapitalization. However, because a common issue in the context of piercing a corporation's veil is failure to have meetings, keep minutes or issue stock, there are fewer instances of LLC piercing than instances of piercing the corporate veil. Assuming the LLC veil is not pierced, members do not have personal liability for the debts of the LLC, regardless of how much they participate in management. Members might have some personal liability for distributions they receive, or vote for, in excess of the amount the LLC needs to retain in order to satisfy its obligations to creditors. Students should be aware that, although LLC members might have liability for improper distributions that they receive from the LLC, in such instances, the personal liability of the member cannot exceed the amount of the improper distribution.

Transferability

Typically, membership interests in an LLC are not transferable without the consent of the other members. An attempted transfer would usually wind up in a transfer of the member's "economic" interest but not her management interest, and the transferee would have no management rights, and could not become a member without the consent of the other members. The transferee would only have the right to receive funds, which would have been distributed to the transferring member on the economic interest transferred.

Dissociation

When a member leaves an LLC, that departure is known as "dissociation". (Note that this same term is used in partnerships.) Dissociation may be voluntary ("I'm leaving") or involuntary ("You've been expelled"). In either instance, the dissociating member is usually entitled to receive the value of her interest, less any damages caused by the dissociation if the dissociation is "wrongful". If the LLC is for a term or for a particular undertaking, the dissociating member may need to wait to receive payment for her interest until the end of the term or undertaking. Rules governing transfers and dissociation are typically dealt with in the Operating Agreement, and may be different than those outlined above.

Dissolution

Most LLC statutes provide that an LLC's existence will continue until it is dissolved. An LLC will typically be dissolved and its affairs wound up, as provided in its Operating Agreement or upon a majority vote of its members. LLCs are subject to judicial dissolutions as well, and the state statutes give courts the power to dissolve an LLC under certain circumstance that vary from state to state.

LIMITED PARTNERSHIPS

A limited partnership is a partnership entity that is required to have at least one limited partner and one general partner. The general partner or partners have personal liability for the debts and obligations of the limited partnership. The limited partners, subject to certain limitations discussed below, are not personally liable for the debts and obligations of the limited partnership. The liability of a limited partner is typically limited to the amount invested (or committed) to the limited partnership.

In a limited partnership the general partner(s), manage the operation of the business and the limited partner(s) are not involved in the day-to-day management of the business. The rules governing the general partner of a general partnership are similar to the rules that govern general partnerships discussed in Chapter 2. Like a general partnership, limited partnerships are governed by a Partnership Agreement. There are "default rules" for limited partnerships as well (although these rules are of course different than the default rules for general partnerships and the default rules for LLCs) that govern the limited partnership, to the extent these rules are not overridden by the Partnership Agreement. A limited partnership is governed by state law and may only be created by a filing with a state regulatory agency, which is usually the Secretary of State.

Limited partners do not take part in the management of the business. As limited partners, they are not subject to personal liability for the debts and obligations of the business. Their liability is limited. Furthermore, a limited partnership is not (at least under existing law) subject to piercing. Therefore, limited partners are protected from unlimited liability to creditors of the firm. However, limited partners may still incur liability for money they receive in the form of improper distributions or fraudulent transfers.

If limited partners do participate in the control of the partnership, they risk losing their "limited" status and being treated as general partners and, as such, may incur personal liability. (This restriction on participation in the business is known as the "**control rule**".) While historically there was a greater risk of a limited partner losing his or her "limited" status by virtue of the control rule, in states that have adopted the Uniform Limited Partnership Act (2001), limited partners will not risk personal liability for participating in management unless they take other action to incur liability. In other states, a limited partner might only incur liability if that limited partner participated in the control of the limited partnership AND a third party is aware of the limited partner's participation in control AND that third party transacts business with the limited partner with the reasonable belief that the limited partner is a general partner. Even under the foregoing circumstances, the limited partner's liability would be only to the specific third party who reasonably believed the limited partner to be a general partner, not to all creditors.

Even in states that have not adopted the protections for limited partners contained in the Uniform Limited Partnership Act of 2001, there are a number of "**safe harbors**" (known as the "**control rule**") that allow limited partners to participate in management on some level without risking liability for participating in the control of the limited partnership. Under the control rule, a general partner does not "participate in control" solely by:

☑ Being a contractor for or an agent or employee of the limited partnership or of a general partner of the limited partnership;

☑   Being an officer, director, or shareholder of a corporate general partner of the limited partnership;

☑   Consulting with and advising a general partner with respect to the limited partnership's business;

☑   Acting as a surety or guarantor of the limited partnership;

☑   Requesting or attending a meeting of the partners;

☑   Voting; or

☑   Winding up the partnership.

In the past, these safe harbors have allowed limited partners to participate on some level without risking liability, but as the "control rule" erodes, the existence of the "safe harbor" becomes less necessary.

Students should also be aware that general partners do not need to be individuals. Often, more sophisticated ventures will form a corporation to serve as the general partner of the limited partnership. This structure allows the general partner in a limited partnership to take advantage of the limited liability protections of a corporation by protecting the shareholder or shareholders in the corporate general partner from the liability they could incur if they were to act as individual general partners. Often, the shareholders in a corporate general partner also serve as officers of that corporation. As officers, acting on behalf of the corporate general partner, these individuals may participate in the management of the limited partnership without risking the personal liability that typically accompanies the management of a limited partnership.

Limited partners do not have the right to bind the limited partnership and, therefore, may not exercise actual or "apparent authority" over the limited partnership while acting in the capacity of a limited partner.

A limited partnership is a pass through entity for tax purposes, so like an LLC, its partners are taxed on the profits from, and may deduct the losses of, the business. Profits, losses and distributions may be allocated among the limited and general partners as provided by the Partnership Agreement. If no provision is made for allocations, they typically will be allocated on a percentage basis, based upon capital contributions (i.e., investments) in the limited partnership.

One difference between limited partnerships and corporations is that partners may contribute a broader range of consideration in exchange for their ownership interest. Partners may generally contribute services, the promise of future services, promissory notes, and any other tangible or intangible property in exchange for their interest in the limited partnership.

General partners have fiduciary duties that are akin to the fiduciary duties of partners in a general partnership discussed earlier in this book. However, limited partners typically do not have fiduciary duties to the limited partnership or to any other partner that arise out of being a limited partner. BUT, limited partners are still bound to discharge all duties to the partnership and to the other partners and to exercise any rights they might have, consistent with the obligation of good faith and fair dealing. Note also that different states may impose different standards, but given the limited role of a limited partners, it is unlikely that fiduciary duties will be implicated, although there may be duties of confidentiality that arise with respect to confidential partnership information.

As in an LLC, a limited partner may only transfer its economic interest without the consent of the other partners. A limited partner may not transfer to a transferee "limited partner" status without the consent of the other partners. However, since limited partner interests are basically economic interests, although the transferee would not have the right to vote, there would be a smaller variation between economic interest and management rights in a limited partnership than there would be in other entities. The transferee would have the right to receive funds, which would have been distributed to the transferring limited partner on the interest transferred. General partners will be more restricted in their rights to transfer their general partner interest in the limited partnership. These restrictions are similar to those found in a general partnership.

Limited partners have the right to dissociate if the partnership is "at will". (Note that some statutes use the term "withdraw" and some the term "dissociate". For these purposes these terms are interchangeable.) However, if the partnership is for a term or a particular undertaking, limited partners may not dissociate without incurring liability for wrongful dissociation. If there is no definite time for the limited partnership to end, then a limited partner may typically withdraw upon six months' notice. A general partner may withdraw by providing notice, but, if the withdrawal violates the partnership agreement, then the withdrawing general partner is liable for damages. Within a reasonable time following withdrawal, and subject to the partnership agreement in all respects, (a) the withdrawing limited partner is entitled to the "fair" value of his or her interest; (b) the withdrawing general partner is entitled to the "fair" value of his or her interest, less any damages arising out of a breach of the partnership agreement.

Limited partnerships have been used as investment vehicles for years. The structure of a pass through entity for passive investors makes the structure very appealing. Students should be aware that limited partnership interests are generally securities and subject to the securities laws. There are a number of interesting structures and uses of limited partnerships in the business world. However, they are beyond the scope of this book.

Final Thoughts

Business Associations covers a broad range of subjects, cases and rules. To make sense of it all, students should remember that the subject is just an effort to answer the initial questions.

- ☑ What responsibilities does one person have to another when they are working together?

- ☑ What responsibilities does a person have to others when she is working on their behalf in the operation of a business enterprise?

- ☑ What are the features, rules and characteristics of various entities that are treated as separate "persons" under the law?

- ☑ What are the rights, protections and obligations of the owners of these business entities and what rules protect and govern the transfer of that ownership?

The students who succeed in this field do so because they understand the structure of the entities, the rules that govern those entities and the rules that govern the people who are involved in the ownership and operation of those entities. In learning this subject, students should focus on the structures involved. Sometimes the structures are fair and logical. Sometimes they don't make much sense. Often just acknowledging that will make an area easier to understand. Finally, when looking at a problem, ask yourself, who is involved, what role are they playing, are they an officer, a director, a shareholder or even a business. The rules in this area are attached to the role a person (or entity) plays, and focusing on that role will help to distinguish which rules should apply.